I0800214

IMAGES
of America

GRANVILLE

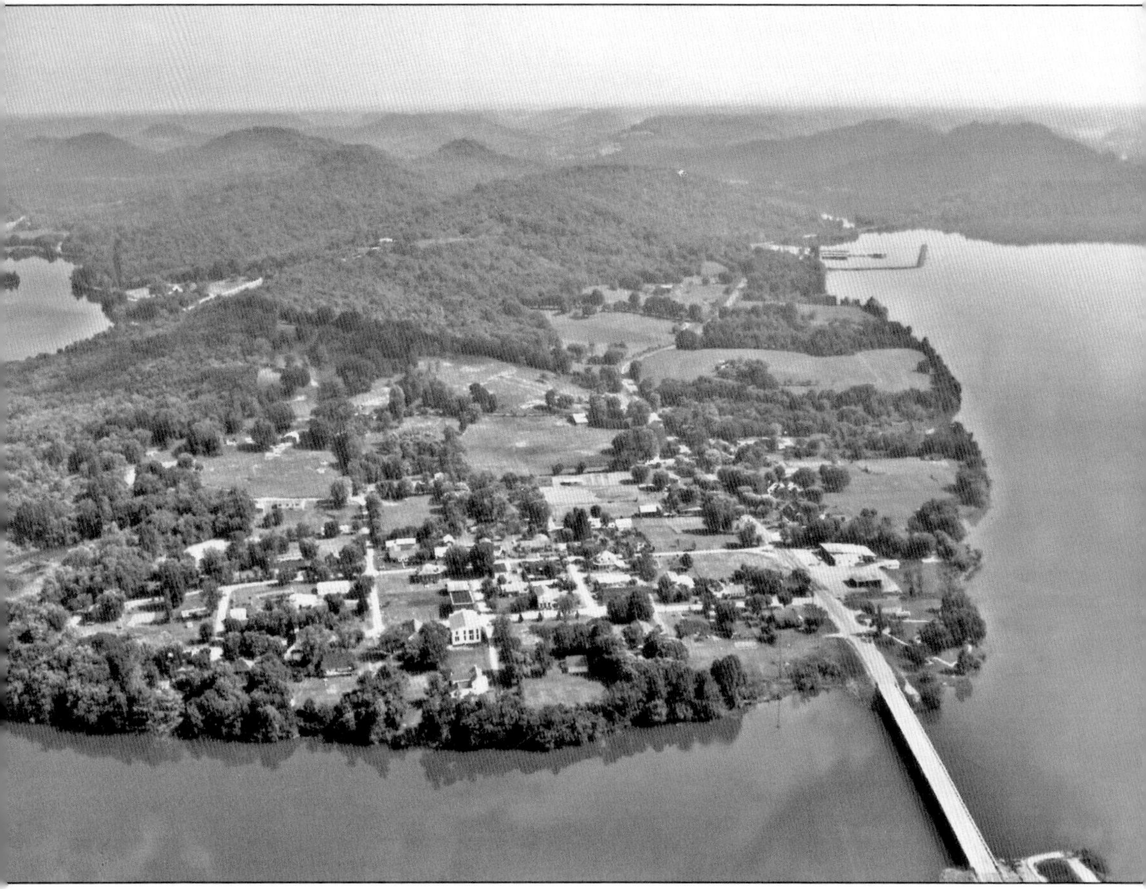

This aerial photograph, taken in 2001, shows how the village of Granville, Tennessee, is surrounded by Cordell Hull Lake and the Cumberland River.

IMAGES
of America

GRANVILLE

Granville Museum, Inc.

ARCADIA
PUBLISHING

ISBN 978-0-7385-1783-4

Published by Arcadia Publishing
Charleston, South Carolina

Printed in the United States of America

Library of Congress Catalog Card Number: 2005921940

For all general information contact Arcadia Publishing at:
Telephone 843-853-2070
Fax 843-853-0044
E-mail sales@arcadiapublishing.com
For customer service and orders:
Toll-Free 1-888-313-2665

Visit us on the Internet at www.arcadiapublishing.com

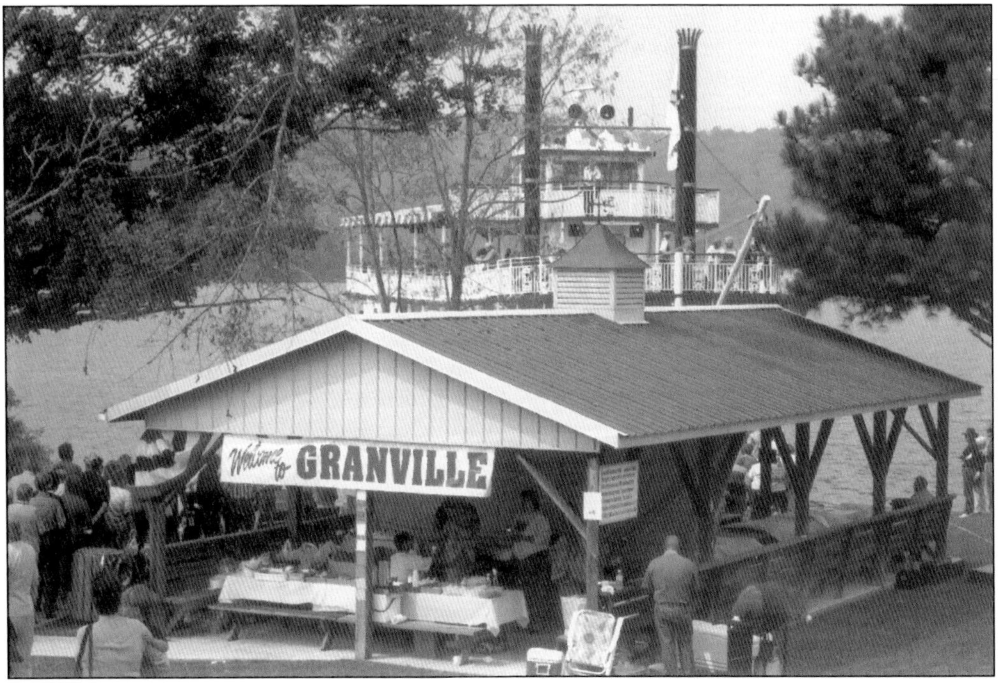

The *Music City Queen*, a steamboat from Nashville, visits the Jazz Festival at Veterans Park in Granville in 2004. Visitors are shown waiting to board the steamboat for sightseeing cruises featuring live jazz bands.

Contents

This book is dedicated to our families for the love, support, and encouragement they have shown us with this project, and to the citizens of Granville, past and present, whose pioneering spirit, determination, and faith make this a wonderful place to live and visit.

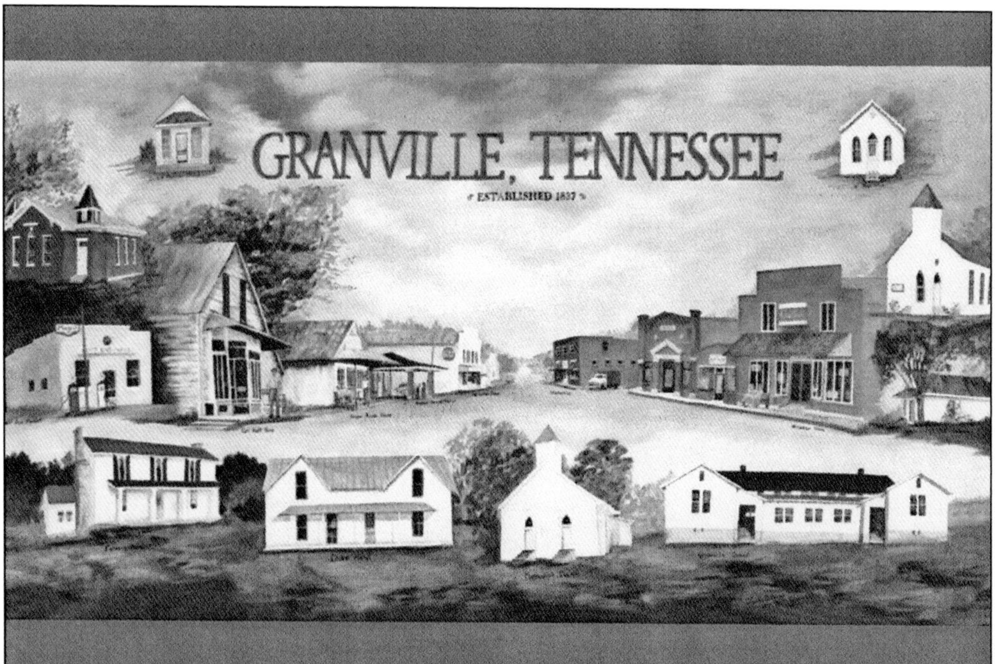

This postcard, copied from a mural now hanging in the museum, depicts most of the well-known buildings in Granville as they looked in the early 1950s. This work of art was used to create an afghan that is now sold in the museum as a piece of history.

Introduction

Granville is located on the Cumberland River in north central Tennessee. It was settled in the early 1800s by Scotch-Irish descendants from Granville County, North Carolina. These family names included Burtons, Dukes, Montgomerys, Pages, Raglands, Sadlers, Shepherds, Smiths, Terrys, Tittles, and Williamsons. The earliest settlers were farmers. Tobacco, corn, hay, cattle, hogs, and lumber were the main products.

On the western edge of the Cumberland Mountains, with rugged hills and narrow valleys, ground travel was difficult and often impossible in bad weather. A river provided transportation to market and a way for settlers to receive goods. Granville became a riverboat town. Warehouses sprang up along a half-mile of river. Furniture, hardware, and groceries arrived by boat. Bob Meadows, a riverboat captain, told his family that Granville was known as Banana Town.

Often, up to 45 paddle wheelers traveled the Cumberland River from Nashville to Burnside, Kentucky. They provided comfortable first-class cabins on the top deck for travelers. Maid service and even childcare was available. Freight going upriver or agricultural products being sent downriver were stowed on the lower decks.

River travel was difficult. It was treacherous in the fall, winter, and spring, when the rains might produce much debris. Large logs floated downriver and shifting sandbars grounded boats. Many boats sank. The *I.T. Rhea* sank and was raised a total of 12 times. The 13th time it sank just a few miles above Granville, and the owners left it there. Divers later brought up treasures including tableware and the ship's bell.

The river provided another means of revenue. Fine old trees were logged and floated down the local creeks to the Cumberland River. Once on the Cumberland, they were tied together for the journey downriver, where they would be sold.

Early settlers brought slaves with them. Houses, rock fences, even roads, as well as the farm labor, flourished thanks to their efforts. This fact contributed to strong sentiments for the Confederacy. Company K of the 17th Tennessee Infantry was active in Granville during the Civil War. In 1890, about 5,000 Company K survivors and friends gathered for a reunion in Granville.

The settlers were education-minded, securing a charter from the state legislature in the mid-1830s for a private school. It was to offer "the finest in education" to local and boarding students. Other private schools flourished before public schools were initiated in 1922.

Residents volunteered to serve with Andrew Jackson, nicknamed "Old Hickory," in the War of 1812. World War I and II saw large numbers serve valiantly. Numerous Gold Stars reflected the loss of lives of local men. An active American Legion chapter flourished in Granville for many years after World War II. Throughout the Cold War, including the Korean and Vietnam Conflicts, locals volunteered to serve their country.

World War II engineering companies trained by building pontoon bridges across the Cumberland during military training maneuvers in 1943 and 1944. Several tent cities sprang up, and local farmland became military locations. This combat training affected both the economy and the lives of locals. Many of these men were invited into local homes. Off-duty time was spent in stores, barbershops, and other establishments. Several local women married men from those units.

The first settlers were Presbyterian. Soon, a log-cabin church, known as the Concord Assembly, was built near the banks of the Cumberland River. Each August for many years a large camp meeting was held. Families came to camp and attended religious services for a week. A second log cabin was built in the village, to be replaced by a large, two-story frame church a few years before 1900. Upstairs were meeting rooms for the local Masonic Lodge, and downstairs was the sanctuary, which was also used as the location of the private high school. In the mid-1800s, a Methodist church was formed, and then a Christian church organized. In 1939, a Baptist church was added to the community. These churches were not only the religious centers of the community, they were the social and educational centers as well. At least two private schools operated in church buildings. Community celebrations of Christmas, Easter, and other holidays were important events. It was there that young people met eligible members of the opposite sex. It was there that babies were christened, and it was definitely there that weddings occurred.

By the early 1900s, in addition to the numerous churches, the town boasted a bank, local doctors, several general stores, a funeral home, post office, hotel, blacksmith shop, barbershop, beauty shop, saloon, and even an icehouse. A local ferry provided transportation across the river for local farmers to do business, seek medical care, or vote in county elections.

Athletic endeavors were a big part of recreation. The junior high school competed in basketball. There were basketball teams in the area as early as 1915. There were sandlot baseball teams also competing with other nearby teams. Many young people who first played basketball in Granville went on to county high-school teams, and five state championship teams have been coached by Granville natives.

In 1972, the Cordell Hull Dam was completed and a TVA lake impounded downstream from Granville. Many homes along the river were moved or destroyed to make way for the lake. The lake brought a marina, fishing, water sports, and retirees who wanted a home near the lake. Granville changed from a thriving farming center to a busy recreation destination with an RV campground, swimming pool, and fishing tournaments. Farms still exist, but few are the sole source of income.

A museum, bank, volunteer fire hall, antique and gift shop, real estate office, post office, and market, in addition to the Granville Marina, Maple Grove Campground, the restored Ben Sutton General Store, and the Granville Bed and Breakfast, now offer services to the community.

One

Travel of Yesteryear

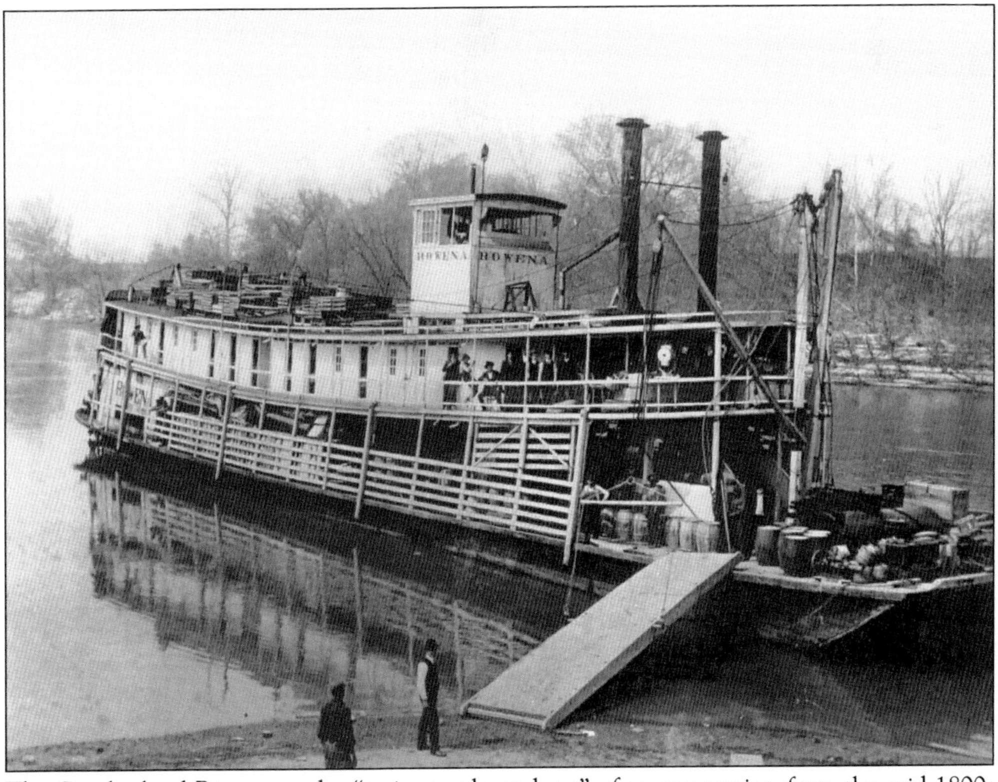

The Cumberland River was the "train, truck, and car" of transportation from the mid-1800s until the time of the Great Depression in the 1930s. The *Rowena*, shown here docking at Granville in 1925, carried supplies into town. Captain Meadows remarked to his children that Granville was known as Banana Town because they ordered more bananas than any other town on his route.

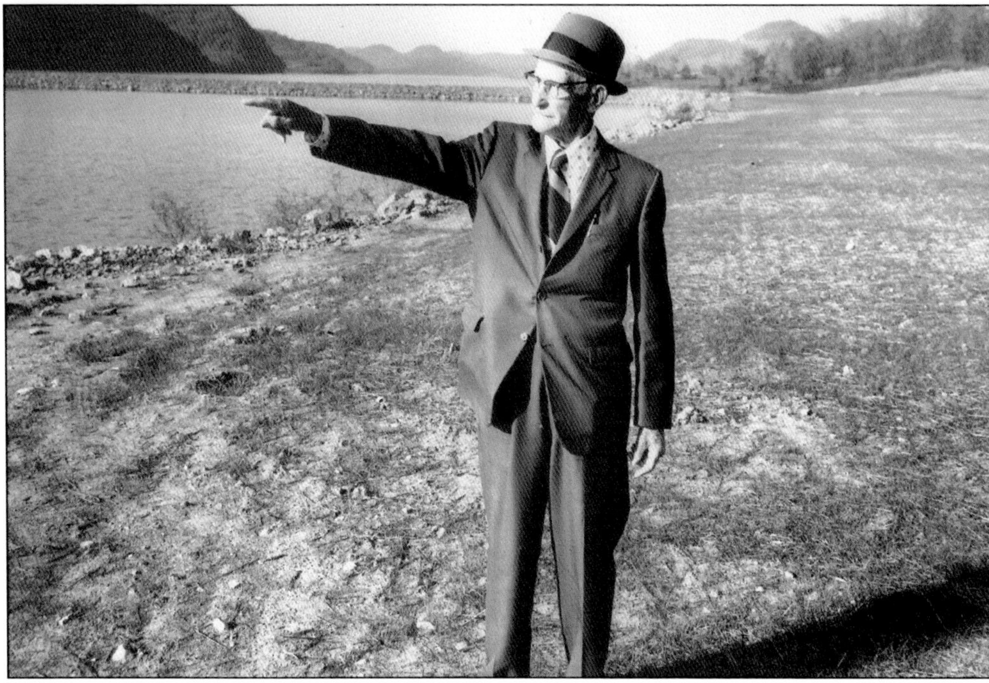

Alonzo Huff points to the location where he operated his Niagara Landing Warehouse from 1906 to 1927, when river traffic was at its peak. Numerous warehouses handled the receipt of freight from the steamboats and delivered the merchandise to businesses in Granville, Enigma, and areas toward Putnam County.

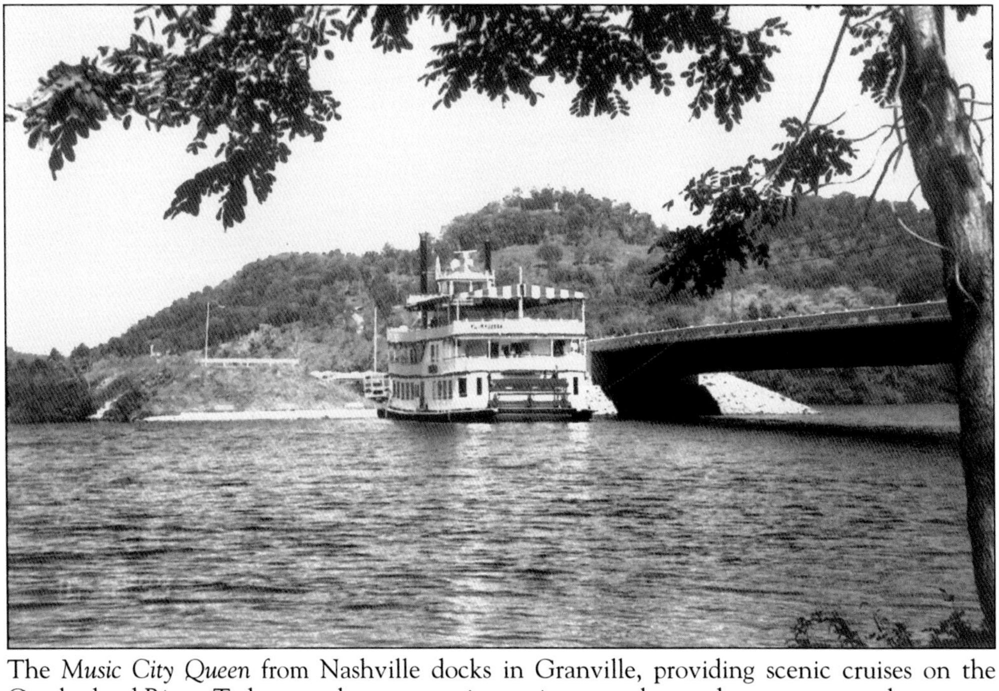

The *Music City Queen* from Nashville docks in Granville, providing scenic cruises on the Cumberland River. Today, people can experience river travel over the same areas where up to 45 steamboats regularly traveled in the early 1900s.

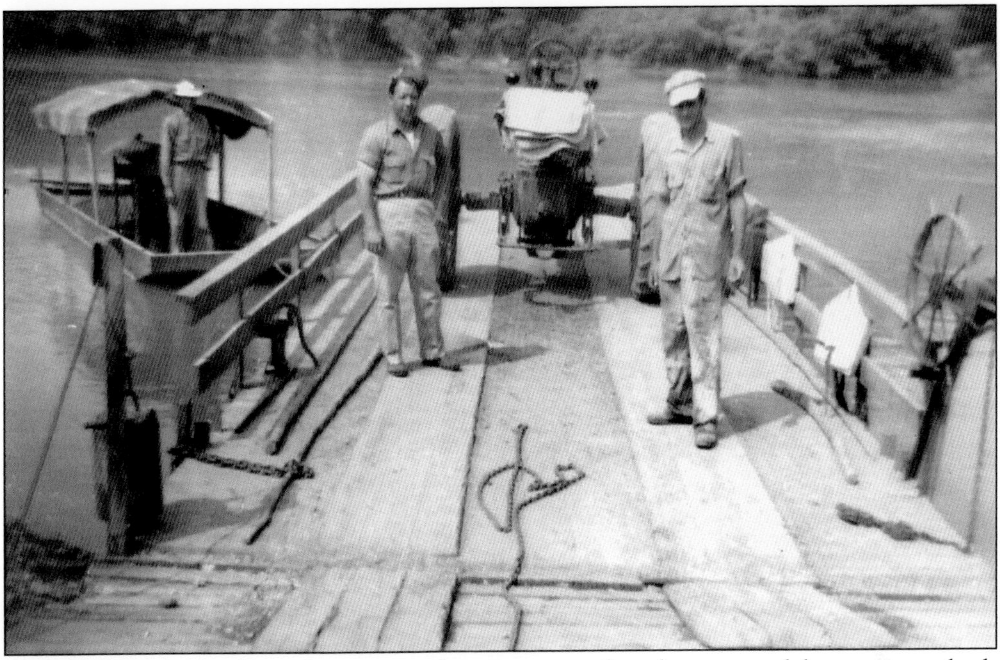

Granville was the banking, shopping, and voting center for a large area of the county on both sides of the river. Until 1971, ferries, like this one operated by Paskel Fields, carried people, animals, buggies, and even automobiles across the river. Mack Austin Carter (center) and Pete Lee (right) are shown preparing to cross.

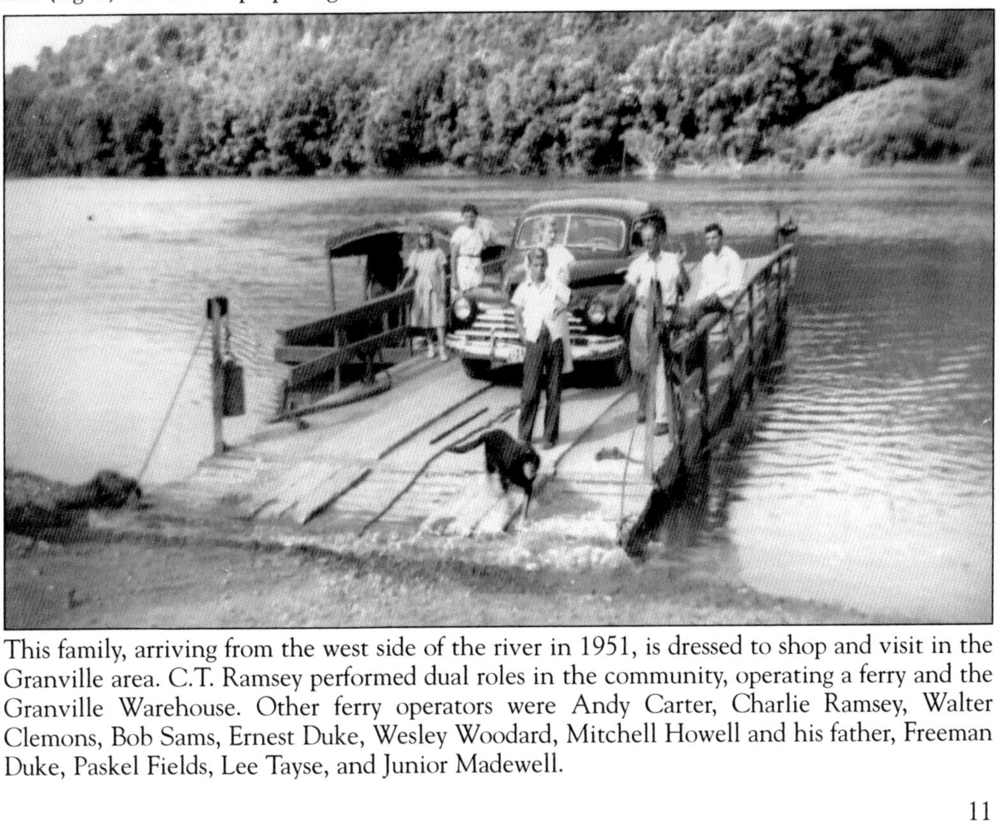

This family, arriving from the west side of the river in 1951, is dressed to shop and visit in the Granville area. C.T. Ramsey performed dual roles in the community, operating a ferry and the Granville Warehouse. Other ferry operators were Andy Carter, Charlie Ramsey, Walter Clemons, Bob Sams, Ernest Duke, Wesley Woodard, Mitchell Howell and his father, Freeman Duke, Paskel Fields, Lee Tayse, and Junior Madewell.

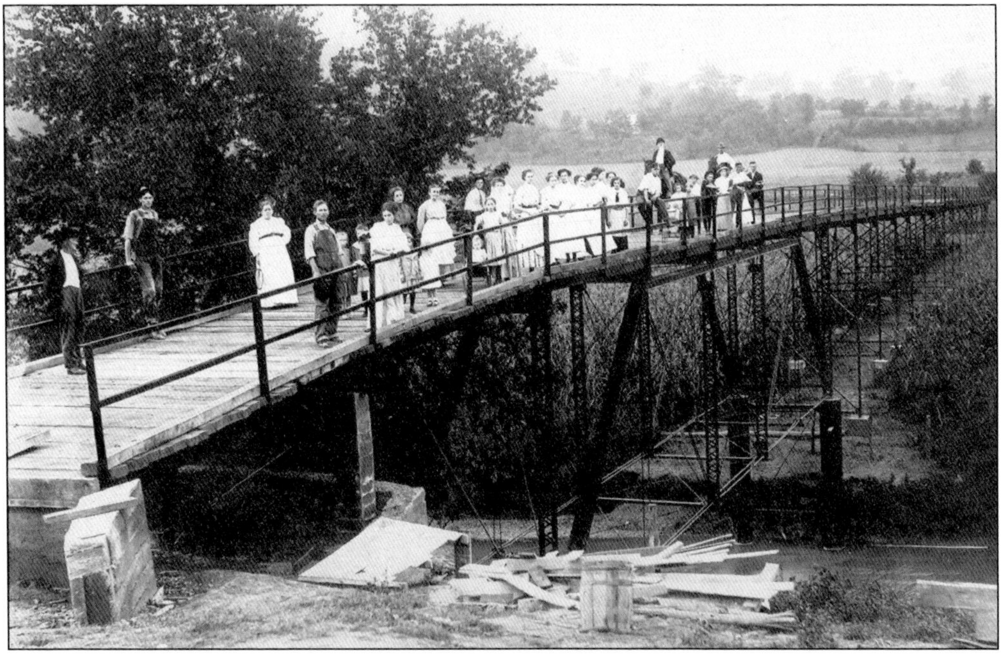

In 1910, the first wooden bridge was completed across Martin's Creek. Dr. William Burchett Page (on horseback), along with many local residents, gathered for the opening, shown in this photo. The bridge was built by Nashville Bridge Company. The committee consisted of R.V. Brooks, S.S. Carver, E.C. Darwin, Daniel Johnson, and W.R. Watts.

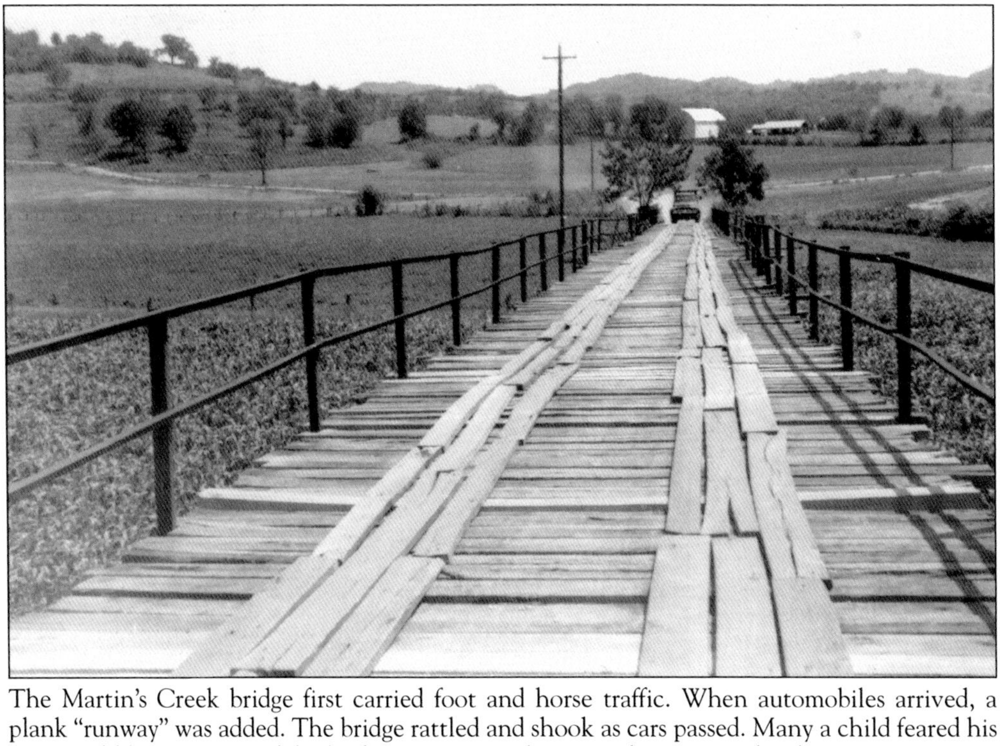

The Martin's Creek bridge first carried foot and horse traffic. When automobiles arrived, a plank "runway" was added. The bridge rattled and shook as cars passed. Many a child feared his foot would hang in one of the bridge openings as he crossed going to school.

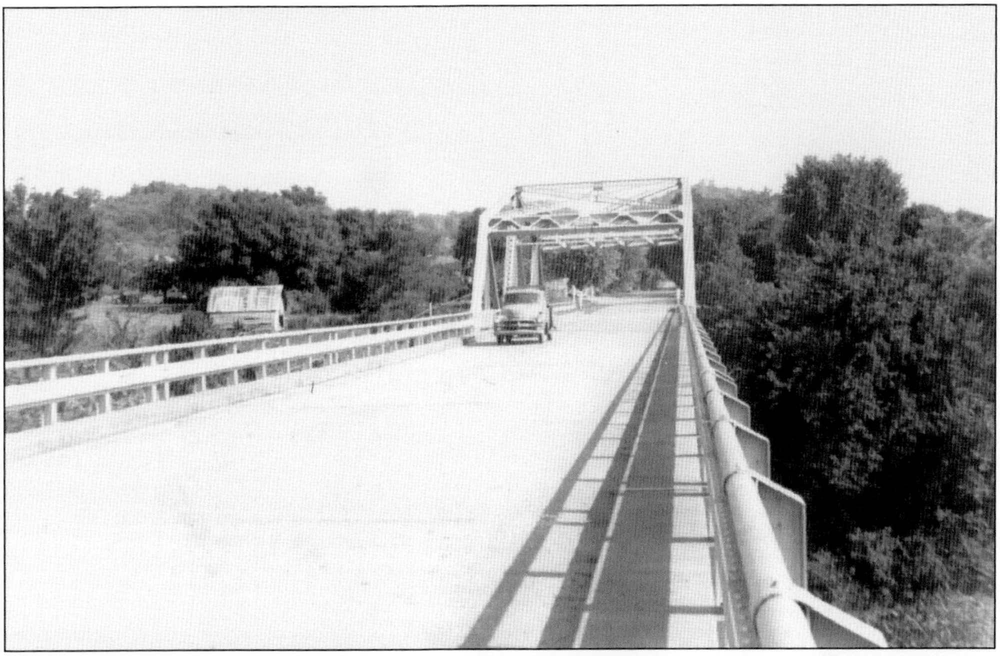

The State of Tennessee replaced the wooden bridge in 1939 with an iron bridge. For almost 60 years, this bridge carried traffic on State Highway 53. In January 1975, the bridge was named for Dr. Luther M. Freeman, a local doctor who delivered babies and served the community from 1906 until just before his death in 1973.

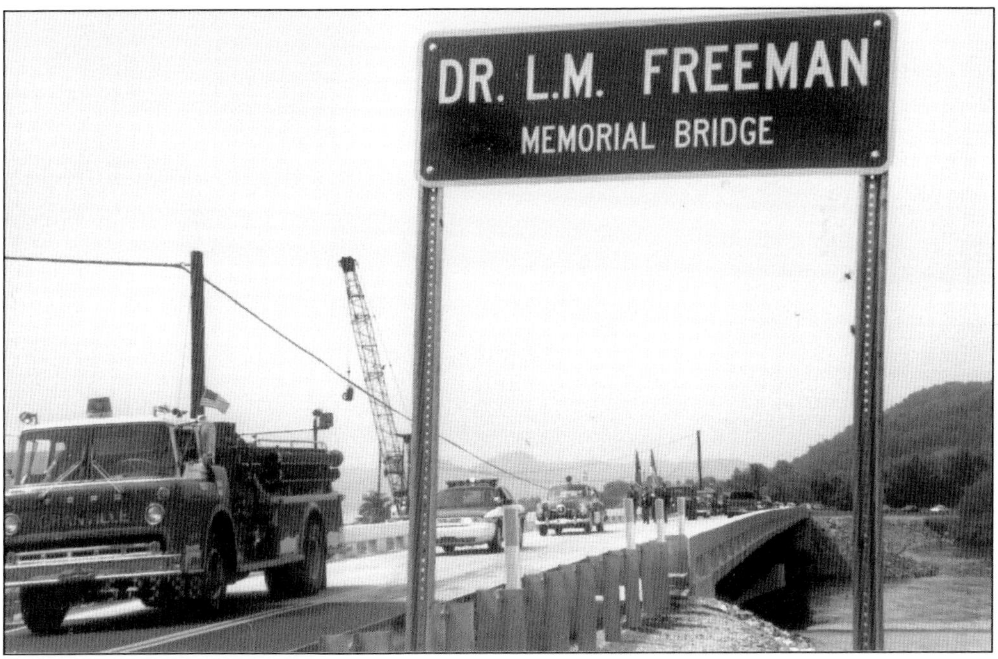

In 1997, the State declared the iron bridge unsafe and replaced it with a new bridge, the first in Tennessee to use high-density steel designed to reduce costs. A dedication for the new bridge, which still bears the name of Dr. Freeman, included the parade seen above, led by local fire and police vehicles, on May 23, 1998.

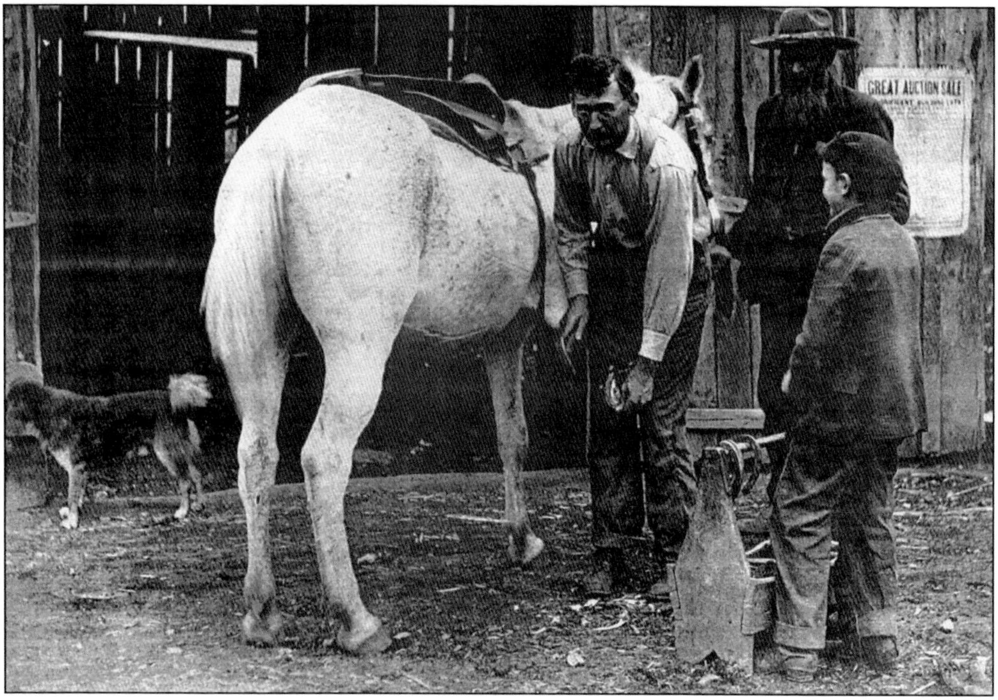

A blacksmith shop was an important asset to the community before motor travel. Pictured here in the 1920s, Morgan Duke operated a blacksmith shop and hotel in the Granville community for many years. Sid Sutton also operated a blacksmith shop on Clover Street.

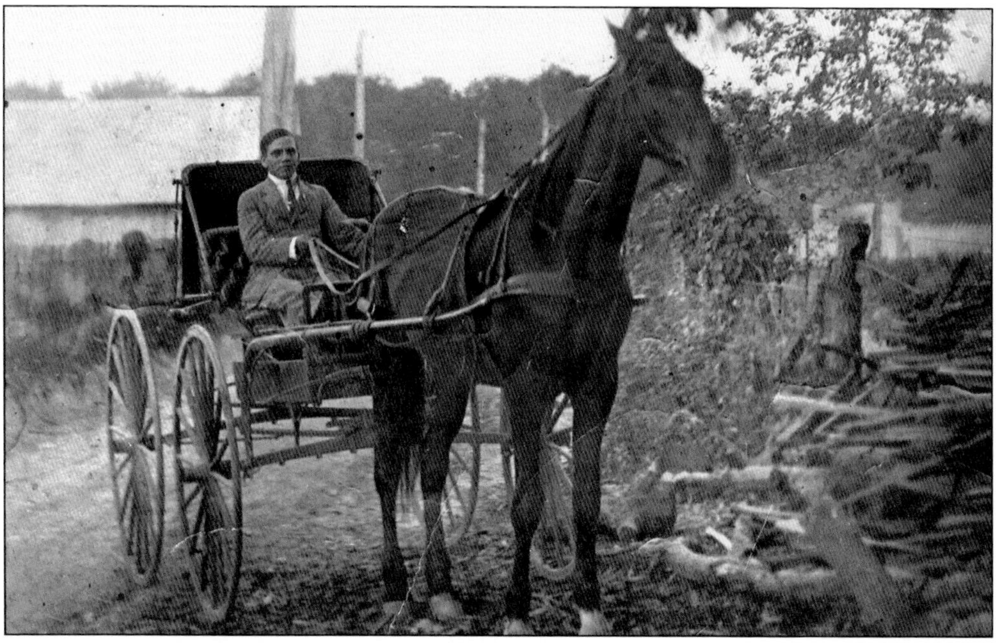

Bradley Huff, dressed in his finery, used a horse and buggy for travel when going to visit. The roads improved as the community joined together to work the roads and haul gravel from the creek beds. Each August, every man over 18 years of age was required by law to work on county roads for five days or hire a replacement to work for him.

In 1915, Howard Daniels purchased the first automobile to be driven into Granville. He always drew a crowd when he traveled through town. He operated a Model T repair shop in the former Sid Sutton blacksmith shop location.

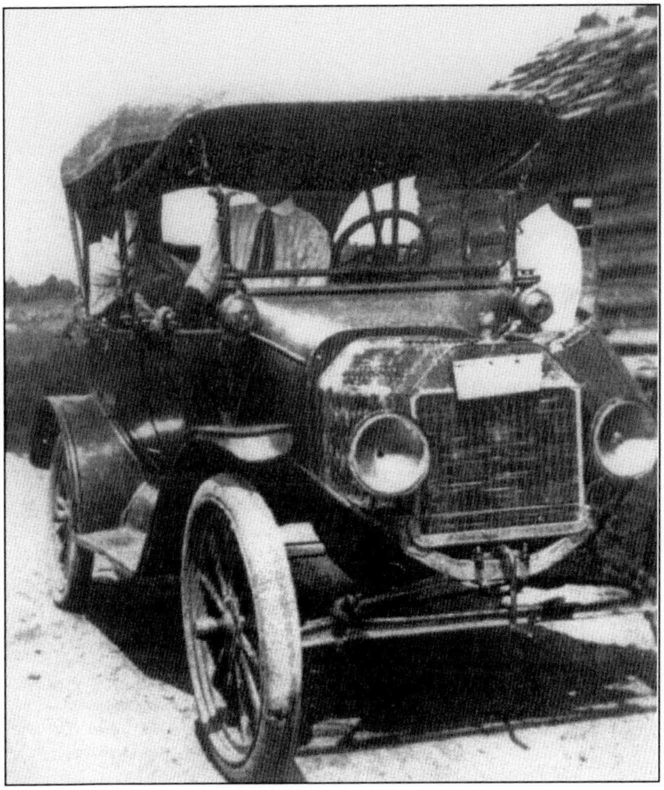

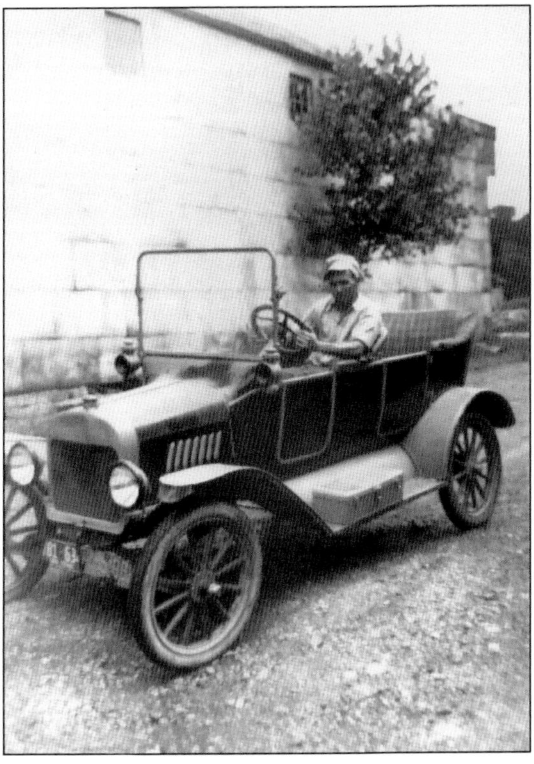

Cars were increasingly popular in the area after World War I. J.N. Carter, shown here with his 1916 Model T Ford, drove Dr. Freeman in the community parade on July 24, 1955, honoring Dr. Freeman's 50 years of medical service to the community. Ben Sutton was the original owner of this vehicle.

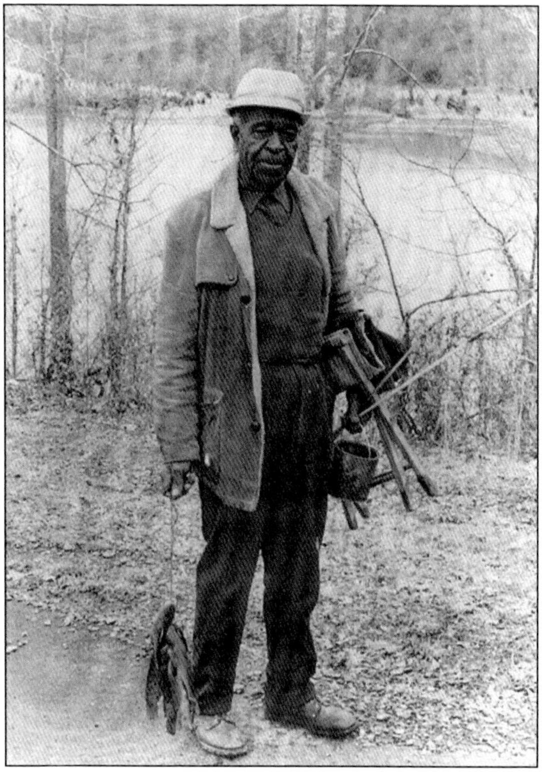

Charlie "Whit" Myers was known to be an avid fisherman on Martin's Creek. Some of the common fish found in Martin's Creek are smallmouth bass, rock bass, yellow suckers, and blue suckers. Whit lived on the Tom McKinley farm with his father, Anthony.

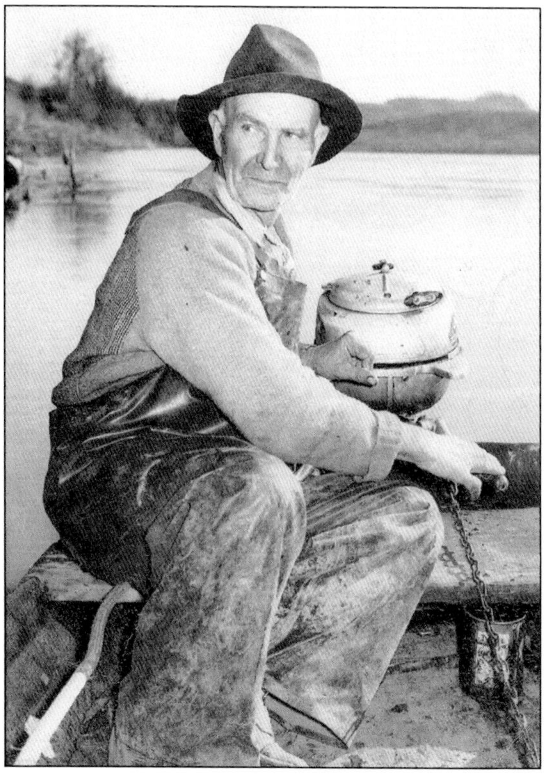

Using a flat-bottom riverboat with a small outboard engine, Robert "Bob" Lee Sams fished up and down the Cumberland River. He was considered one of the best fishermen in the area, catching catfish and sturgeon weighing from 90 to over 100 pounds.

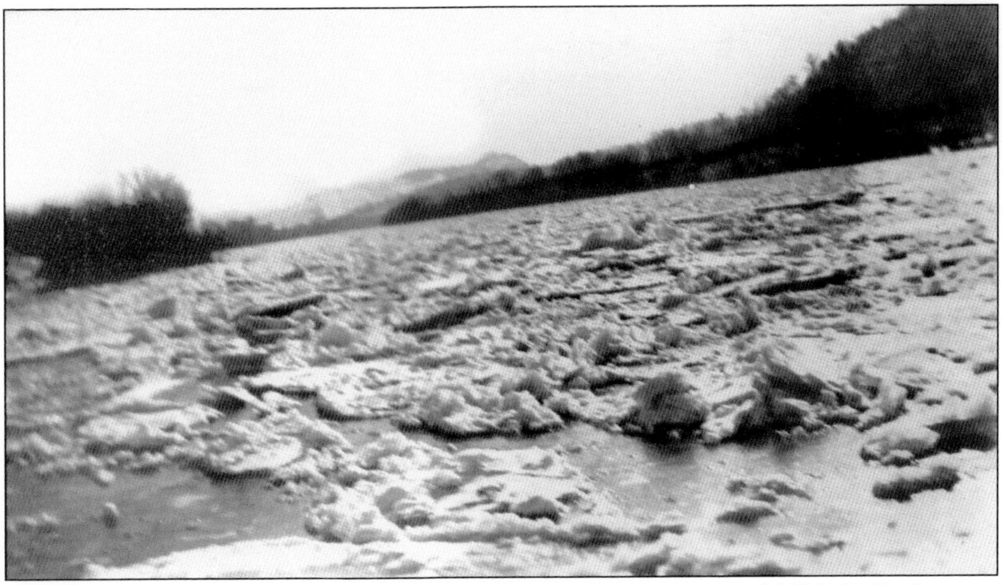

The Cumberland River has frozen over several times. In the winter of 1939–1940, the river froze solid enough that Farmer Carter actually drove his car across it, and people walked across the river instead of taking the ferry.

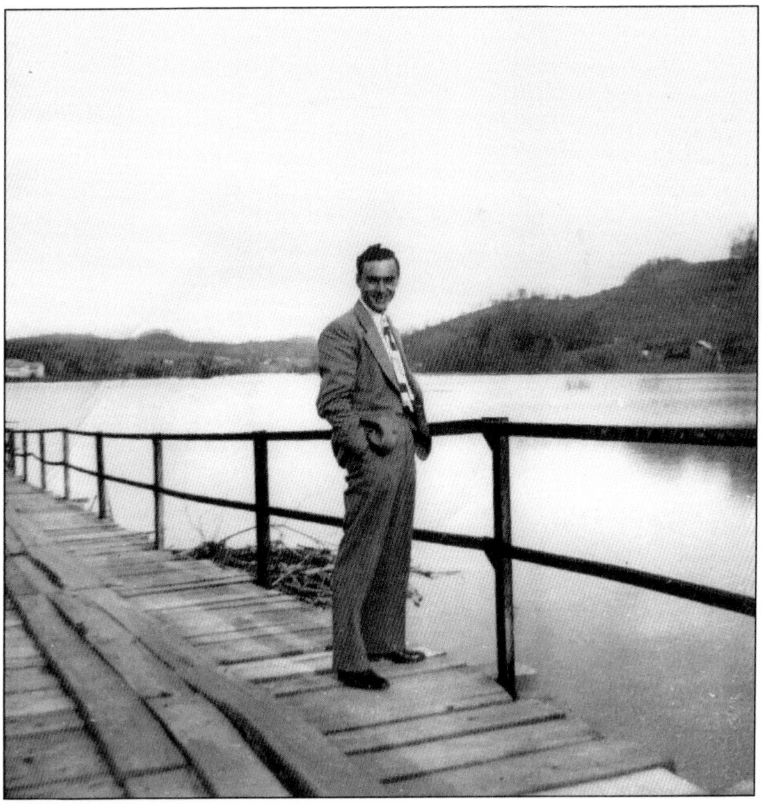

Before the Tennessee Valley Authority intervened, the Cumberland River flooded almost every spring. In this picture, Loyd Kelly Stout looks at the backwater that covers one end of the wooden bridge, making travel impossible without a canoe.

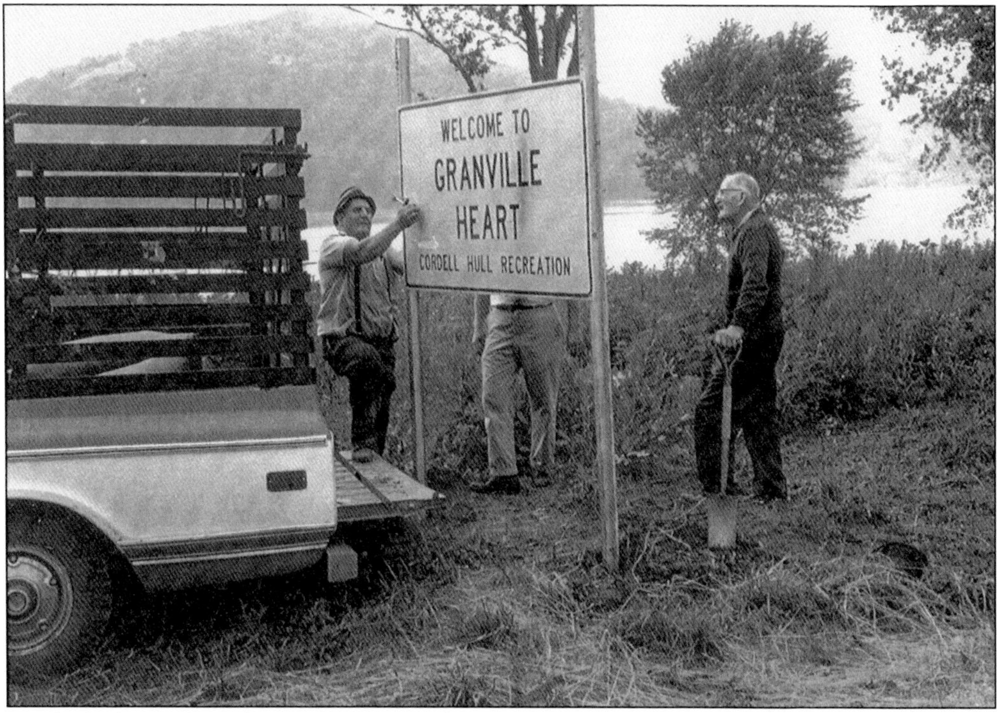

On the highway through town, Everett Halfacre, Hooper Brown, and Cecil Williamson installed a sign reading "Granville, the Heart of Cordell Hull Recreation" after the lake was impounded.

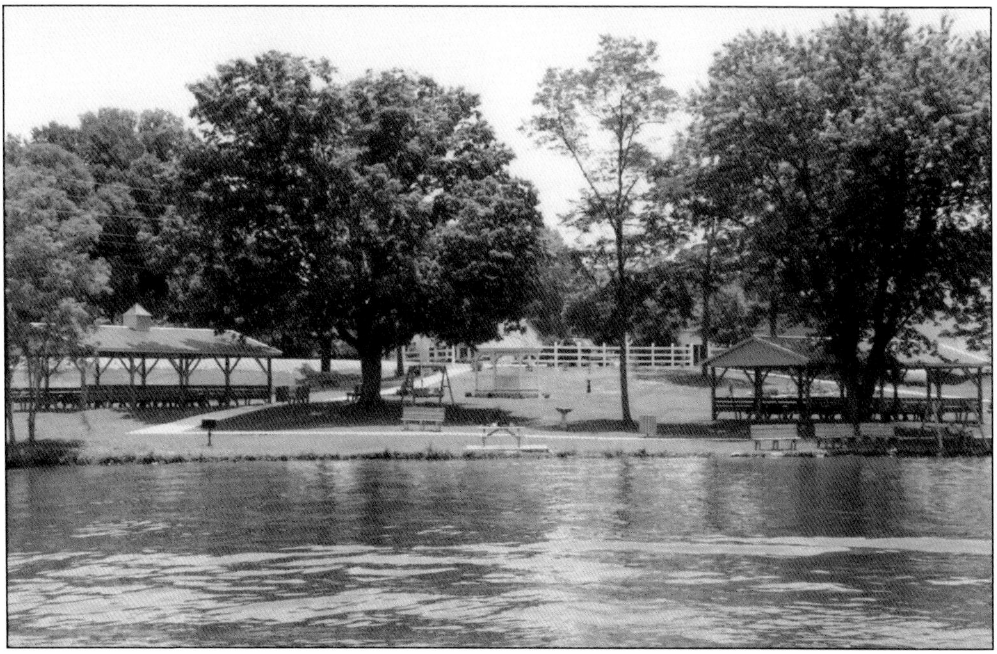
The Granville Veterans Park was dedicated on May 23, 1998, on the banks of the Cumberland River and Martin's Creek, close to the original town spring. The park was built as a result of donations and grants sponsored by the Granville Community Club, which meets monthly today.

Two

LIVING OFF THE LAND

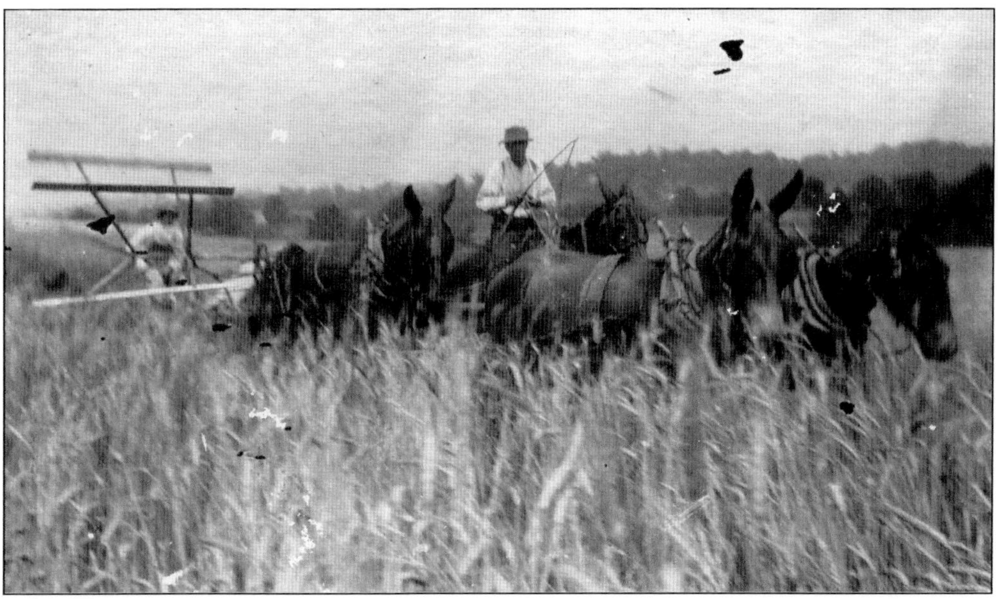

Agriculture was the mainstay of the Granville community for many years. The fertile bottomland enabled farmers to harvest many crops. Joseph R. Carver is shown binding wheat with horse-drawn equipment in this 1910 photograph.

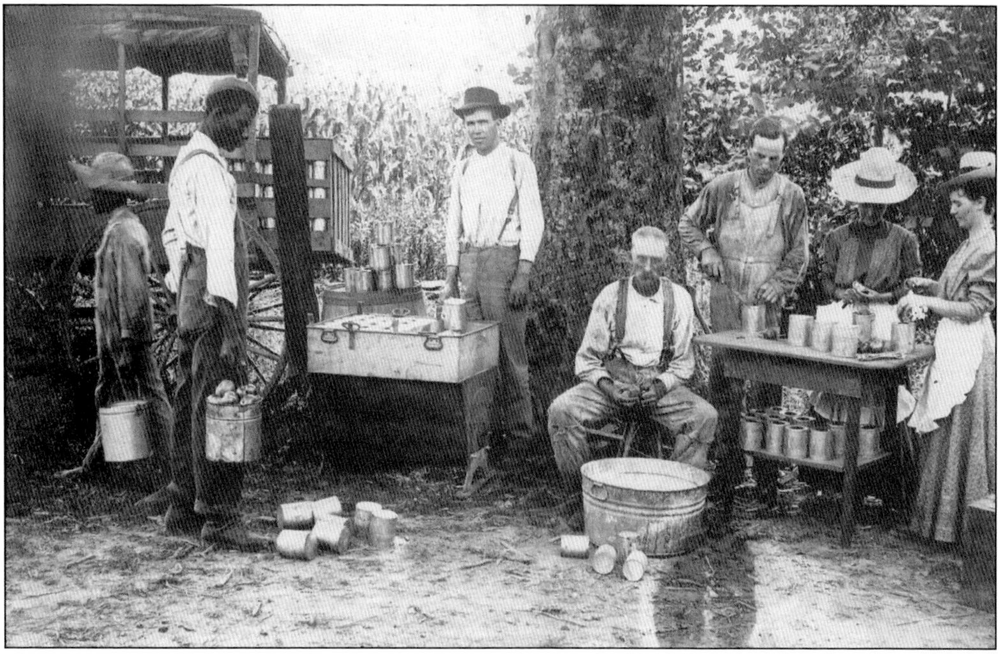

Most farms were family affairs with everyone participating when harvest time arrived. Canning tomatoes at the Carver Farm around 1910 are the family and friends shown here. From left to right are Andress Williamson, Jim Pharris, Joseph Carver, Roy Willoughby, Noah Fox, Nellie Myers Fox, and Lillie Fox Carver.

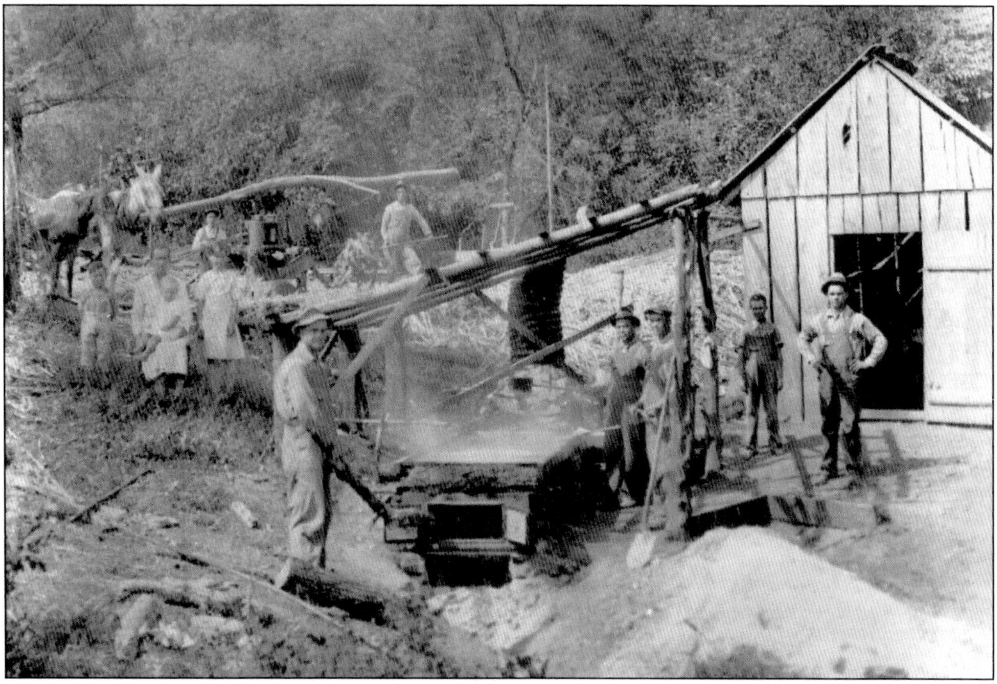

The Herman Woodard family ran a molasses mill for 22 years in the Enigma community to serve Granville and the surrounding areas. This photograph shows family members at the mill using sugar cane in the molasses-making process.

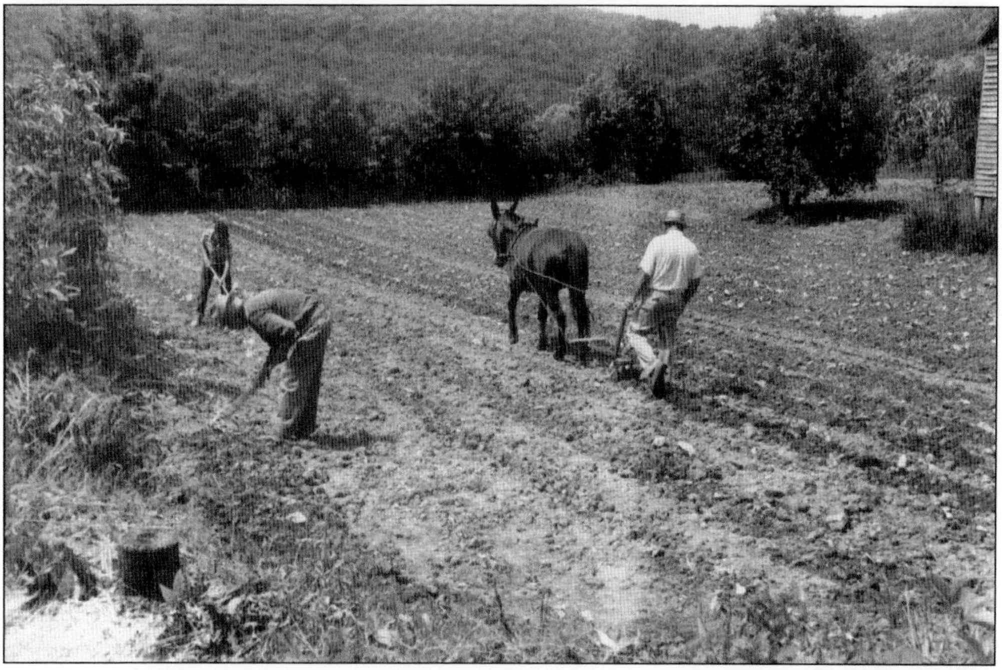

Few farmers in the area owned tractors before World War I. Clyde Eller used a plow pulled by a mule to cultivate his tobacco base as Ress Eller worked the dirt with a hoe.

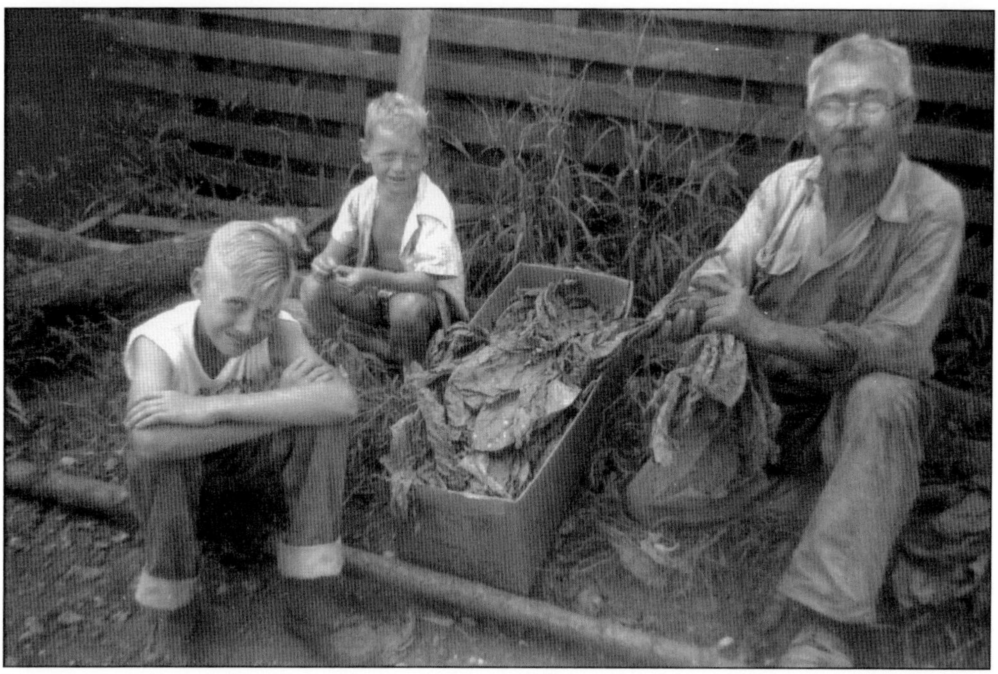

Tobacco was the number one cash crop in the area for most of the 20th century. Lee Carter is working his tobacco as youngsters look on in this picture.

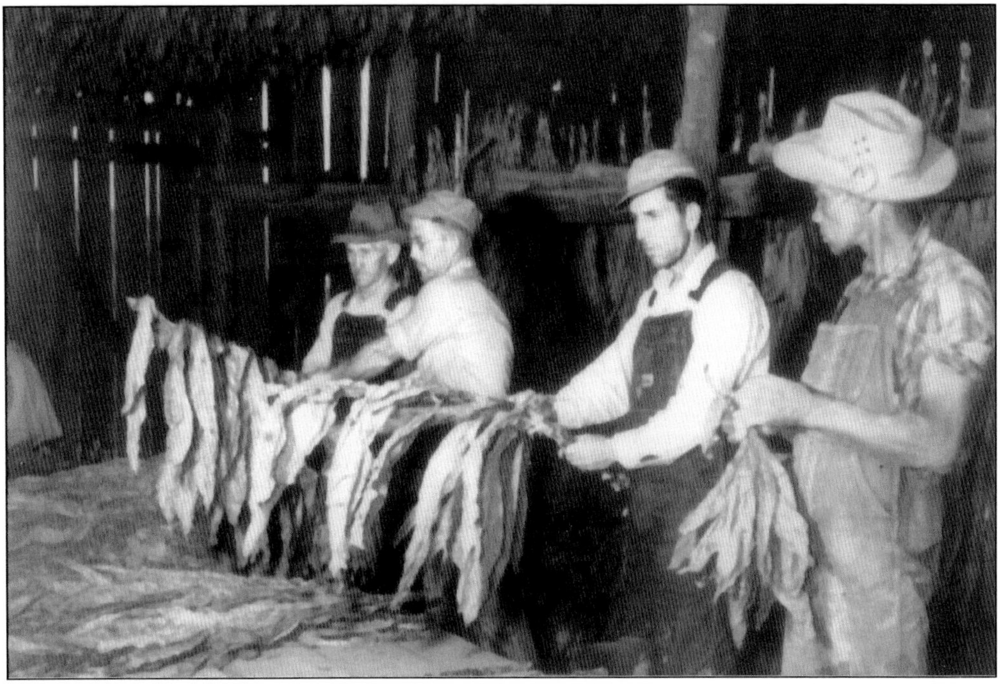

Tobacco was stripped by removing the leaves by hand. This photo from the Carver farm shows, from left to right, John Tack Carter, Albert Gillespie, Charles Carter, and Zonie Williamson stripping tobacco and tying the leaves into sections called hands.

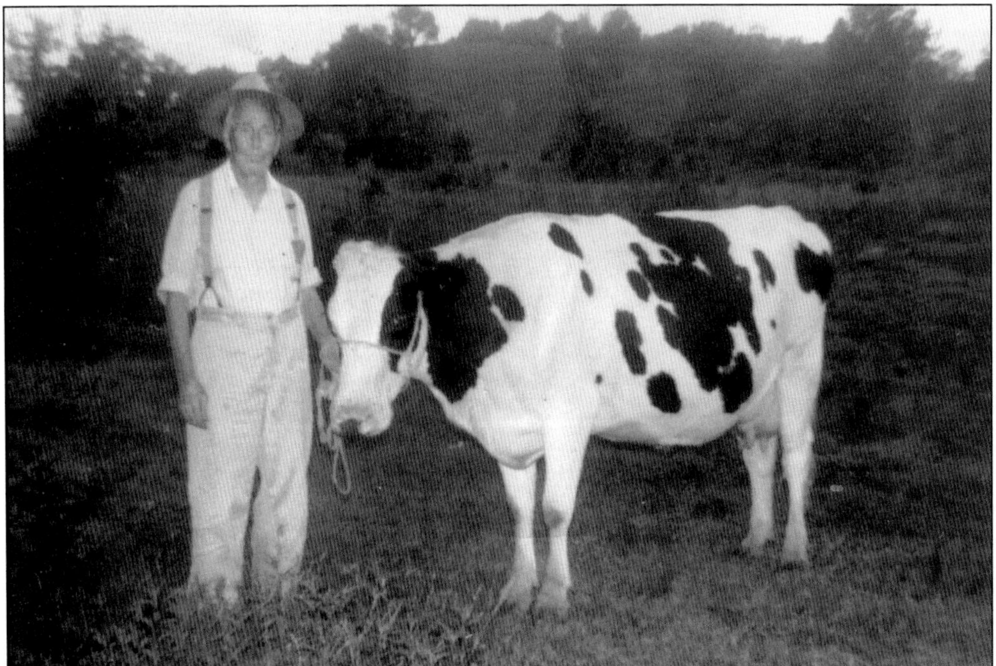

Ress Eller is seen leading his milk cow through the pasture in this picture. Before refrigeration, families depended upon cows to supply milk, butter, and cream. Often, neighbors would barter goods and services for fresh milk.

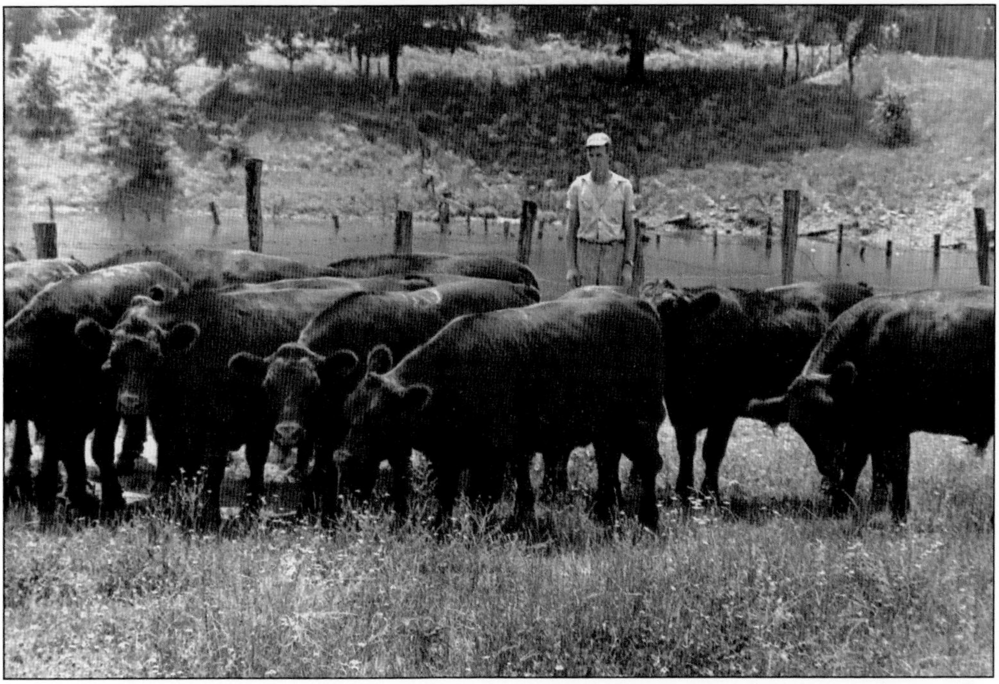

Beef cattle were the second largest cash crop in Middle Tennessee. This "car lot" of cattle, raised by Joe Moore, is shown ready to go to market. Angus, Herefords, and Black Baldies were popular cattle brands raised here for beef. Milk farmers often raised Jerseys and Holsteins, along with a few Red Durham cattle.

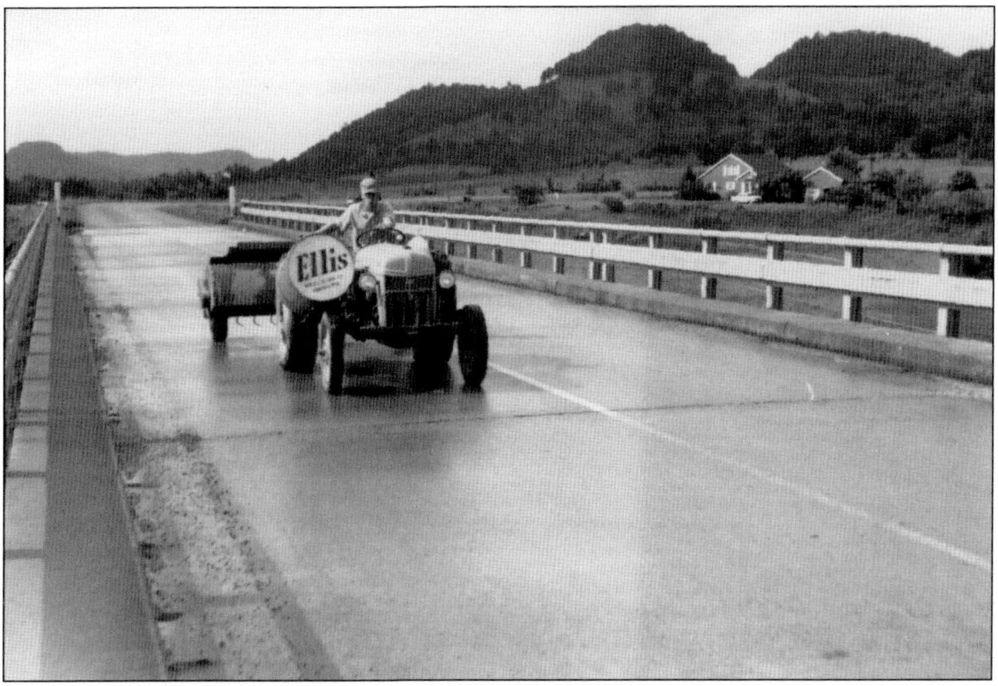

Ralph Maddux, pictured on his Ford tractor with an Ellis tobacco setter and pulling a hay baler, crosses the Granville bridge, with the Dowell home in the background.

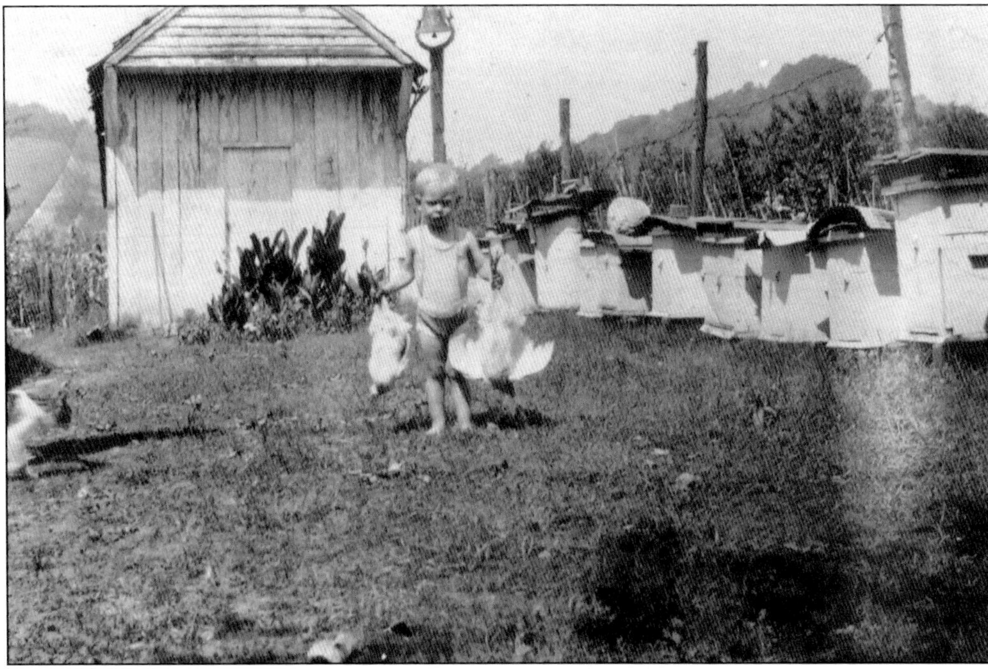

Earl Grisham holds two fryers ready to pluck and cook for dinner. Farmers raised most of their own food. Beehives can be seen in the background on the right.

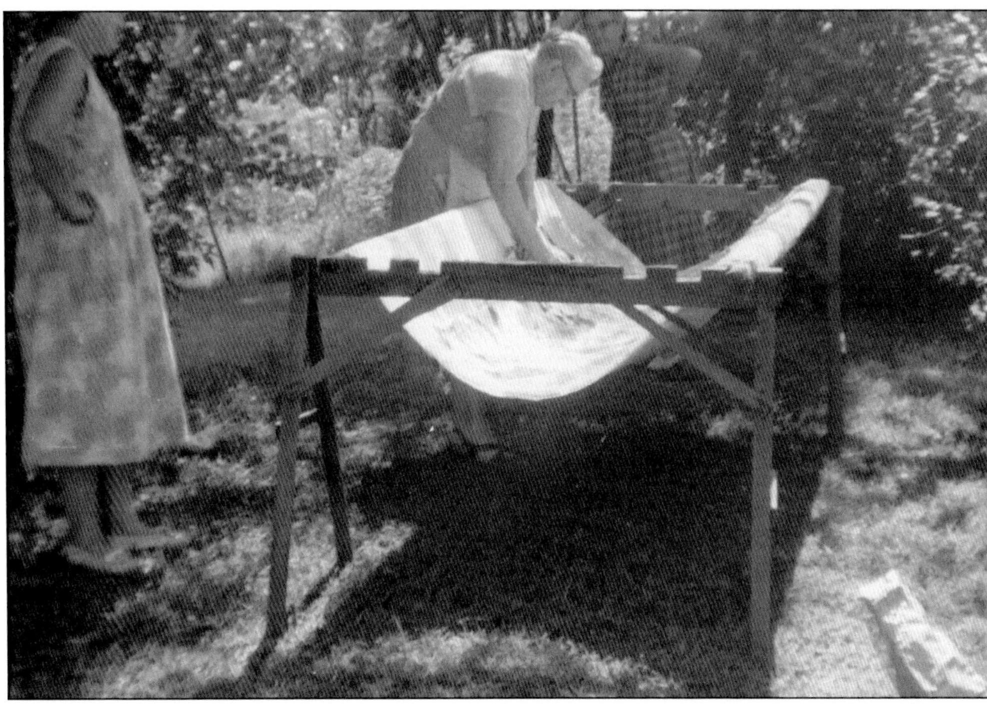

As a way to preserve fruit, ladies would lay apples out to dry on a quilt or cloth hung between two sawhorses. Metal roofs were also used for drying food. Mrs. Snowie Fields is shown laying out the apples in this photograph.

Joe Moore of Granville was named the Star Farmer of America in 1955 by the Future Farmers of America. A reporter from *Time* magazine came and spent a week with Moore on his farm. He was one of only two farmers to ever grace the cover of *Time*. He also appeared on the Arthur Godfrey show.

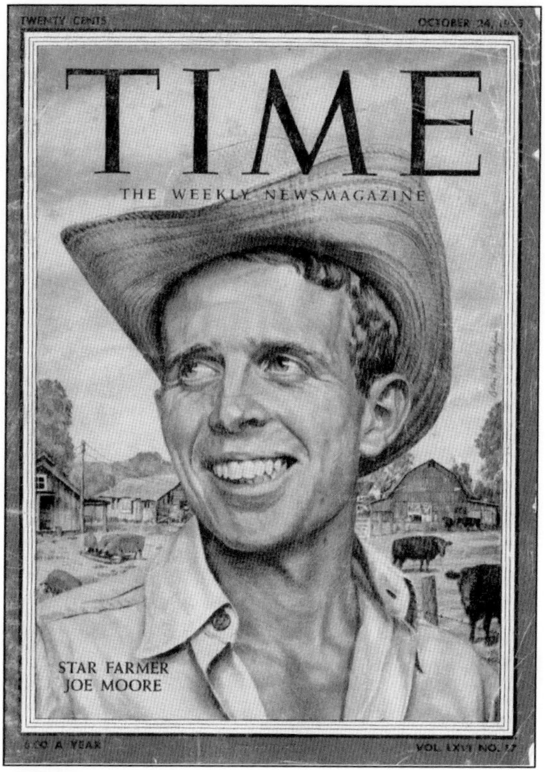

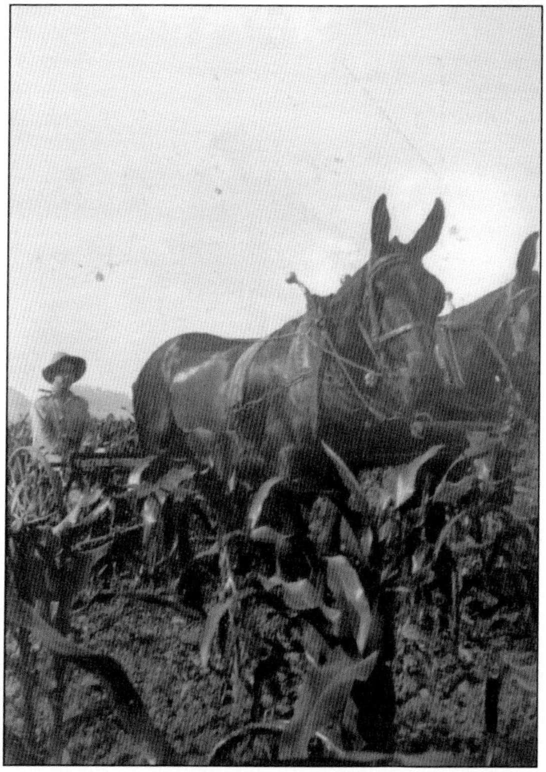

Across the river from Granville, Harrison H. Woodard is shown riding a cultivator on the Hugh Philpot place in 1943. Corn was an important source of food for people as well as farm animals.

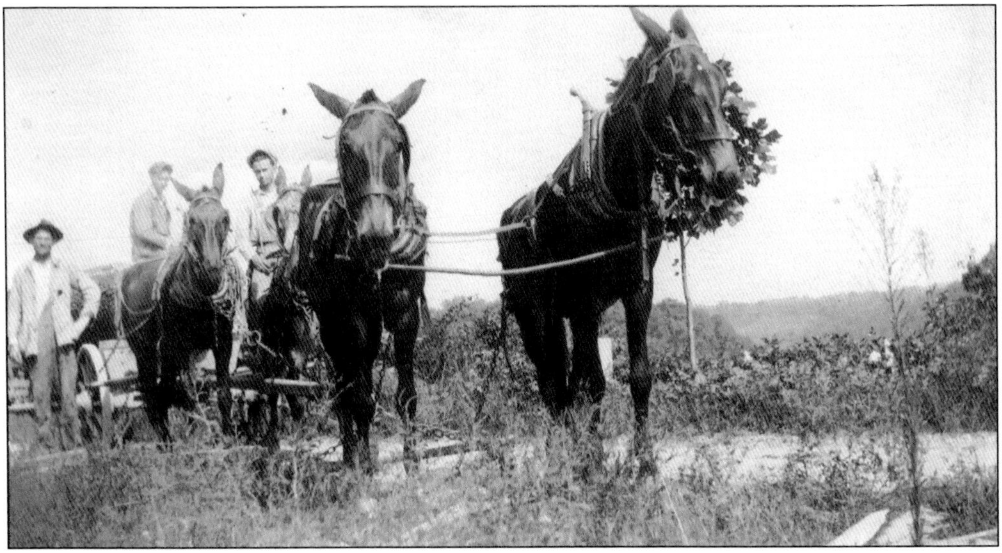

This picture shows Sid Ragland with his log wagon and mules as his sons, Savage and Lester Ragland, help out.

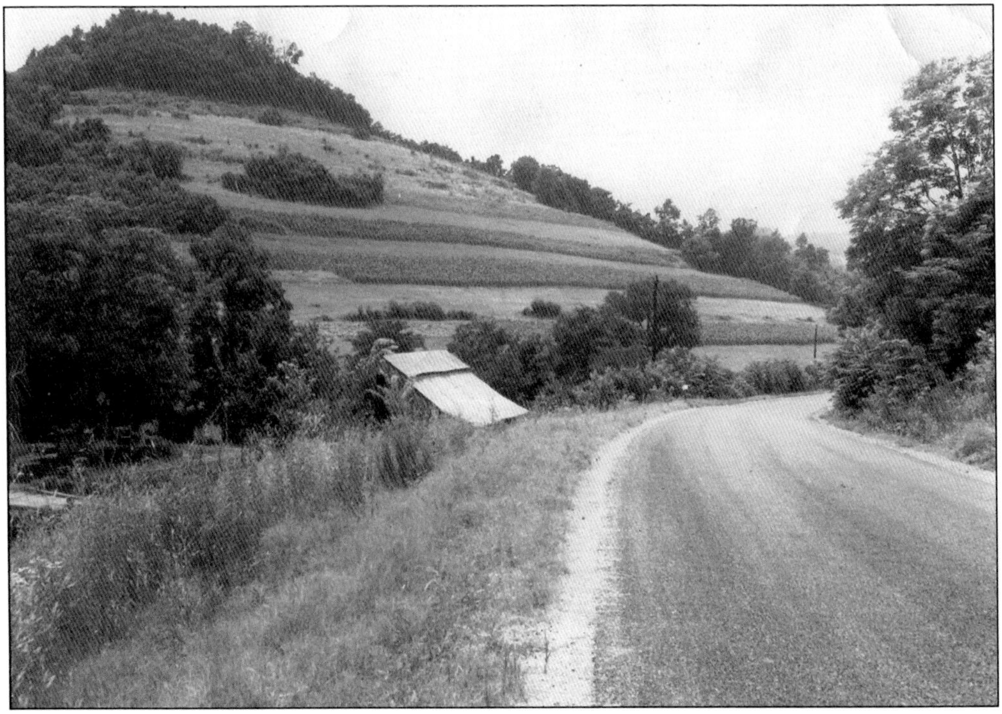

Henry Harris participated in the Soil Conservation strip crop program. This Soil Conservation photo, taken on July 5, 1949, features the Harris farm near Liberty.

Three

FOUNDATION OF THE COMMUNITY

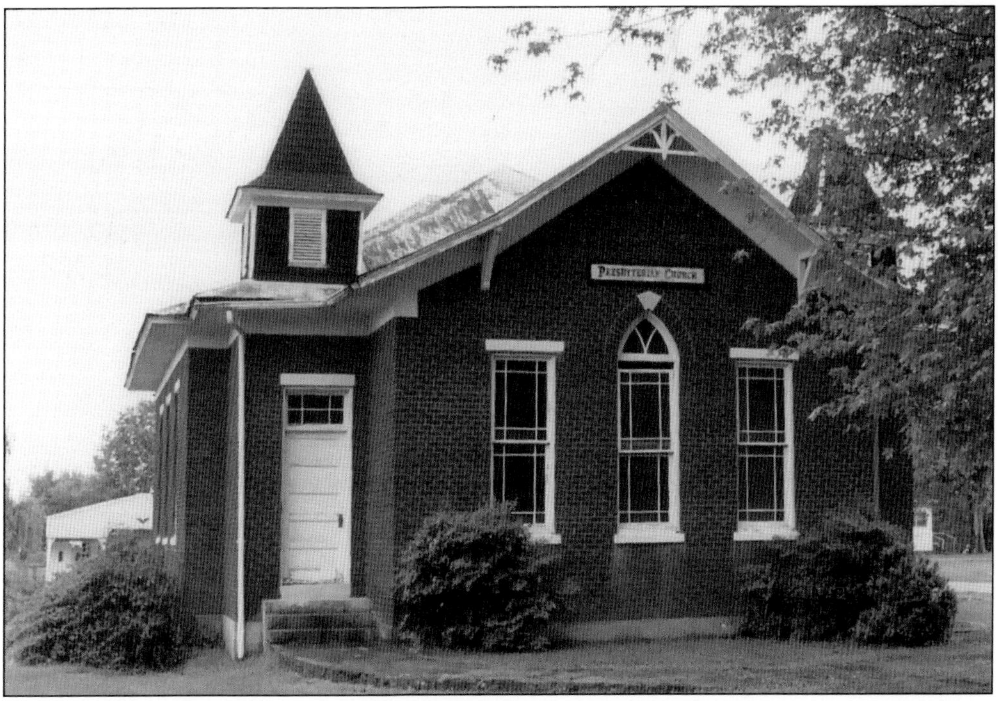

Early settlers to this area worshiped as Presbyterians. The first log church was the Granville Presbyterian Church, built in the early 1800s. That building was replaced with a frame building in 1890 and with this brick building in 1924. The church closed in 1997.

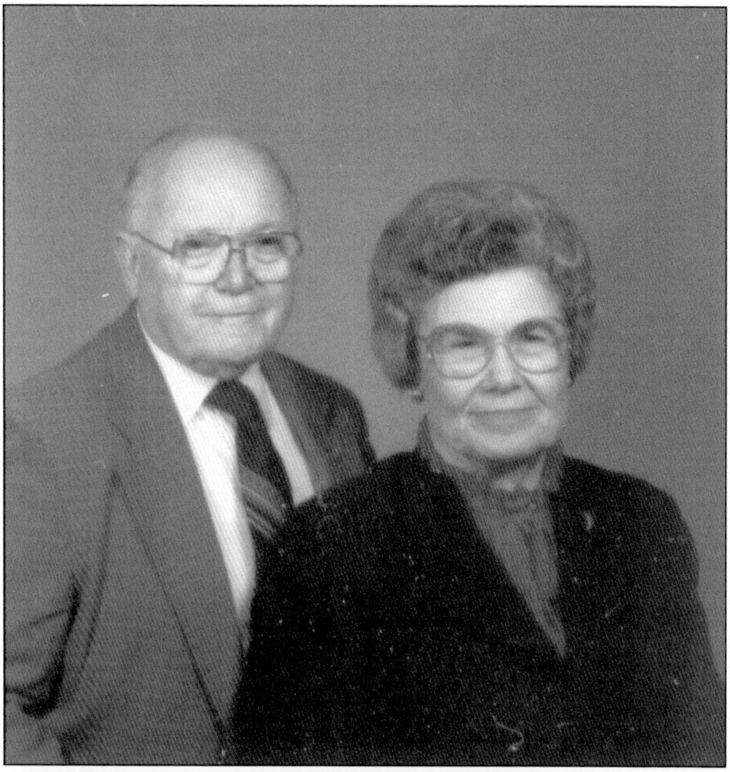

Brother Andrews J. Albert—with his wife, Inez, at his side—served the Granville Presbyterian Church for almost 40 years, preaching one Sunday a month. He also served rural churches in Double Springs, Bloomington Springs, and Union Grove. He was noted for helping churches in the Upper Cumberland area with Sunday schools and vacation Bible schools and was said to have been a blessing to all in the Granville community.

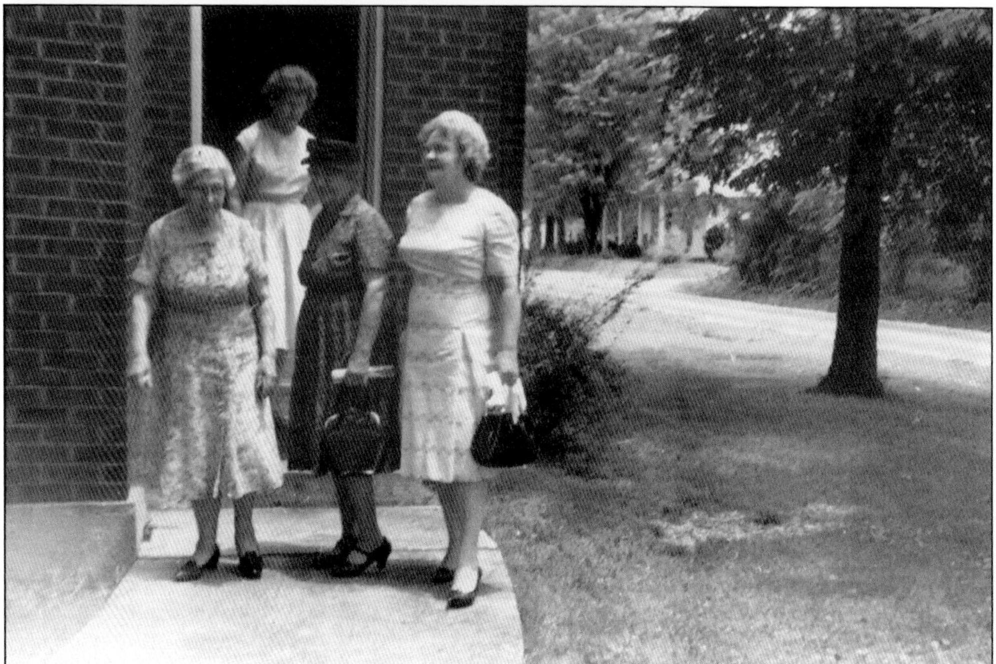

In this picture, from left to right, Minnie Flatt, Lennie Fields, Lola Eller, and Melissa Bailey are shown leaving the Granville Presbyterian Church. Small churches had Sunday school each week, with sermons preached by traveling ministers every other Sunday.

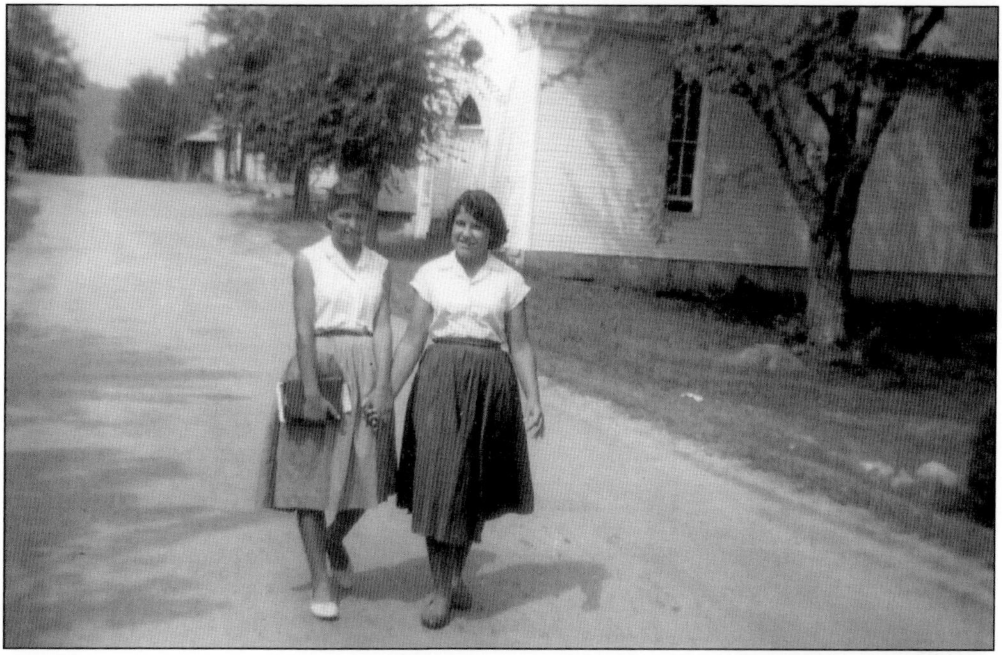

The Granville Church of Christ building, seen in the background behind Tennie and Betty Petty, was constructed in 1873. It was located across from the field from the Presbyterian Church and two doors down from the Methodist Church on Clover Street. In 1912, the Granville Private School was operated in this building by Dr. B.L. Simmons. The church stopped worshiping here in June 1987, and the building now houses the Granville Museum.

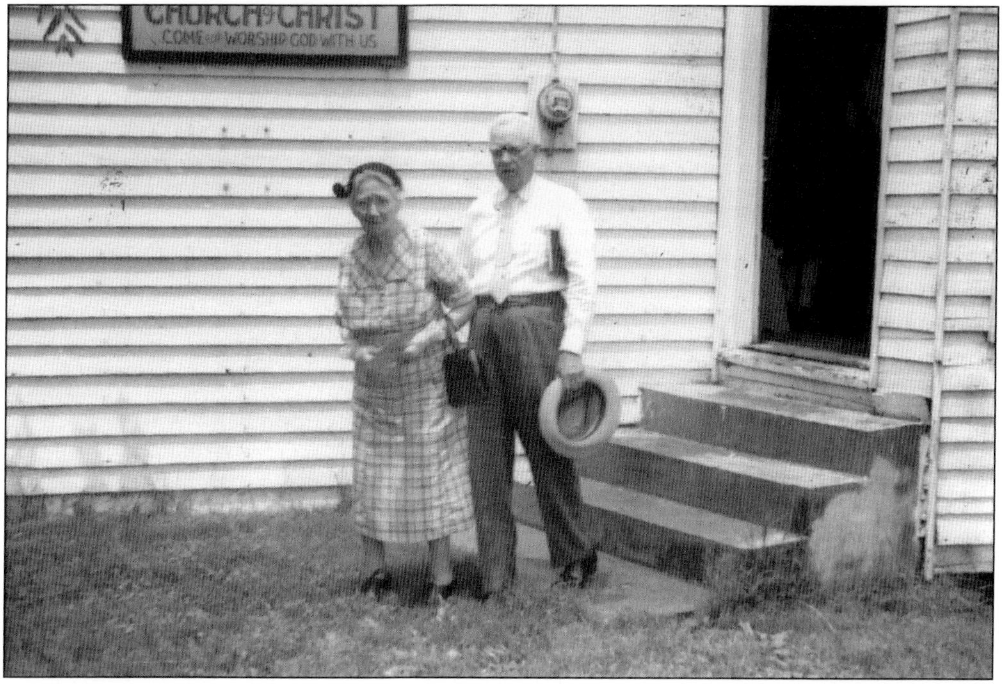

Arthur Willoughby, a local banker and church leader, is shown here assisting his mother, Maude Byrne Willoughby, from the original Granville Church of Christ building.

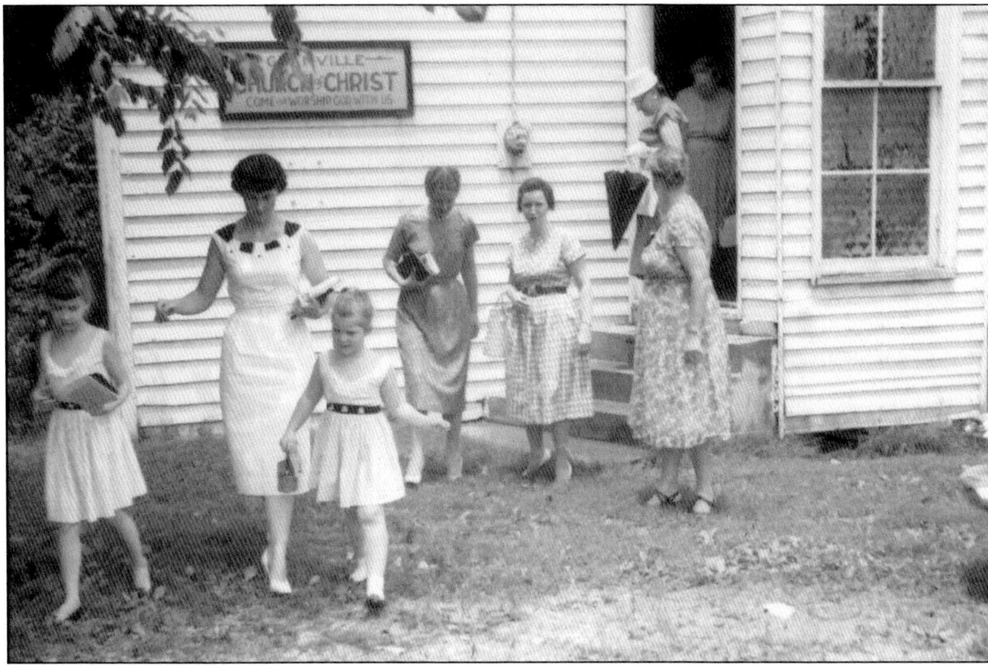

Shown from left to right, Carolyn, Mildred, and Jennie Carter lead the exit from church services while Tootie Willoughby, Sue Halfacre, Willie Clark, and Mrs. Bee Chaffin (with umbrella) follow. Hallie Philpot is shown in the doorway.

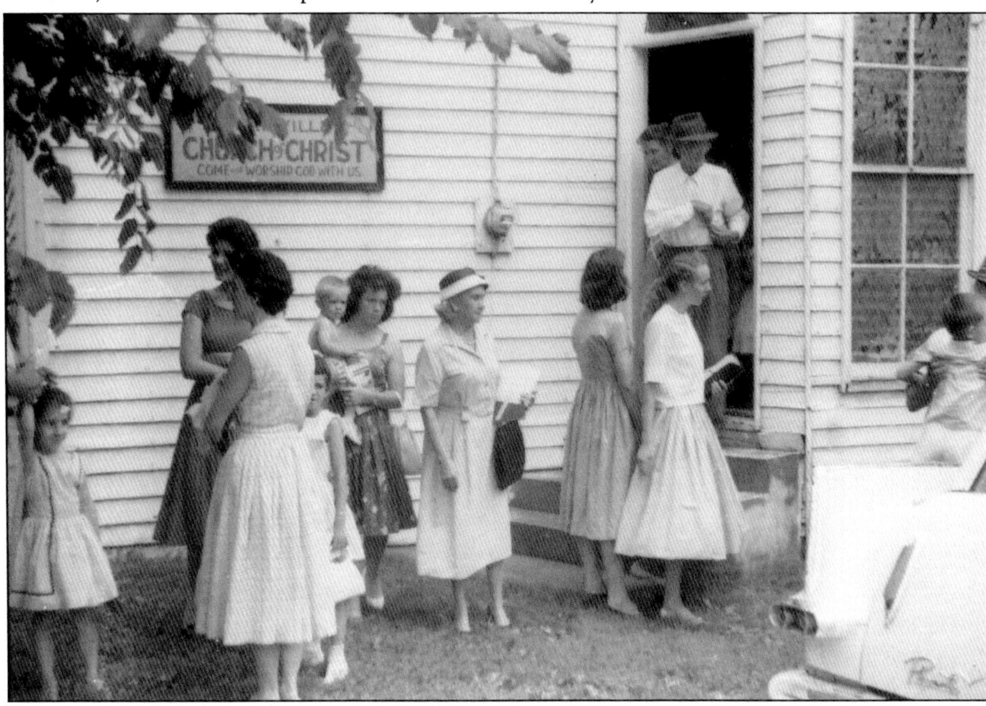

After services at the Granville Church of Christ, Mary Ann Halfacre, Kerry Fields, Kay Fields, Mrs. Lynch (in hat), Margaret Tayse, Anna Tayse, and Milton "Lee" Tayse can be seen visiting in this picture from the 1950s.

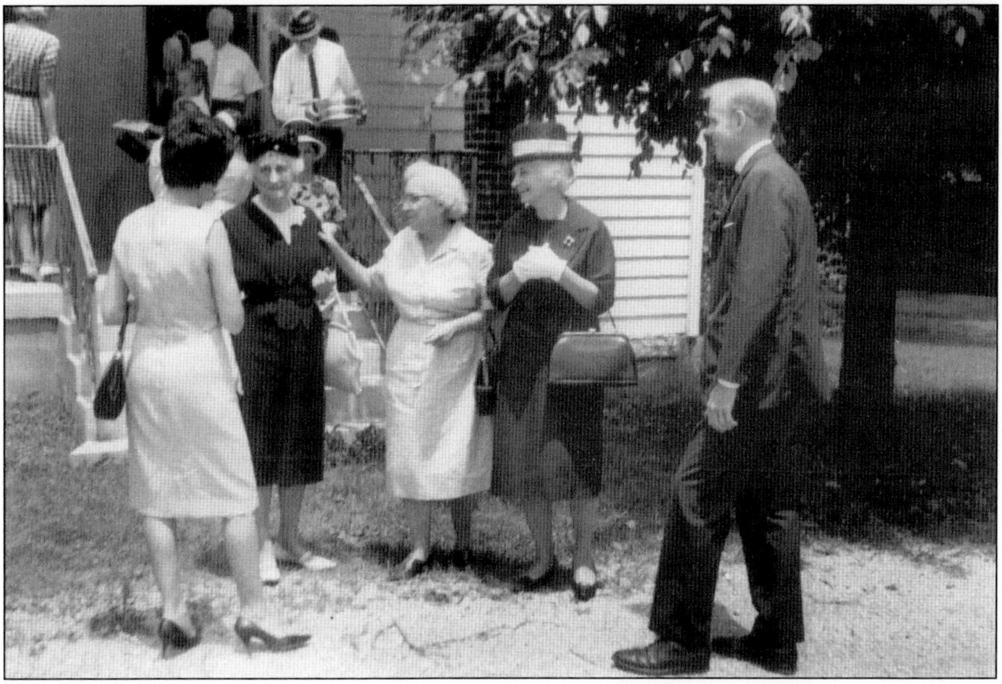

The remodeled front of the Granville Church of Christ building can be seen in the background of this photo showing, from left to right in front, Faye Halfacre, Mrs. J.W. Jellicourse, Georgia Halfacre, Mrs. Walter Dowell, and unidentified. Bee Halfacre is seen carrying the communion from the building.

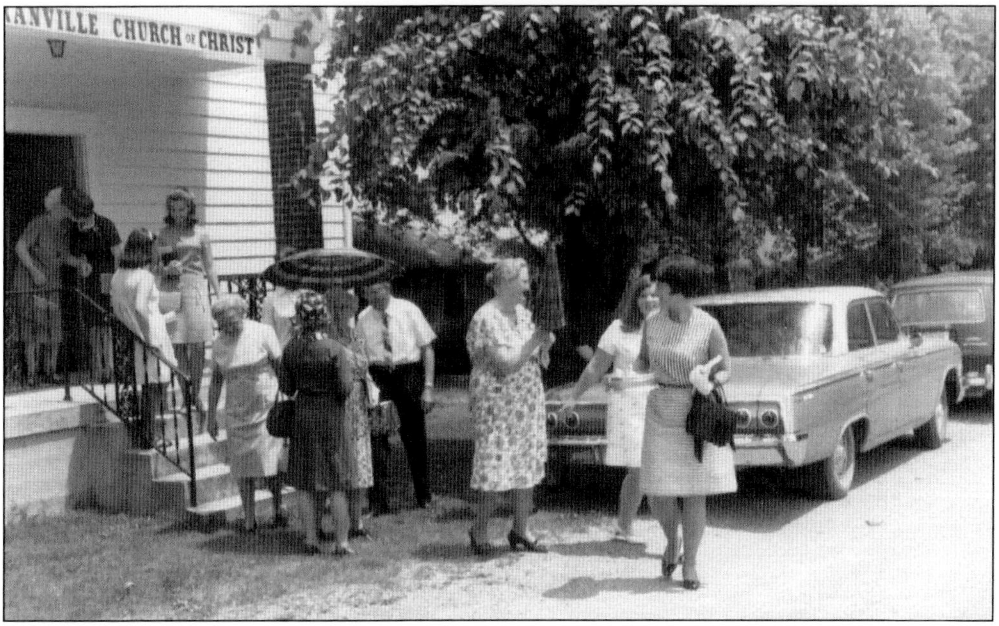

Coming down the steps after a morning service at the Granville Church of Christ are, from left to right, Carolyn Carter, Mary Ann Halfacre, Jennie Huff, Georgia Halfacre, two unidentified, Willie Clark, Jennie Carter, and Mildred Carter. Umbrellas were carried to shield the walkers from the noonday sun.

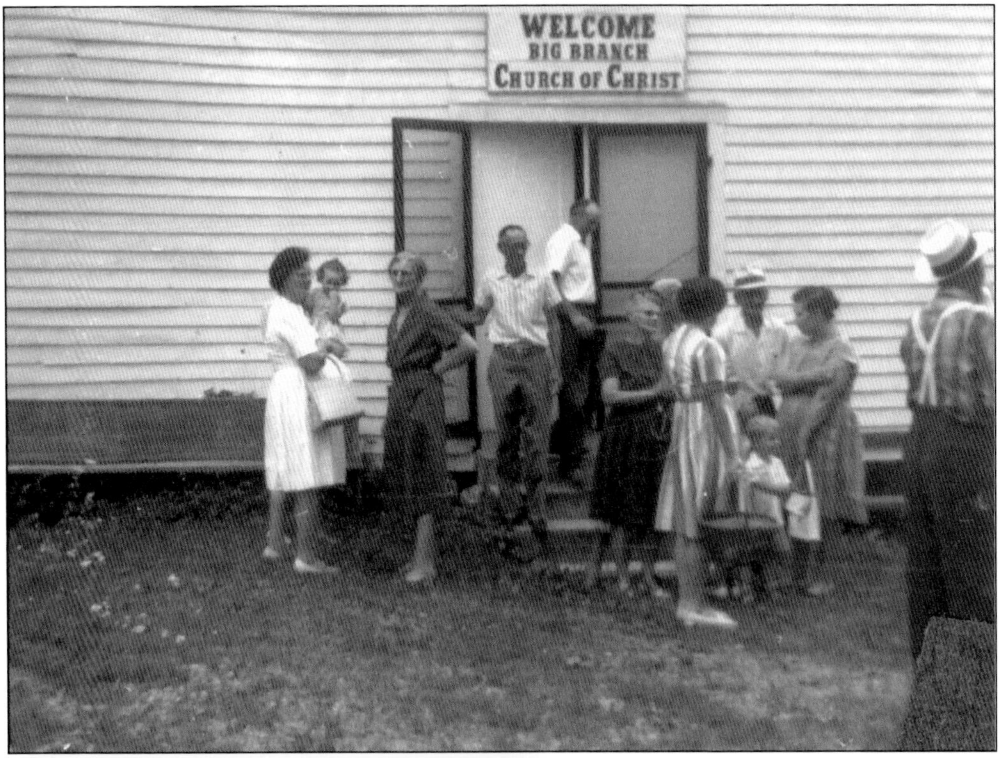

The Big Branch Church of Christ closed on April 18, 2004. The memories are lasting, and the lives affected are many. Pictured here, from left to right, are Mary Collier holding Lisa Huff, Vennie Huff, Dave Guess, Davy Collier, Dorie Frizzell, Mary Tayse, Nell Guess, Floyd Anderson, Vola Huff, and G.W. (George) Guess.

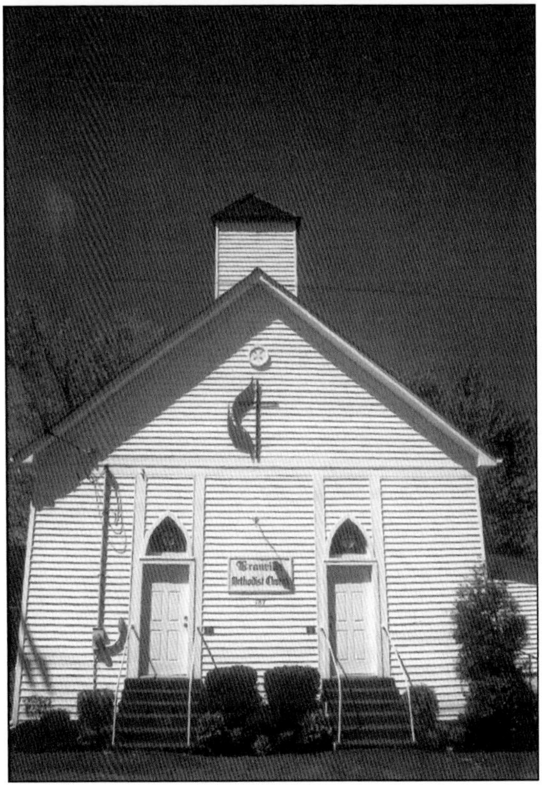

The first congregation of the United Methodist Church was organized in Granville in 1840. Their first building was located two blocks from the present building, which was built in 1896. In 1954, Sunday school rooms were added. The church has been remodeled several times over the years and is still holding services regularly today.

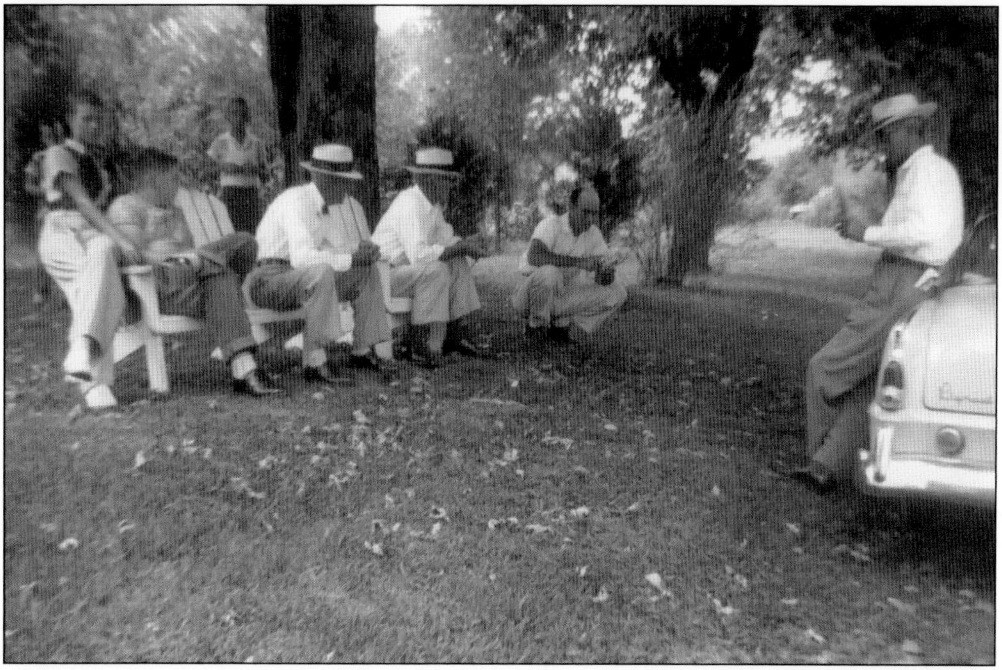

After services, the gentlemen gathered to talk apart from the womenfolk. This group includes, from left to right, Paul Huff, Junior Harris, Tom McKinley, Bob Hargis, Ralph Maddux, Buddy Myers (beside tree), and Cecil Harris (leaning on the car).

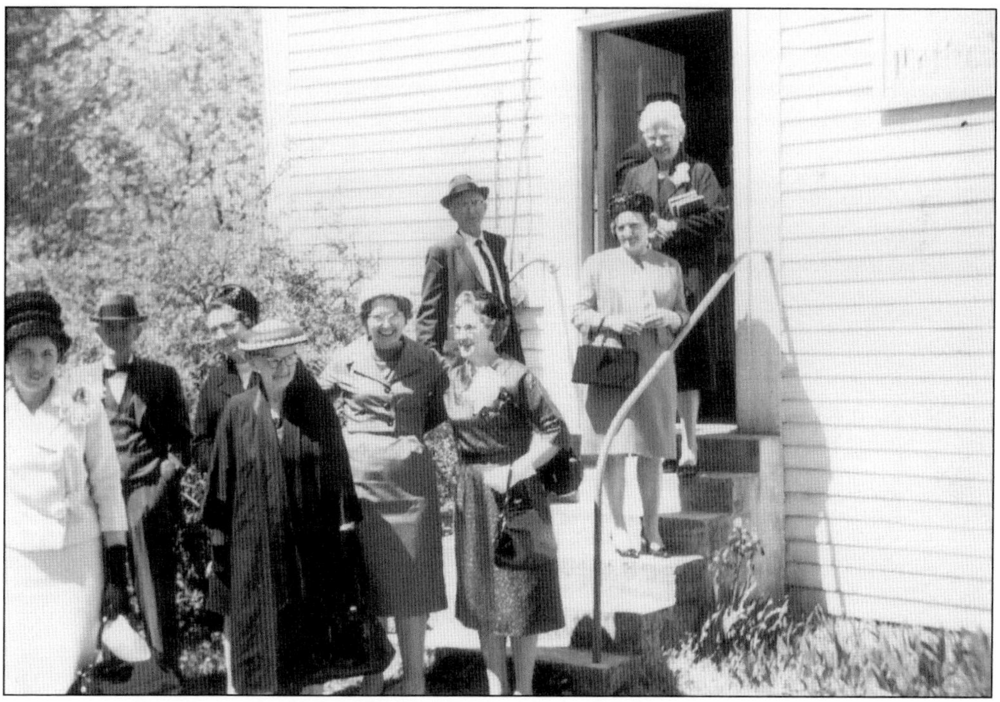

Leaving an Easter service at the Methodist church in the early 1960s are, from left to right, Tommie Clemons, Tom McKinley, Hattie Myers, Lois Cornwell, Lennie Fields, Hallie Mai Clemons, Jimmie Clemons, Ruth Brown, and Mrs. Cliff King.

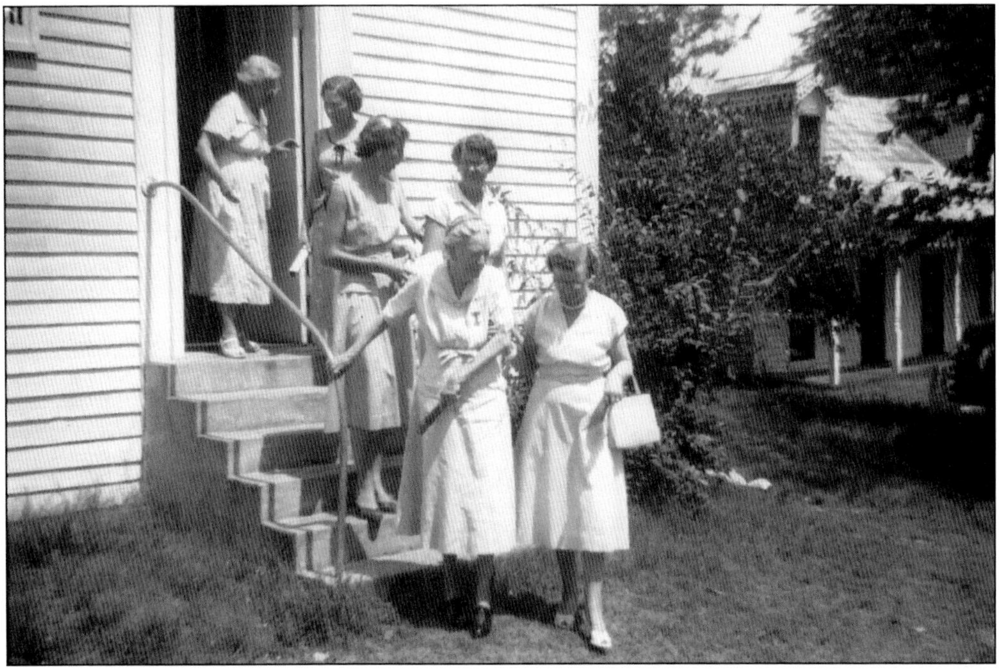

Pictured, from left to right, are Lethie Clemons, Louise Ragland, Helen Reynolds, Lennie Fields, Della Holleman, and Mable Dowell leaving Granville Methodist Church. Mrs. Reynolds and Mrs. Fields were previously members of the Granville Baptist Church, which was organized in 1939 next to the bank. The church closed in the late 1950's, and members joined other local churches.

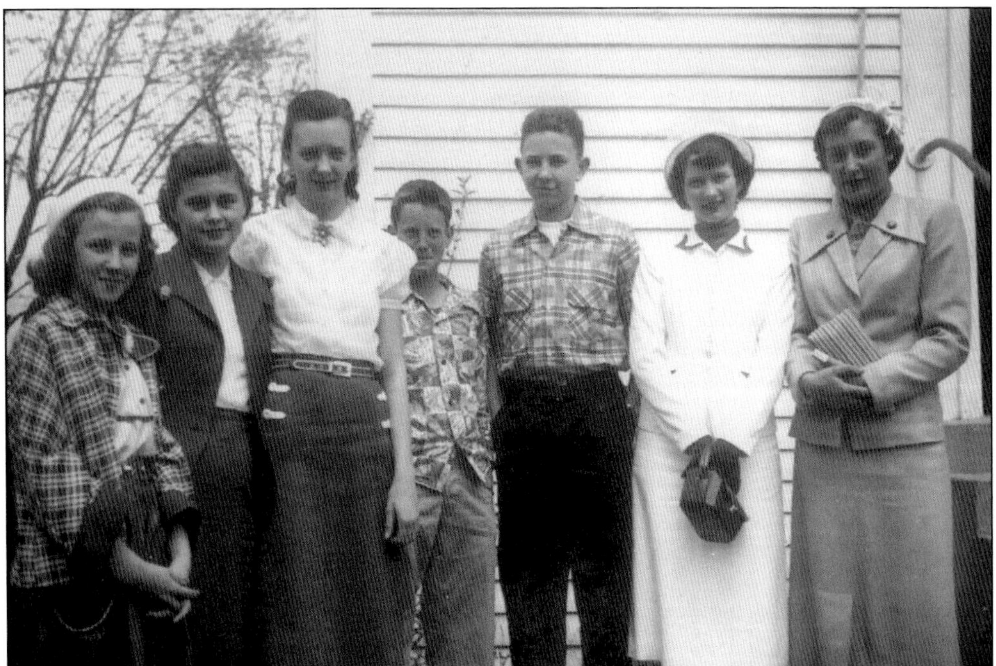

This group attending the Granville Methodist Church is, from left to right, Sandra Jo Pharris, ? Vickers, Louise Duke, Eugene Duke, Buddy Brown, Ann Huff, and Shirley Jean Carter.

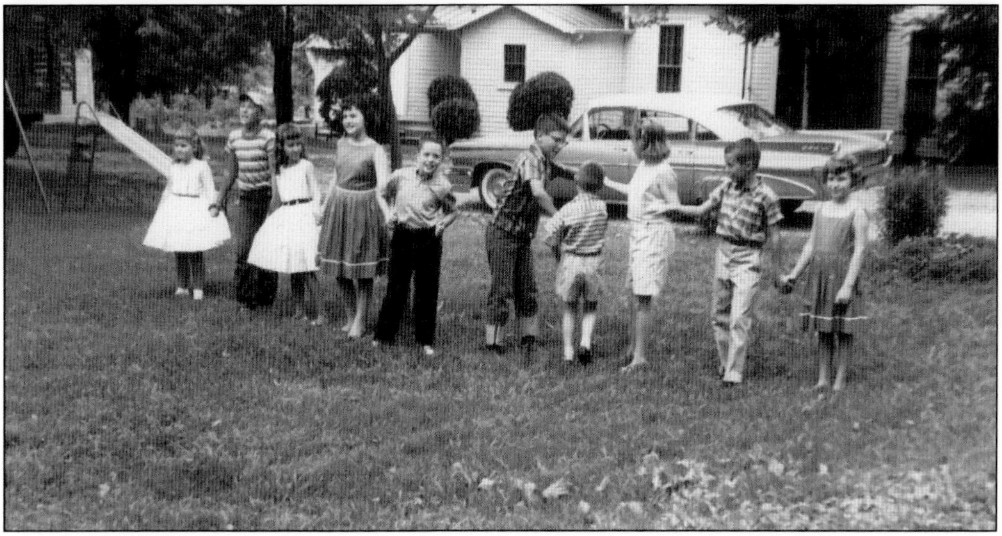

During Granville Methodist Church's Vacation Bible School, the children gathered on the lawn to play games. Shown in this photograph from the 1960s are, from left to right, Jeanie Carter, Marion Halfacre, Carolyn Carter, Teresa Halfacre, Randall Clemons, Pat Reynolds, Mike Reynolds, Linda Brown, Bruce Carter, and Sarah Halfacre.

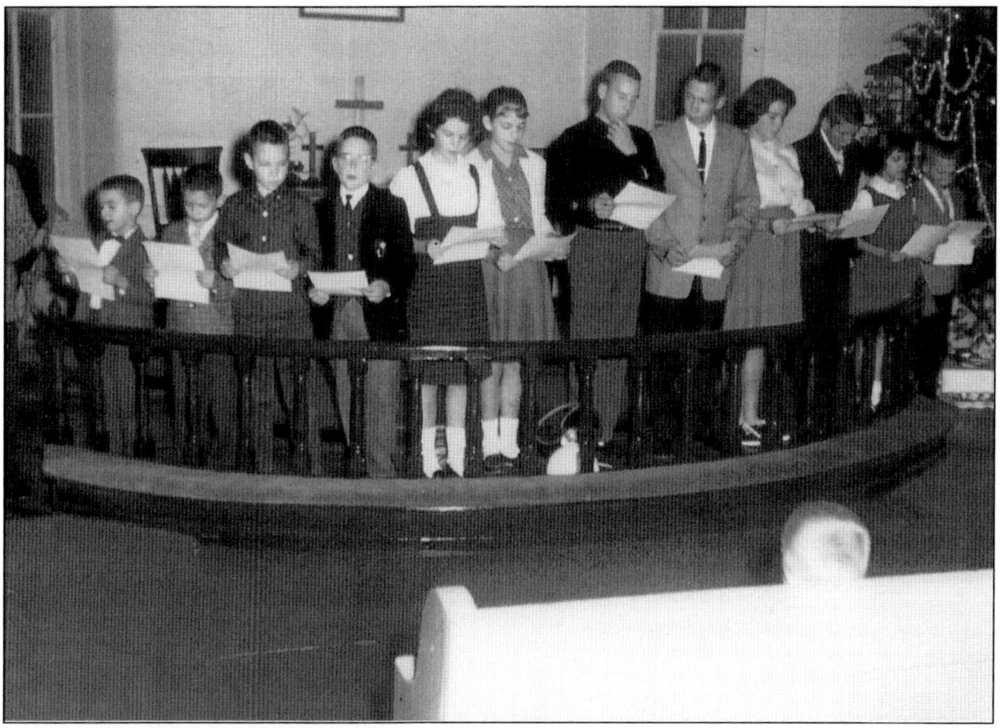

In the early 1960s, a Christmas program was performed at the Granville Methodist Church by, from left to right, James Lee Wright, Mike Reynolds, Dale Brown, Randall Clemons, Linda Brown, Martha Sue Maddux, Marion Halfacre, Larry Montgomery, Nancy Maddux, Steve Ragland, Kay Fields, and David Eller.

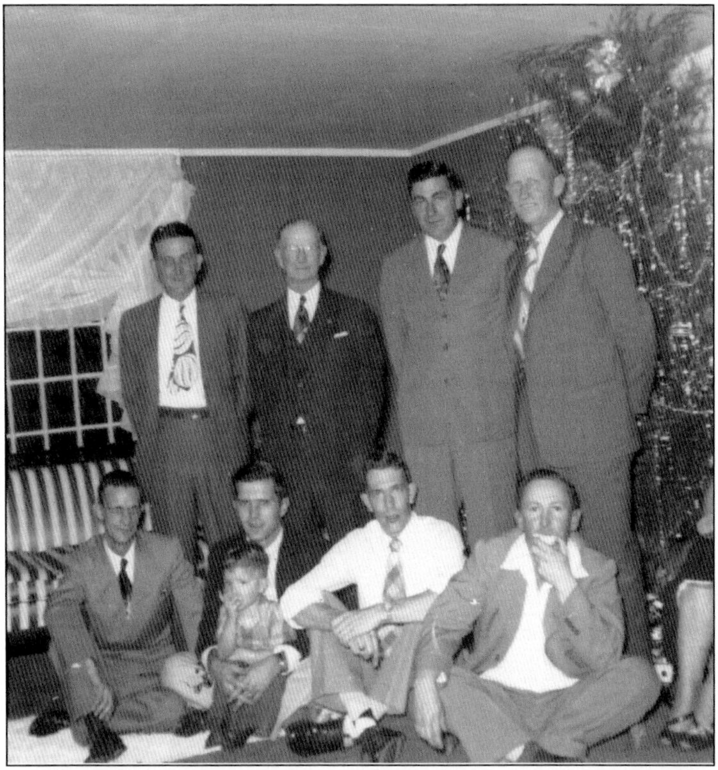

Ruth Huff hosted her church friends for a Christmas party in 1952. The gentlemen attending were, from left to right, (seated) Brother Walter Schaerer, Arnold Reynolds holding Pat, Edward Clemons, and Hugh Lee Pharris; (standing) Comer Clemons, Guy Maddux, Clyde Eller, and Lester Ragland.

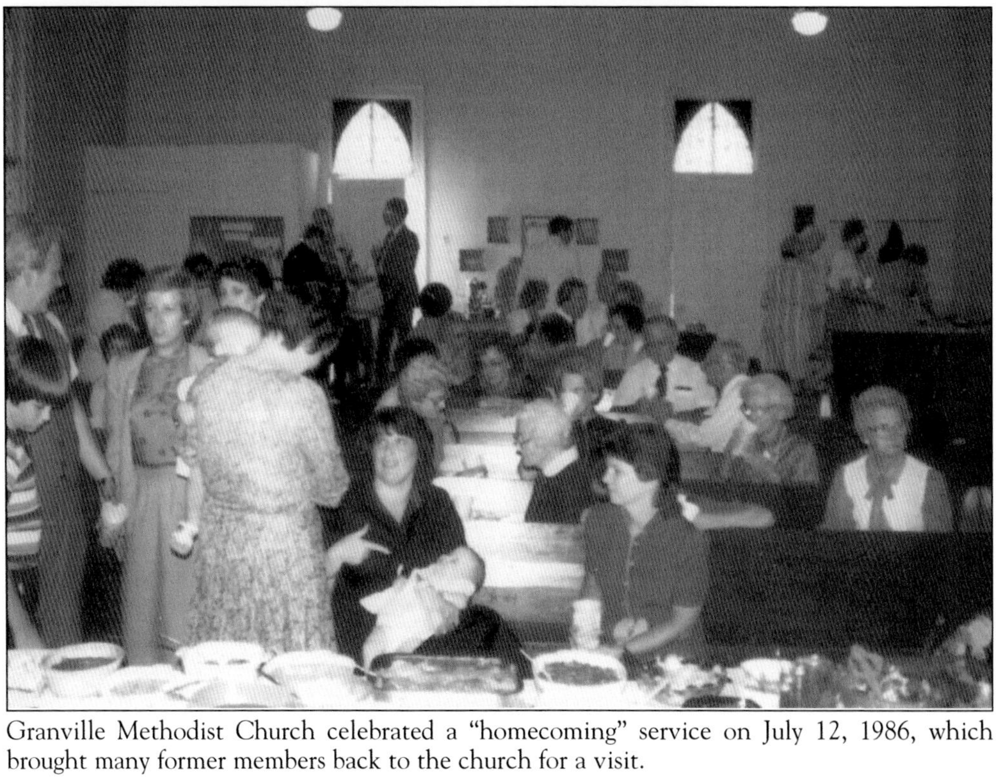

Granville Methodist Church celebrated a "homecoming" service on July 12, 1986, which brought many former members back to the church for a visit.

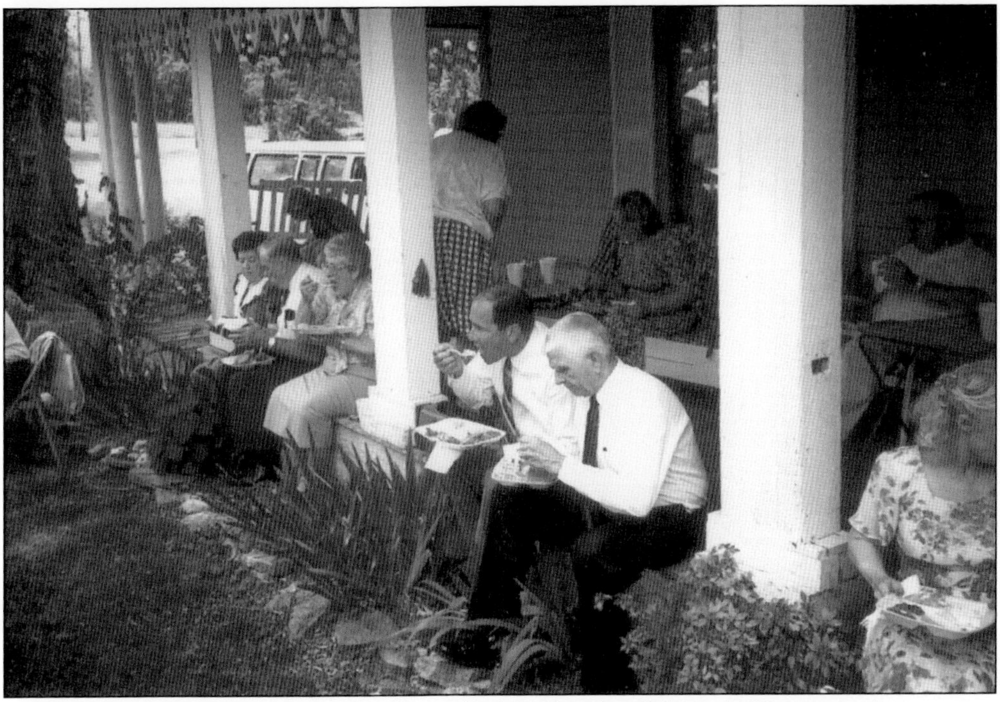

In May 1996, members of the Granville Methodist Church celebrated 100 years in their current building and dedicated the new stained-glass windows that had been added to the building. Enjoying dinner on the grounds after the worship service are, from left to right, Dorothy Harris, Robert Harris, Janie Bockman, Pat Reynolds, Sonny Reynolds, and Mary Reynolds.

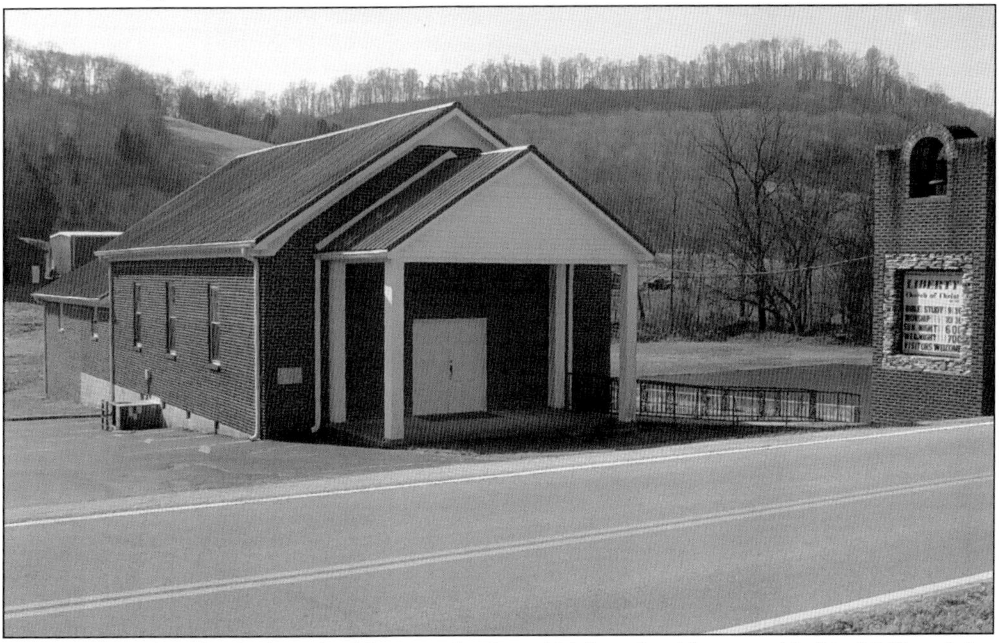

The Liberty Church of Christ building was built in 1916, with additions added in 1960 and the 1970s. The first service was held on January 14, 1917, led by Bascom Byrne, S.S. Carver, J.R. Carver, and Ben Fox.

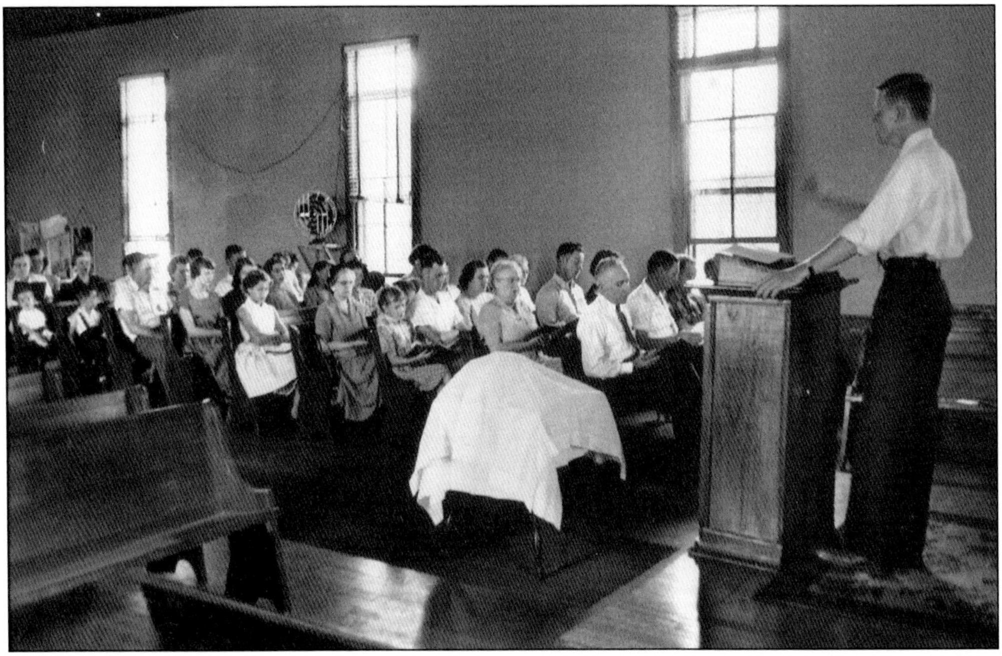

The Liberty Church of Christ congregation still meets today in this same building, shown here in 1955. Communion, which is served each Sunday, is shown covered by a linen cloth in the front of the room.

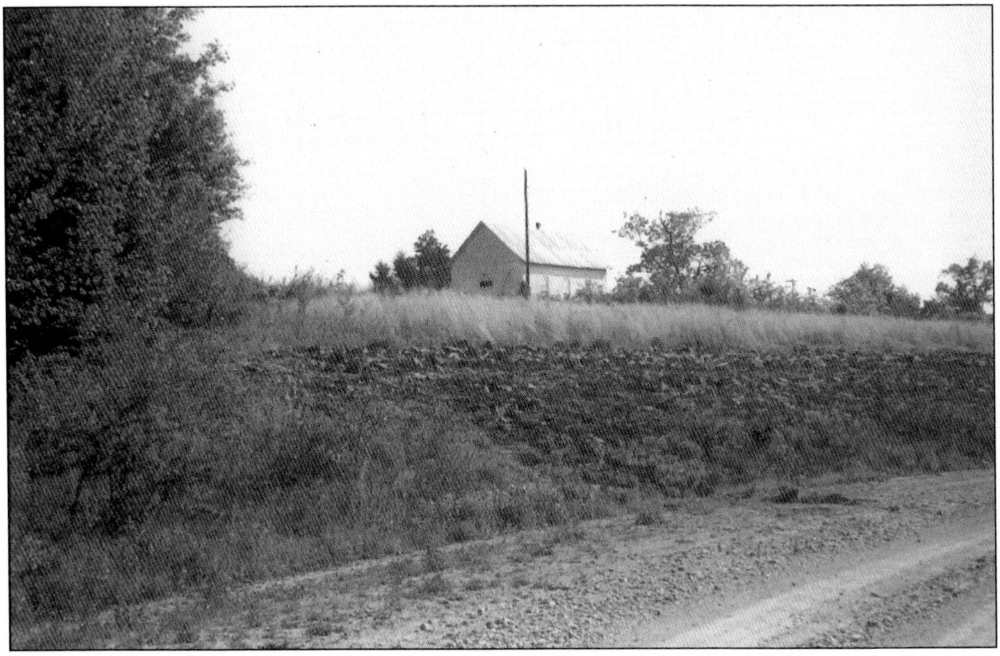

The Corinth Methodist Church was across the river from Granville on the Dycus Circuit in the Cumberland District. In 1950, the membership numbered 40. In 1966, the church was closed with the flooding of Cordell Hull Lake, and the members were transferred to another church on the charge, Ensor's Chapel. Brother Okla Hopper was the last pastor. The Liberty Methodist Church was another local community church until it closed in 1964.

Four

Reading, Writing, and Arithmetic

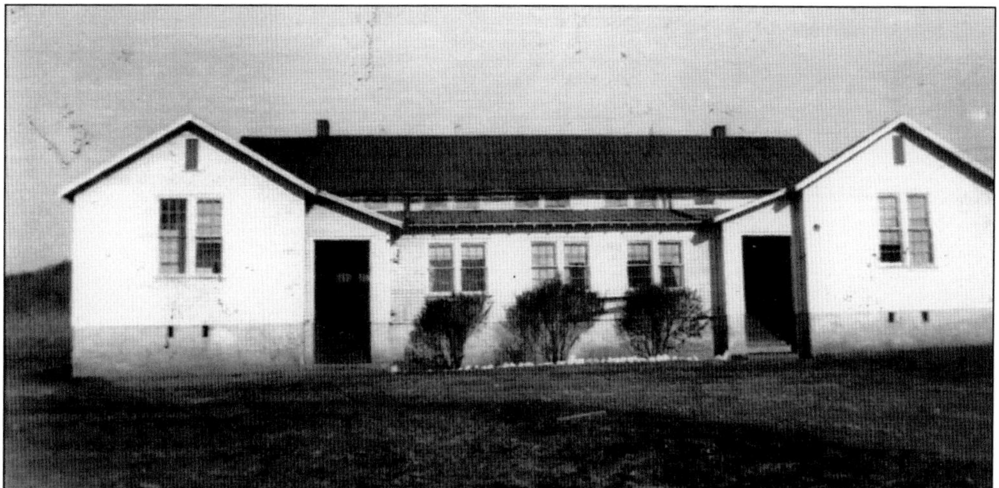

This white frame building, constructed in 1927 on the banks of Martin's Creek, housed Granville students until 1956, when a brick school was built. The junior high students left in 1951 when the junior high was dissolved. Students rode on horseback, crossed the river by canoe or ferry, or walked. The building's auditorium was used for assemblies, plays, a Saturday night movie, and a show featuring Grand Ole Opry performers who traveled from Nashville.

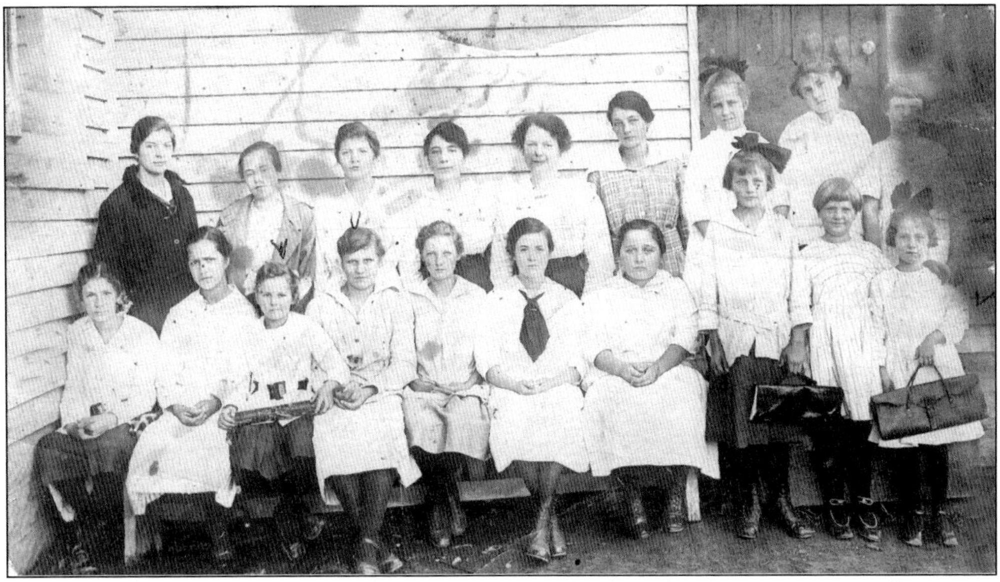

Miss Fisher's 1916 piano class was, from left to right, (front row) Margaret Hargis Collier, Mary Emma Cooper, Katherine Hargis Birdwell, Sallie Huff Stout, Dimple Jones, Nellie Grisham, Lorene Green, Bonnie Huff Patton, Dimple Grisham Mullinax, and Eliza Freeman Thompson; (back row) Hallie Williamson Johnson, Francis Maddux, Dona Mai Williamson Lee, Sallie Jones Stout, Miss Fisher, Hallie Mae Burton Fox, Asbula Huff Rector, Vallie Gold Smith, and Lillie Grisham.

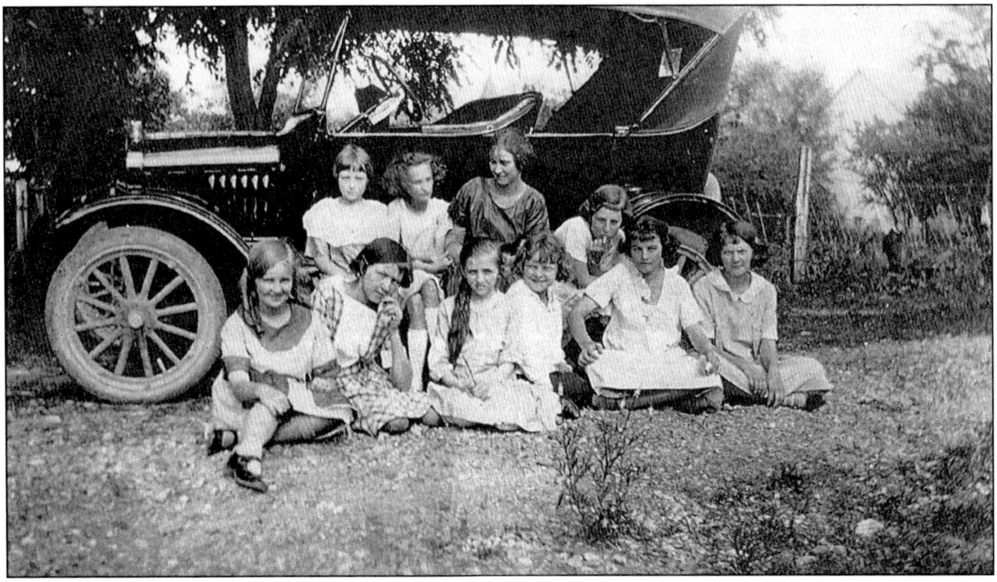

Mary Nell Ferrell Watts taught piano in Granville for over 50 years. This picture is of her first class in 1920 and includes, from left to right, (front row) Thelma Carver, Elsie Draper, unidentified, Elizabeth Sutton, Bonnie Huff, and Alice Bush; (back row) Louise Huff, Evelyn Maddux, Mary Nell Ferrell, and Eliza Freeman.

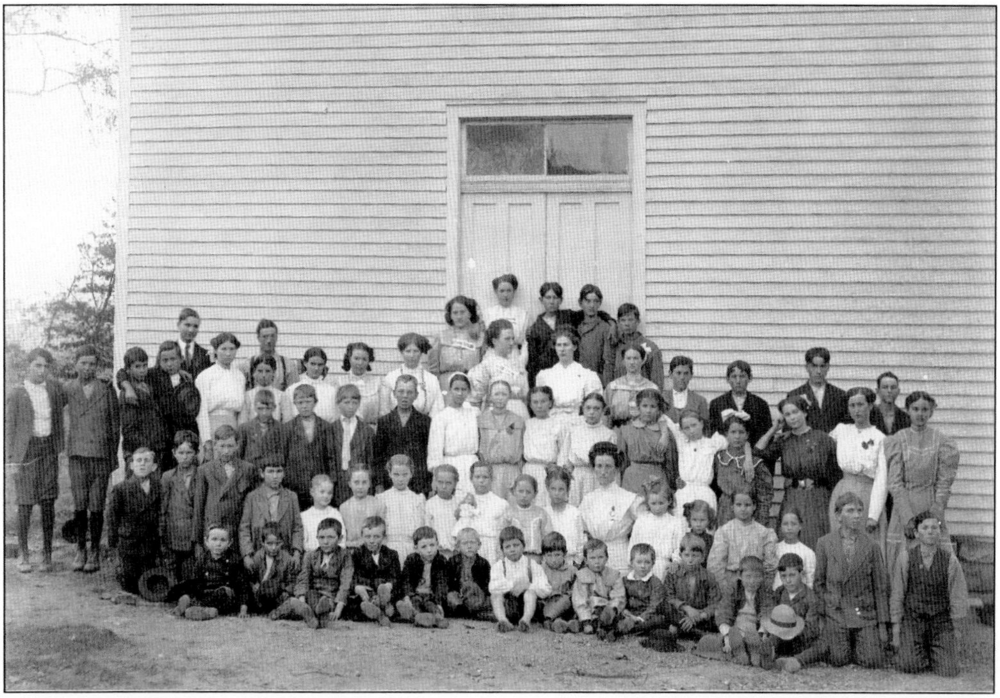

The Corinth School in Brooks Bend was a private school. Parents paid a monthly fee for their children to attend classes taught by Avo McGlasson and Vallie Maggart Barnett. This school photo was taken around 1910 or 1911.

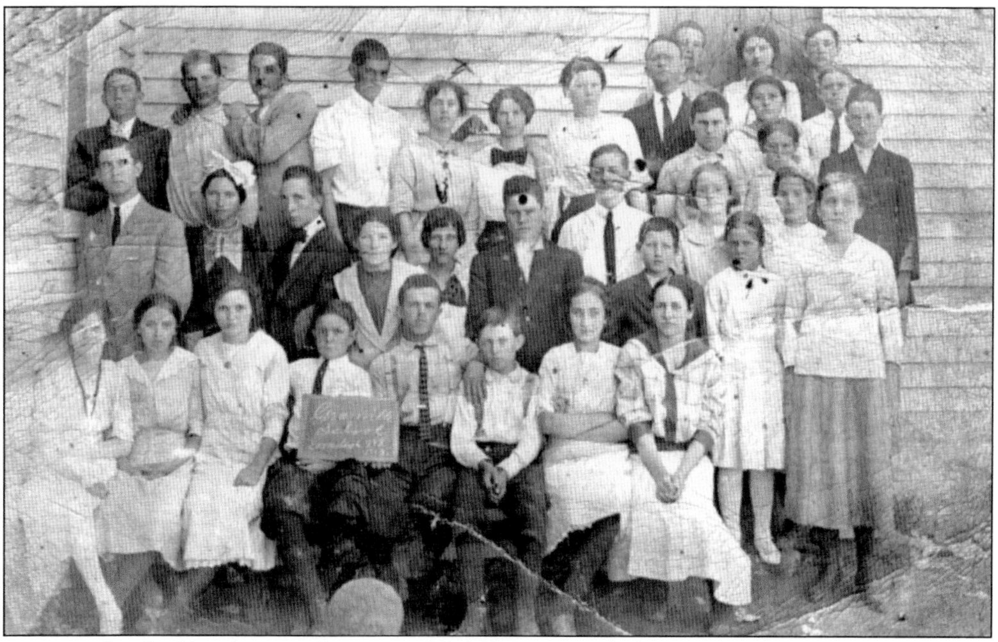

Private schools, like the one this group of students attended around 1913, operated for nearly 100 years before public education was available. The school building that these students attended was converted to a private home and still stands to the north of what was once Ragland's Campground in Granville.

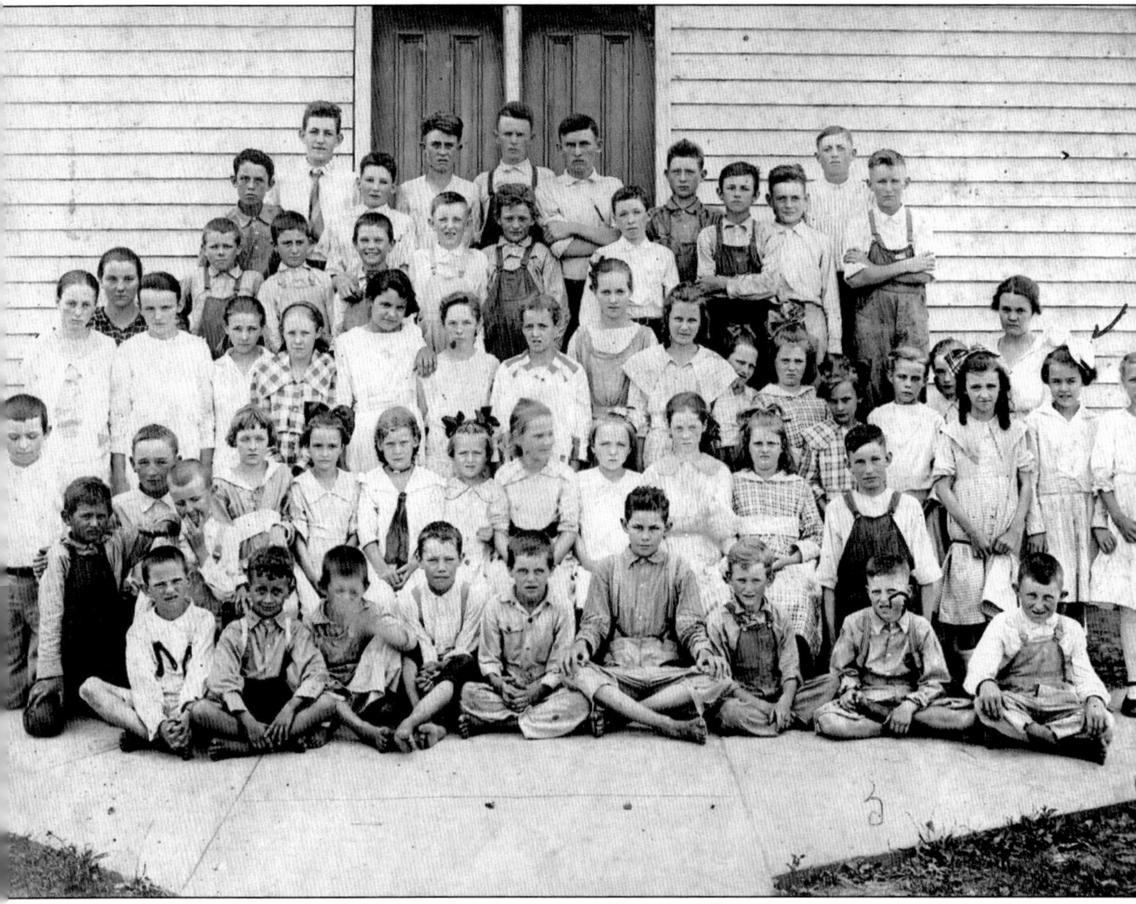

This photograph, taken in front of the Granville School, is dated approximately 1915. The students are, from left to right, (first row) Thomas Simpson, Carl Daniel, Lutrell Cornwell, Robert H. Huff, two unidentified students, Walter Agee, Willie Tittle, and Frank Holleman; (second row) unidentified, Frank Williamson, Howard Green, Sam T. Brown, Mattie Byrne, Vallie Byrne, Fannie B. Agee, Amanda F. Brown, Asbula Huff, Virginia Green, Rubye Tittle, Lillie Grisham, Josh Kent, Carrie Byrne, Eleanor Maddux, and Bonnie Huff; (third row) Birdie M. Tittle, Lois Carter, Ruby Byrne, Lera Lambert, Emma Williamson, Fannie M. Willoughby, ? Myers, ? Holleman, Claude Mensor, Vallie Simpson, Dimple Grisham, Ruby Nell Daniel, and teacher Flora Willoughby; (fourth row) Easter Mayberry, Raymond Myers, John Eller, Richmond Hargis, Douglas Holleman, Clarence Williamson, Carmack Clemons, unidentified, Charles Grisham, and Allen Manier; (fifth row) Gladdice Mayberry, unidentified, Walter Burton, Charles Sadler, Bob Carter, Will Carter, Willis Carter, Mule Reece, and Lon Tittle.

James Webb Smith, a descendant of one of the first land-grant families, taught school at Holleman's Bend. His 1913 contract with the board of education was for seven months and called for Smith to furnish his own wood for heating, chalk, buckets to carry out ashes, and brooms to sweep up. He was paid $42.50 per month to teach.

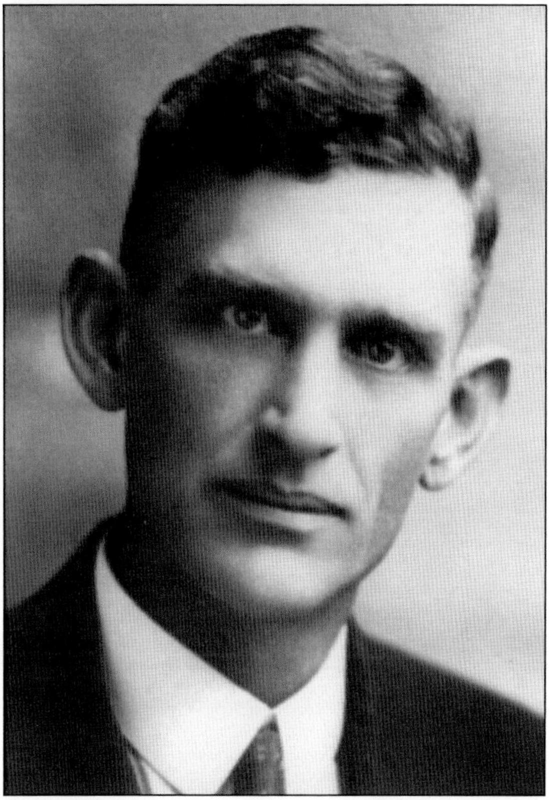

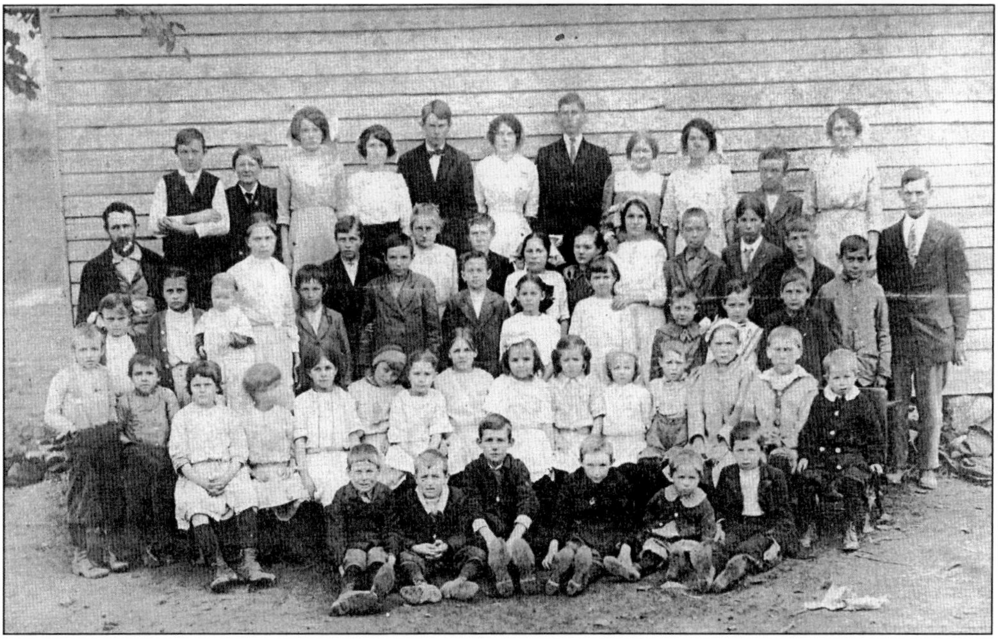

Holleman's Bend School was a subscription, or private, school about three miles from Granville. This photo from the early 1900s shows Webb Smith on the right, along with another male teacher on the left, and their students.

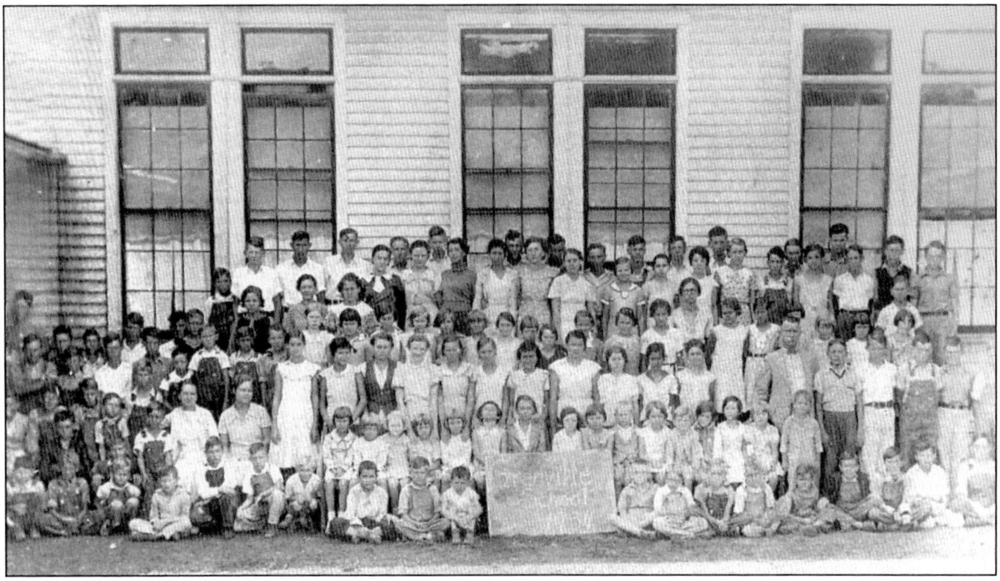

In 1927, a large, multi-room building was constructed in Granville to house elementary grades 1 through 8 and a junior high school, which contained grades 9 and 10. The entire student body is shown in this photo behind a sign stating "Granville School 1934."

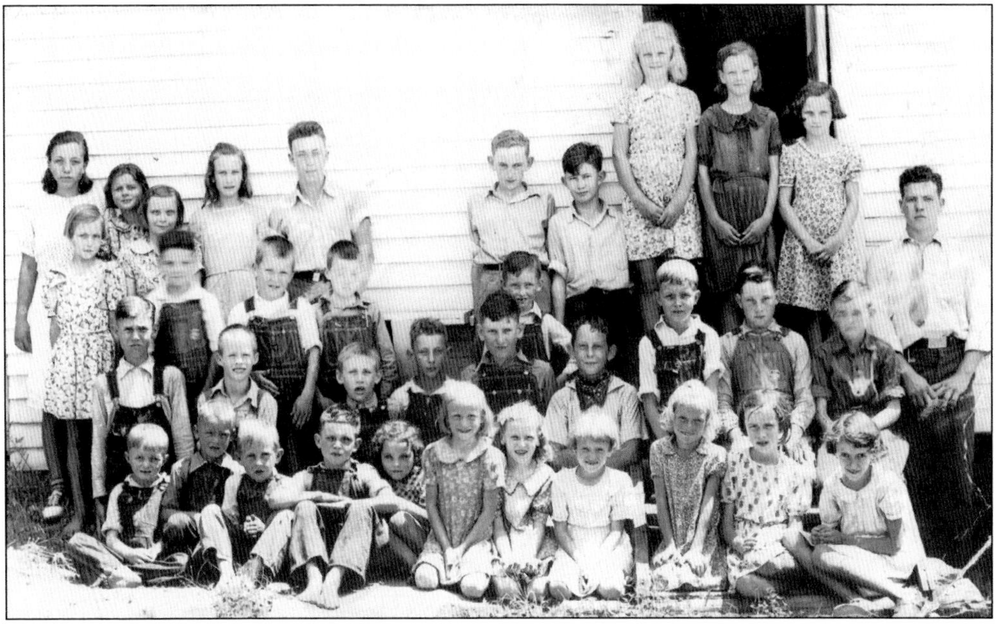

Brooks Bend School students in 1939 are, from left to right, (first row) Glendon Woodard, Billy Fields, Billy Sullivan, Donald Green, ? Woodard, Geneva Gentry, Dorothy Allen, Anna Duke, Elizabeth Wade, Willa Clemons, and Ida Duke; (second row) Raleigh Duke, Harold Clemons, Donald Sullivan, Frank Maggart, Freeman Duke, Dexter Hamilton, Bernice Woodard, Junior Green, and Dalton Green; (third row) Willodean Burgess, Jason Woodard, Junior Clemons, Bobby Fields, and Lemon Kent; (fourth row) Marie Woodard, Wilene Fields, Modene Burgess, Bula Allen, Elvis Woodard, Jessie Duke, Junior Duke, Adell Wade, Opal Woodard, and teacher Mac Carter.

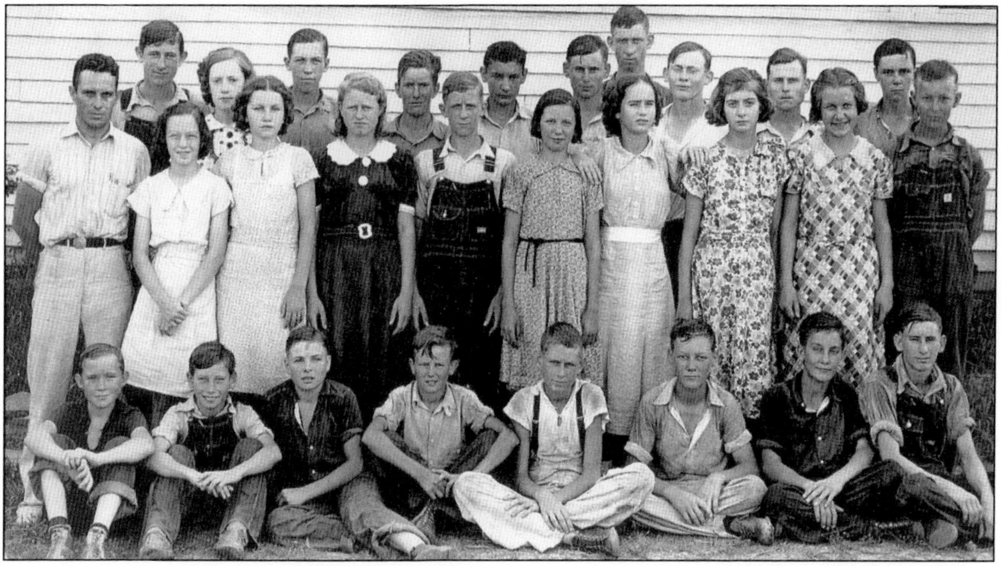

This Granville School seventh- and eighth-grade class of 1938–1939 contains, from left to right, (front row) Bobby Dowell, Dow Carter, Donald Maddux, Charles Duke, John Burton, L.B. Carter, Lewis Jackson, and Lloyd Hargis; (middle row) teacher Edgar Halfacre, Ogeal Halfacre, Inez Russell, Clara Mathis, Isham Keith, Helen Fields, Lilly Ann Clemons, Evelyn Haile, Bonnie Butler, and Joe R. Pharris; (back row) Joe Mathis, Bethel Vinson, David Montgomery, Carl Manier, Henry Daniel, Harvey Hargis, Carl Burton, Douglas Collier, Garland Collier, and Freeman Green.

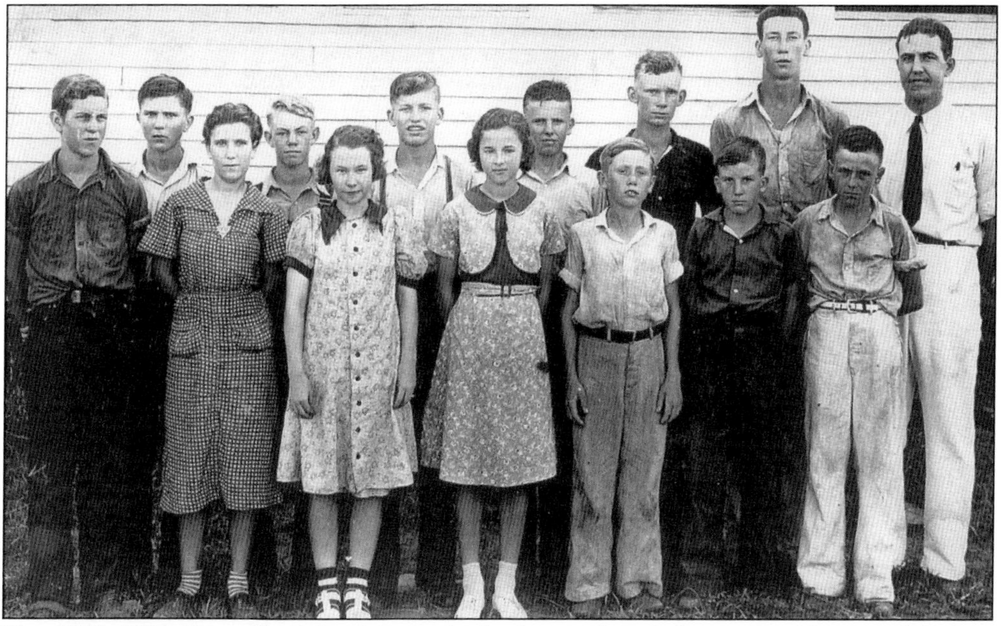

The 1938–1939 Granville School junior high class is, from left to right, (front row) Robert Grisham, Hazel Allen, Magdalene Carter, Eva Harris, Preston Wade, Lloyd Halfacre, and Thomas Bockman; (back row) Arnold Reynolds, Thurman Vinson, Odus Pruett, Willie Billingsley, Gartha Agee, Eugene Carter, and teacher John W. Brown. Brown later became the county high school principal and school superintendent.

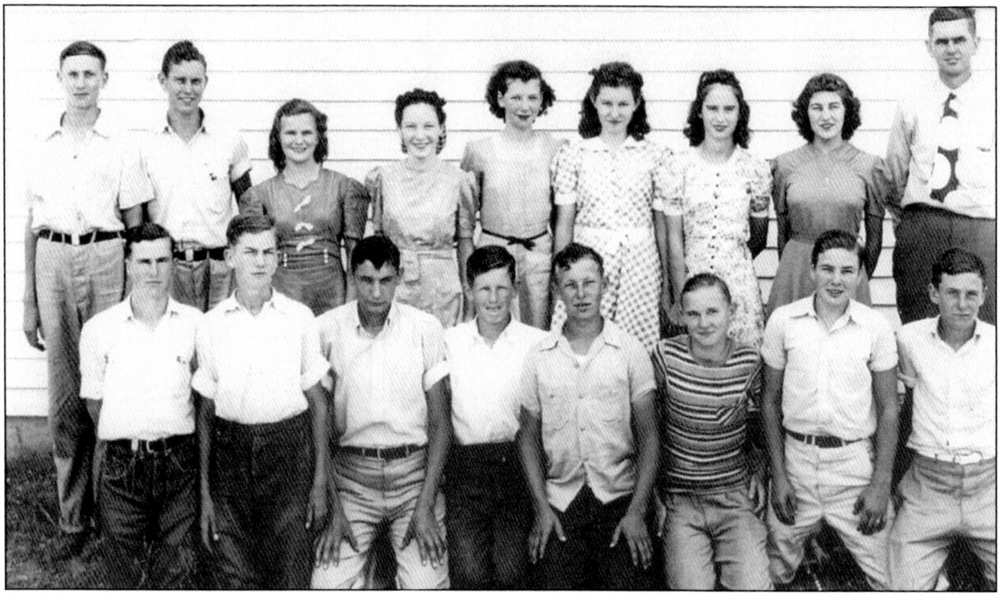

The 1940–1941 Granville School junior high sophomore class was taught by R.V. Reynolds, who also went on to become county school superintendent. Students in his class are, from left to right, (front row) Finis Brown, Willie Frank Wheeler, Henry Harrison Daniel, Harry Spurlock, Joe Ridley Pharris, Bobby Dowell, Donald Richmond Maddux, and Tommy Bockman; (back row) Russell Pippin, Robert Grisham, Marie Scott, Ogeal Halfacre, Helen Fields, Inez Russell, Lillie Ann Clemons, and Ola Jane Sams.

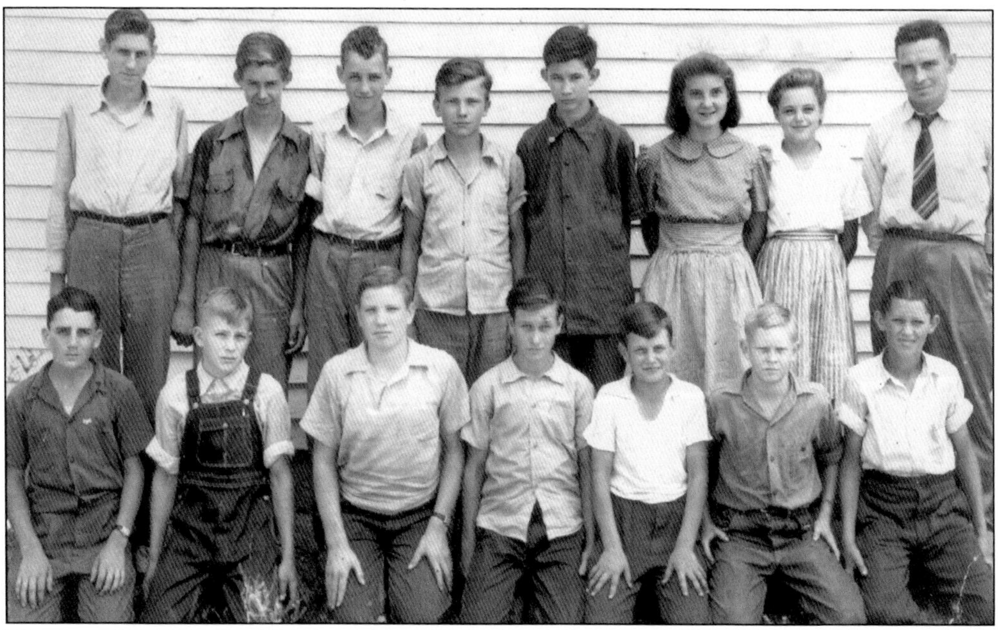

This list of 1941 Granville School seventh- and eighth-grade students reads like a phone book of Granville families. Shown here from left to right are (front row) Everett Halfacre, Albert Ragland, Glenn Ferrell Watts, Dow Carter, Charles Williamson, Earl Grisham, and Erastus Duke; (back row) John Burton, Charles Clemons, Martin Burton, unidentified, Allison Duke Jr., Mildred Haile, Katherine Willoughby, and teacher Edgar Halfacre.

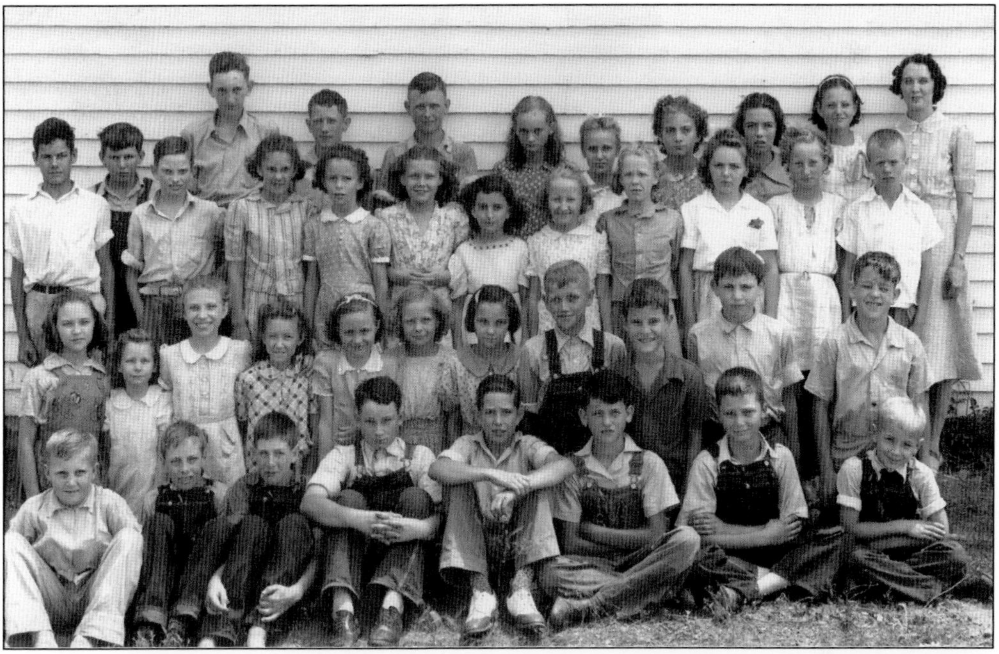

Granville School's fourth, fifth, and sixth grades in 1941–1942 are, from left to right, (first row) James Haile, Billie Wade, Bobbie Wade, Raymond Woodard, James Clemons, Dois Fields, Hubert Eller, and Edmond Ragland; (second row) Juanita Carter, Nell Carter, Margaret Watts, Robbie Robinson, Dorothy Brown, Juanita Elrod, Opal Woodard, Jonas Ragland, Donald Ramsey, Donald Collier, and Lee Mathis; (third row) Johnnie Dickson, Loyd Chaffin, Pauline Burton, Willadean Clemons, Virginia Elrod, Geraldine Halfacre, Evelyn Pharris, Betty Burton, Tommie McKinley, Dolan Pryor, and Harold Clemons; (fourth row) Maglon Burgess, Jessie Duke, Garland Mathis, Raymond Burgess, Janie Tayse, Sue Pharris, Avo Haile, Beatrice Maberry, Nell Wade, and teacher Jewell Whitaker.

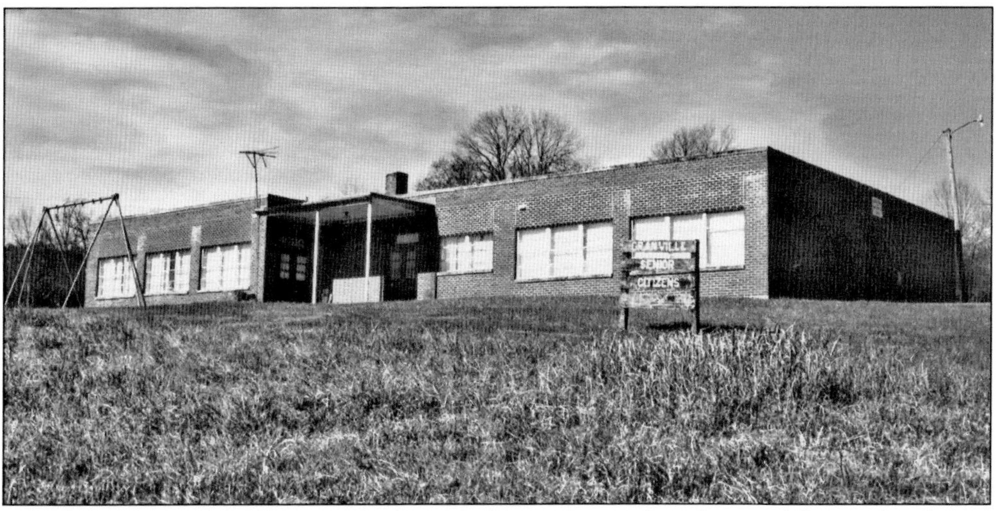

In 1956, a new brick building was built on Highway 53 to replace the wood-frame schoolhouse. Students attended this Granville Elementary School until 1981, when it was closed and students were bussed to the county-seat schools in Gainesboro. Today, it serves as a community center and a senior citizens nutrition site and also houses an archive of Granville historical information.

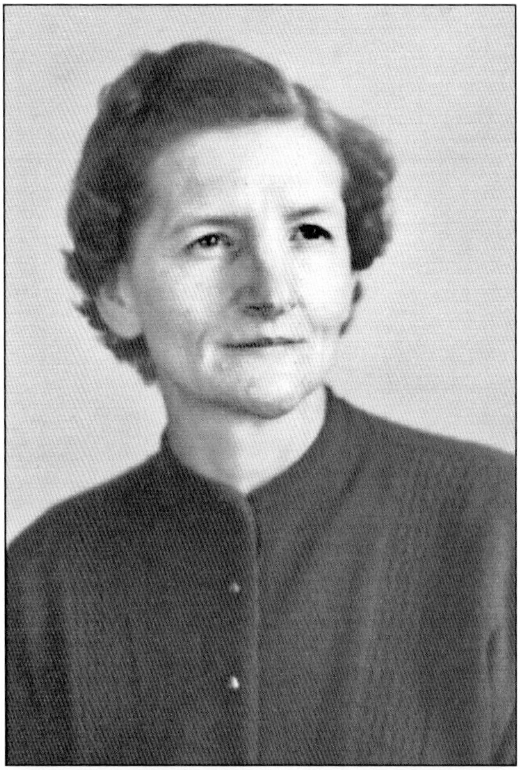

Minnie Ada Williamson Holleman began teaching in this area in 1931. She served as principal from 1953 until 1972, longer than any other person in Granville schools' history. She was one of the organizers of the local senior citizens group, the secretary of the Granville Cemetery Association for many years, an elder in the Presbyterian church, and an active leader of the Granville Home Demonstration Club.

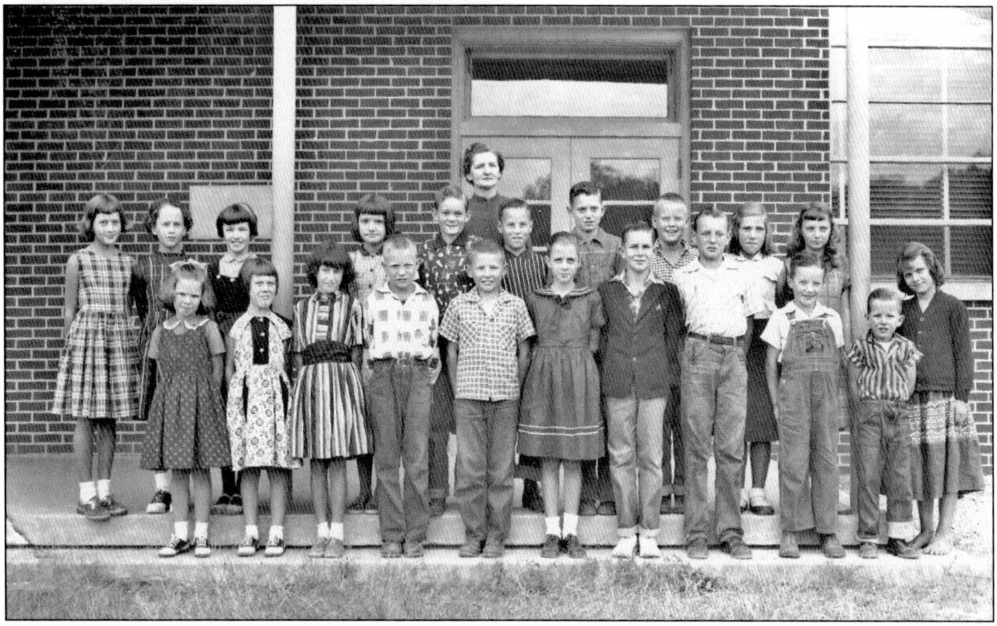

This photo from Granville Elementary School in the late 1950s shows Mrs. Holleman with students, from left to right, (front row) Linda Brown, Nell McBroom, Sharon Guess, Tommy Tayse, Steve Ragland, Ginger Huff, Jerry Carter, Freddie Wade, Billy Wade, Ricky Lambert, and Linda Petty; (back row) Eloise Collier, Judy Collier, Betty Neal, Judy Manier, Sonny Tayse, Marion Halfacre, Roy Case, Brownie Manier, Susie Petty, and Frances Wade.

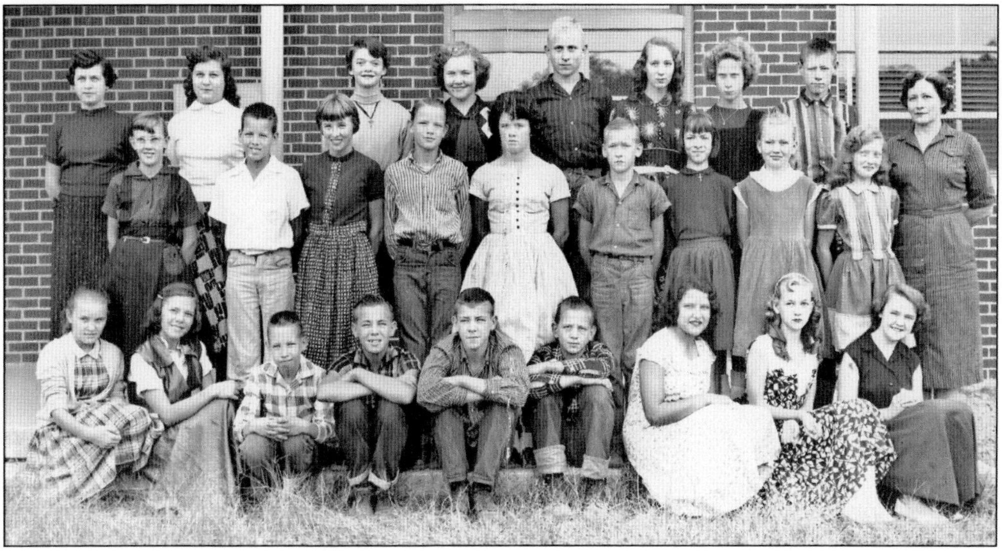

This Granville Elementary School fourth-, fifth-, and sixth-grade picture from the late 1950s contains, from left to right, (front row) Sandra Flatt, Tennie Petty, Larry Montgomery, Paul Myers, Mickey Myers, Buddy Myers, Betty Petty, Margaret Tayse, and Velma Loftis; (middle row) Betty McBroom, Jacky Huff, Paulette Neal, Jimmie Loftis, Helen Myers, Roy Philpot, Linda Harris, Carmella Philpot, Jeneal Philpot, and teacher Louise Ragland; (back row) Judy Dawes, Suzanne Clemons, Linda Manier, Wanda Collier, Raydean Collier, Anna Tayse, Lois Collier, and Carlos Rich.

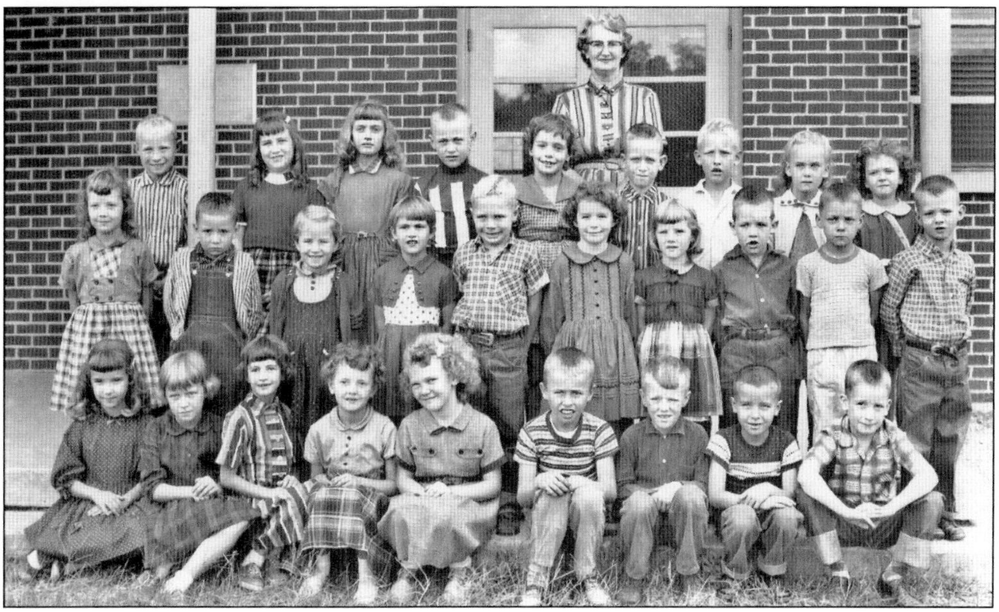

Granville Elementary School's first, second, and third graders in 1959 are, from left to right, (front row) Carolyn Carter, Judy Anderson, Sherry Guess, Sylvia Jones, Minnie Ada Case, Gerald Neal, Fred Myers, Bruce Carter, and Robert Halfacre; (middle row) Joy Clark, Stanley Huff, Sarah Halfacre, Diane Loftis, David Eller, Betsy Halfacre, Daffolene Brown, Robbie Clark, Tony Wade, and Wayne Harris; (back row) Jackie Loftis, Teresa Halfacre, Sheila Wade, Buddy Collier, Charlotte Manier, Billy Dawes, Fred Case, Gail Tayse, and Patricia Ragland.

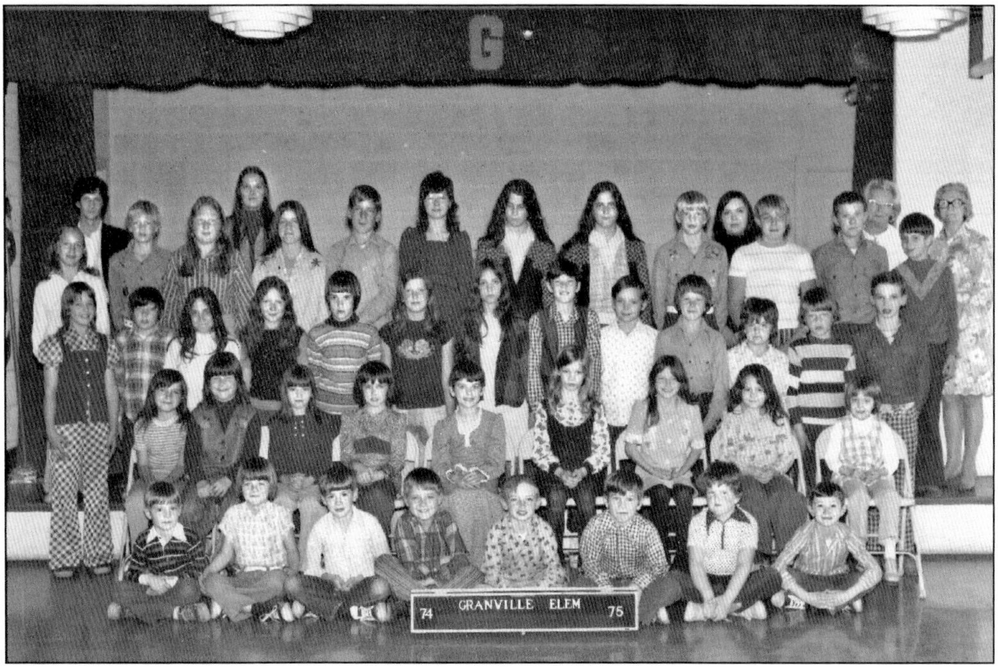

Ruth Stout Huff and Patsy Jo Lee taught this class for Granville Elementary School the year of 1974–1975. Just a few years later in 1981, the school was closed permanently when the county school board consolidated all Granville students into the large elementary school in Gainesboro.

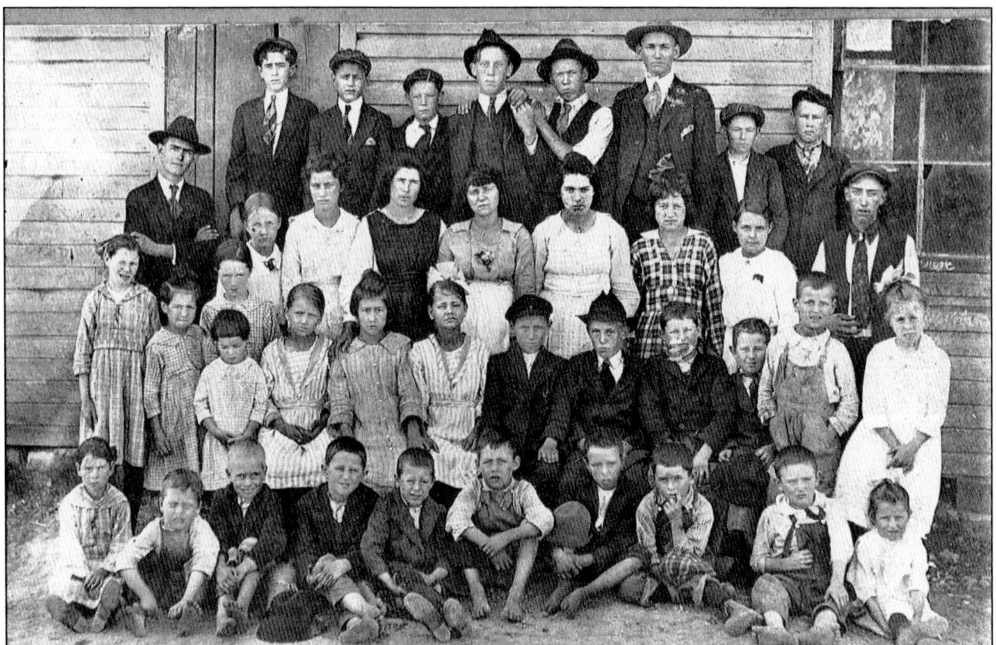

Although the Granville School provided education to many residents, there were also rural schools located throughout the area. The Spring Fork School shown in this picture was located just four miles from Granville off Martin's Creek Road on Spring Fork Road. A close look at the students' clothing dates this picture to the early 1900s.

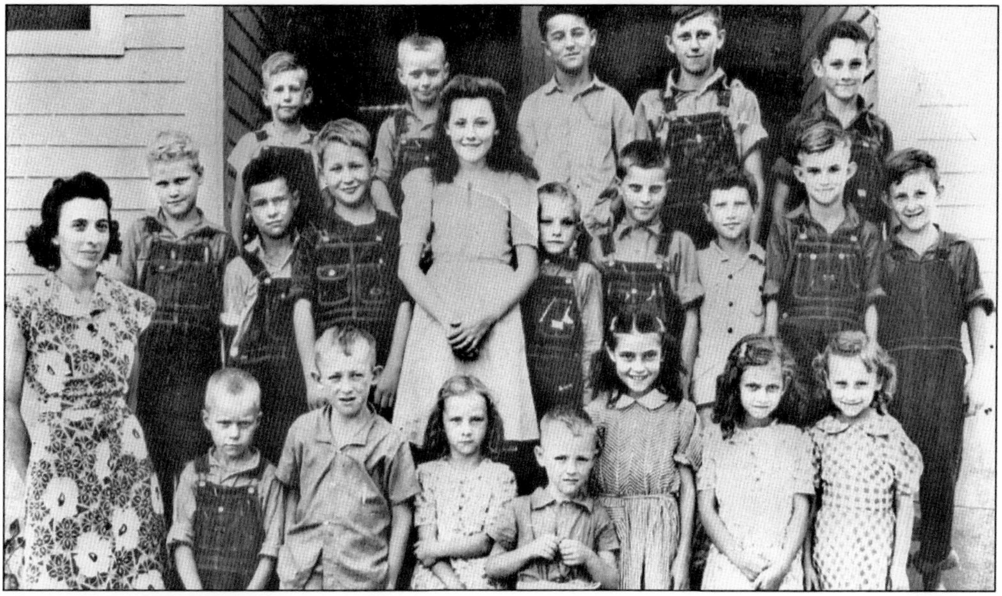

This early 1940s photo from Sadler School on Martin's Creek shows first through fourth graders, from left to right, (front row) teacher Mary Freeman Maddux, Joe Carter, unidentified, Peggy Keith, unidentified, Mamie Loftis, Ella May Keith, and Ruby Bryant; (middle row) Joe Stout, Ralph Manier, Ernest Lloyd Burgess, Estell Boyd, unidentified, Harold Carter, Kenneth "Turtle" Bryant, Henry Phillips, and Frank Jared; (back row) unidentified, Charles Carter, Ernest "Cowboy" Manier, Jessie Hargis, and Earl Stout.

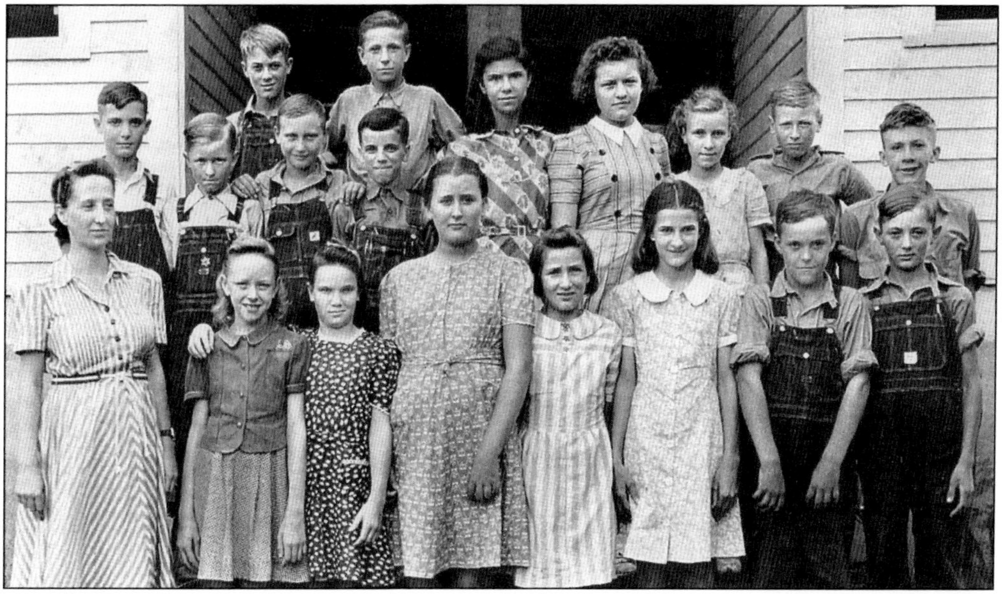

The "big" room of the Sadler School contained fifth through eighth grades. This photo from the 1940s shows, from left to right, (front row) teacher Eliza Freeman, Mattie Franklyn Rogers, Magdalene Pulley, Emorne Burgess, Bernice Bryant, Ruth Phillips, Elton McBroom, and Ernest Sadler; (middle row) Ralph Bandy, Robert Halfacre, Dewey Stout, Eldon Carter, A.V. Manier, Margaret Halfacre, Bobbie Sue Carter, Douglas Bryant, and William Stout; (back row) Robert Sadler and Junior Johnson.

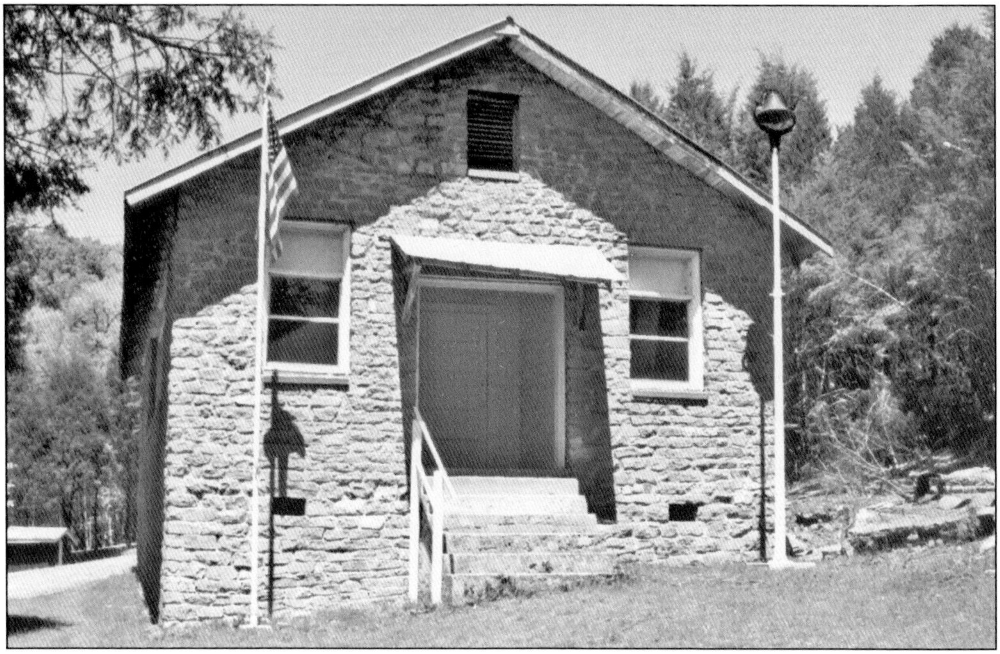

Until the 1964 Civil Rights Act, separate schools existed for black and white children. This building was constructed by the Civilian Conservation Corps in the mid-1930s. It was made of local stone and provided one room and one teacher to educate elementary students. Local African Americans used it for church services. Jonas and Anna Ragland restored this building. It is now used as a living history museum.

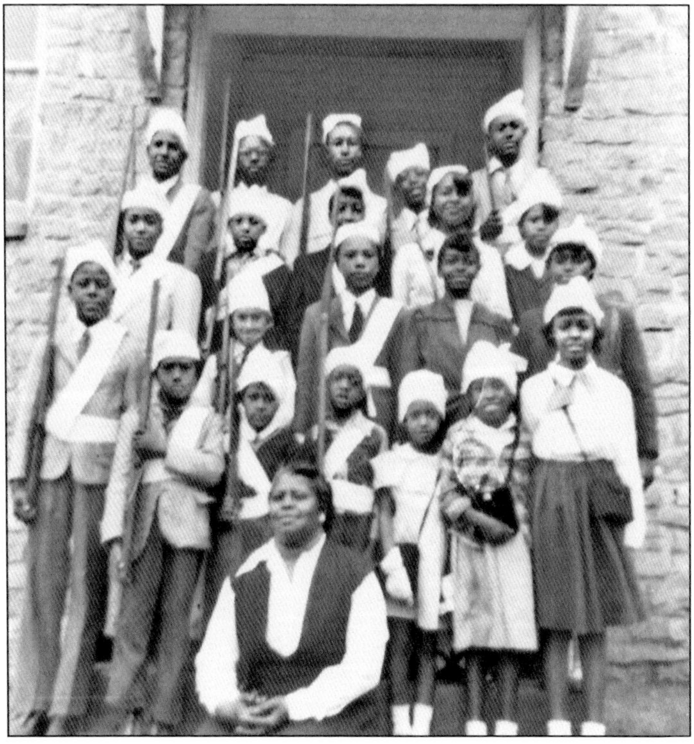

Sallie Blackmon and her students are shown dressed up for a musical pageant directed by Granville resident Fowler Stanton, who was also the band director at Jackson County High School. Before 1964, any African-American students wanting to continue their education past the eighth grade were bussed 25 miles to attend high school.

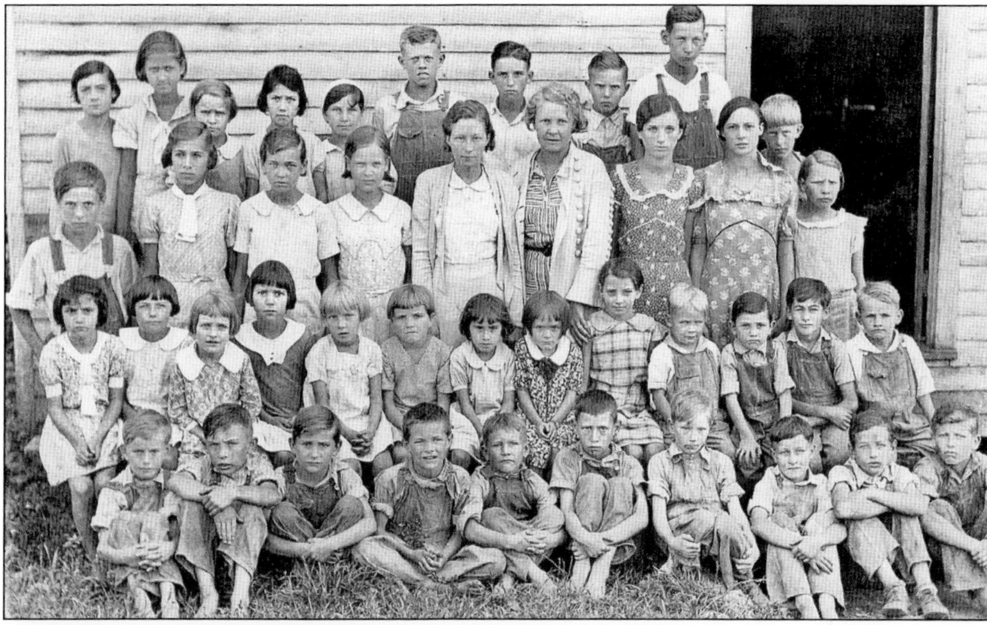

Liberty Elementary School was located just a few miles from Granville. This 1934 picture shows 42 of the students who attended this two-room school. To continue their education, they would go on to the Granville School for junior high and to Gainesboro for high school. Louise Huff and Melissa Sutton, seen in the center, wearing sweaters, were the teachers.

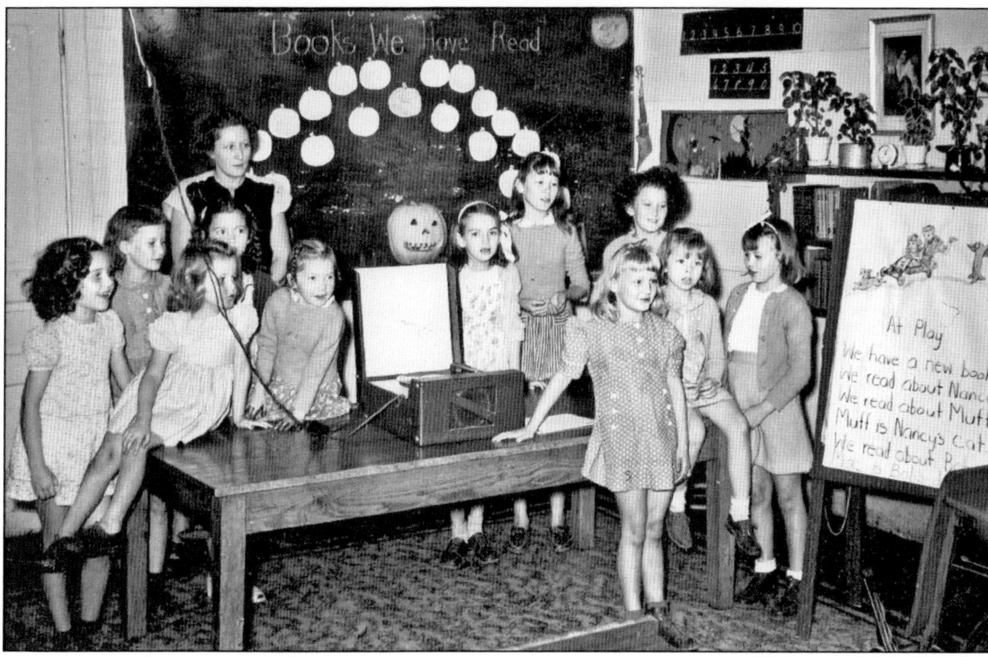

Liberty School received their first record player in 1948. This photo features, from left to right, (in front of table) Katherine Kirby, Elizabeth Huff, and Peggy Carter; (first row behind table) Meta Sue Reynolds, Sandra Jo Pharris, Mable Wade, Susie Pruett, Bonnie Jean Carter, and Elizabeth Johnson; (back row) Marie Johnson and Frankie Ruth Pruett; teacher Louise Ragland stands behind them.

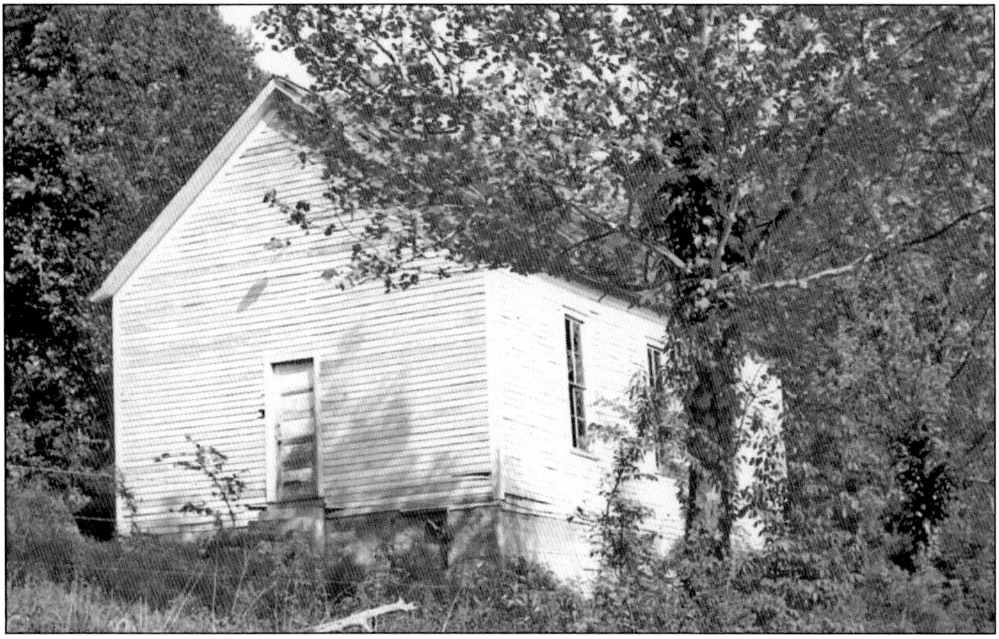

This one-room schoolhouse located in the Fifth District across the river from Granville was known as the Corinth School. Students attended classes in this building from around 1915 until the school closed in 1955, when the students transferred to Funns Branch School.

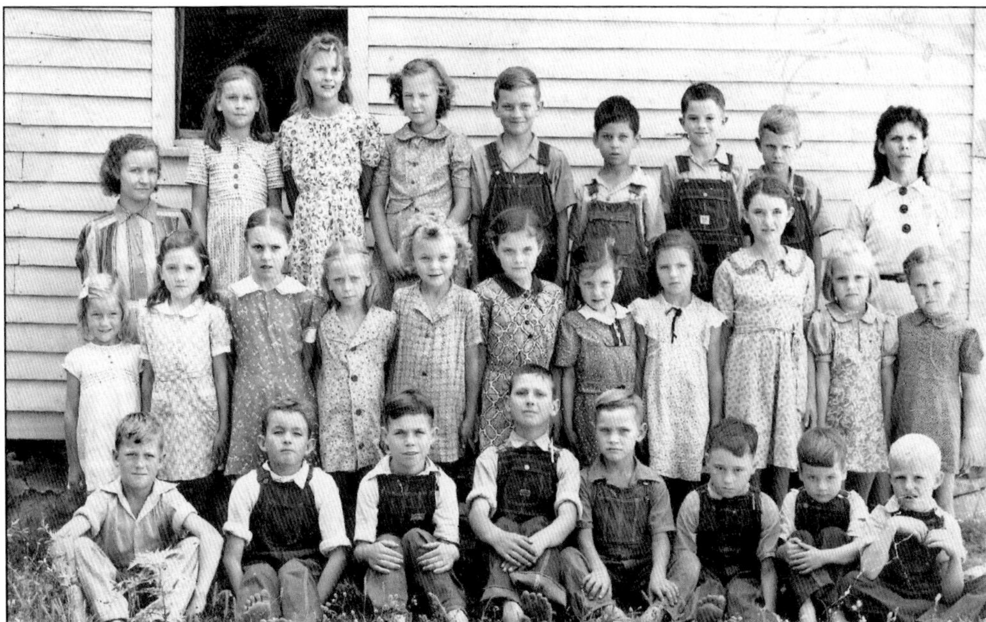

This picture shows a class from the Nameless School. After the Civil War, the locals in this small village applied for a post office. Their first choice for a name, Morgan, after a Confederate colonel, was rejected as that name was already in use in Tennessee. The residents could not agree on another name, so they sent the application to Washington without a name. It was approved and someone stamped "Nameless" on it, and the post office, school, and community have gone by Nameless ever since.

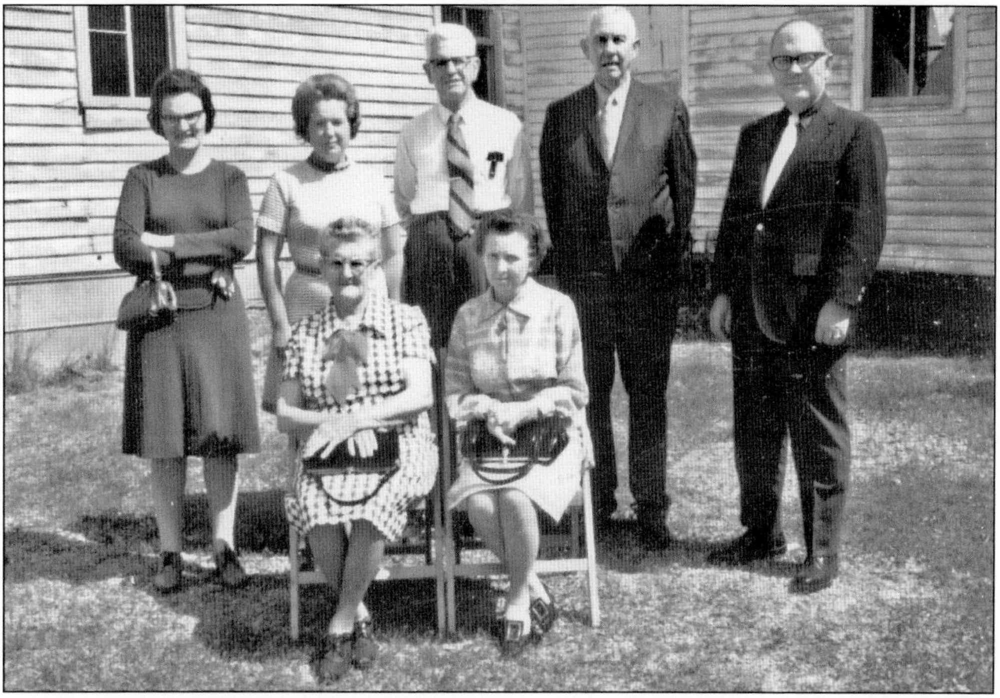

Retired teachers gathered at the Nameless School, where they taught, are, from left to right, (front row) Jennie Huff and Eula Wheeler; (back row) Mable Carter Stout, ? Way, Vestle Reynolds, O.C. Wheeler, and Guy Ragland.

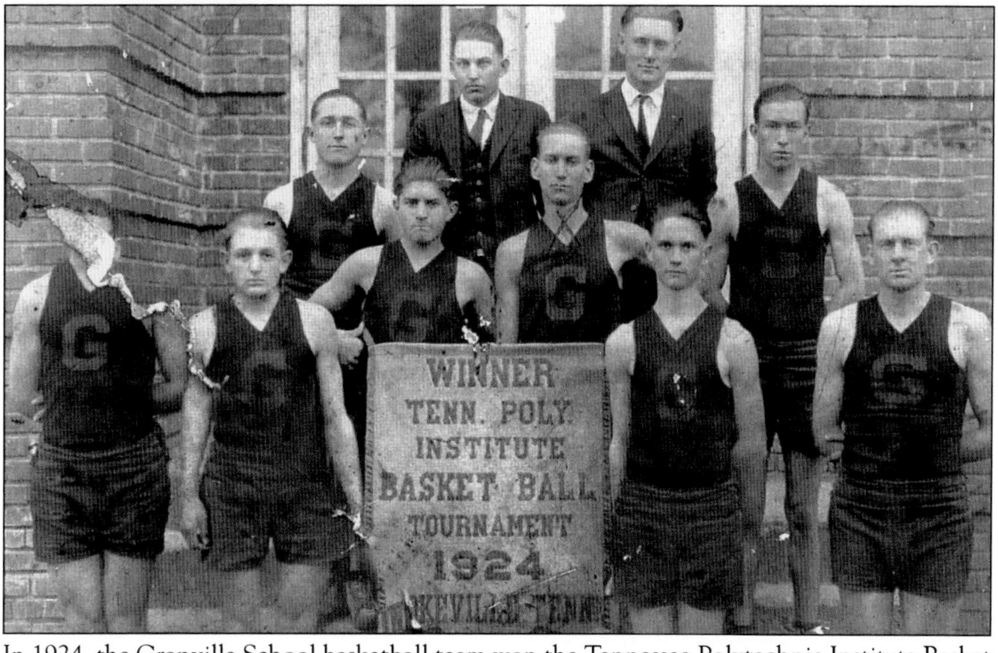

In 1924, the Granville School basketball team won the Tennessee Polytechnic Institute Basket Ball Tournament in Cookeville. Only the second and fourth players from left in the first row—Pete Williamson and Albert Clark—are known. Others who played for this team and may be in the picture above are Bowser Williamson, Cordell Meadows, and Hamp McDonald.

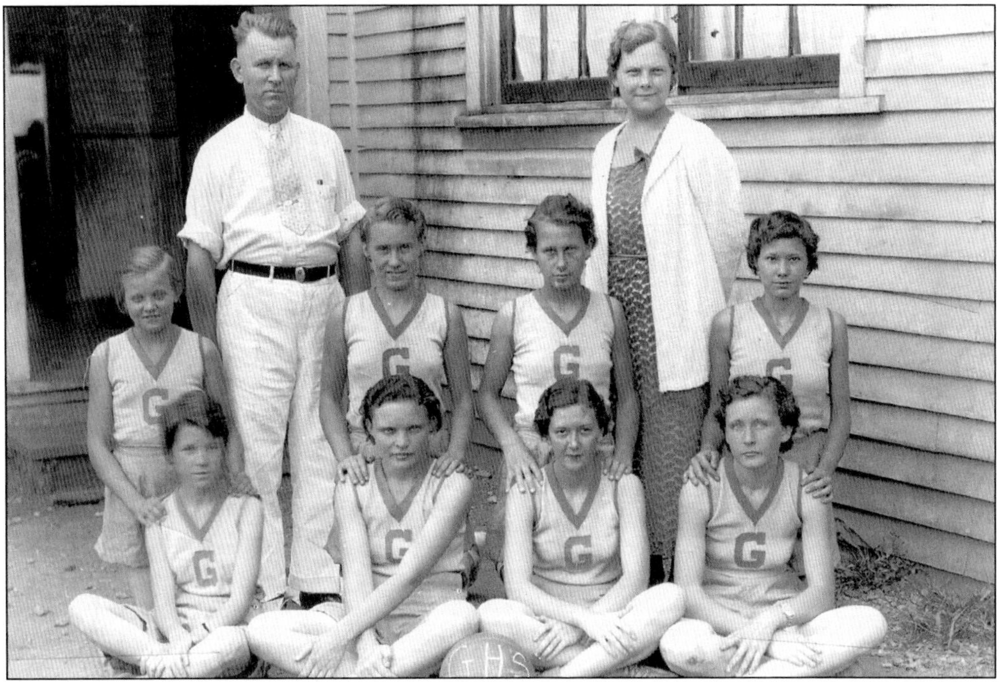

This group of girls from Granville Junior High School in 1934–1935 purchased their own basketball uniforms and played other girls' teams from the surrounding counties. They were, from left to right, (front row) Irene Halfacre, unidentified, Frances Ditty, and Ernestine Dixon; (back row) Mary Nan Huff, Star Clemons, Ada Myers, and Maggie Lou Pruett. A.C. Whitefield and Elizabeth Sutton were teachers and coaches.

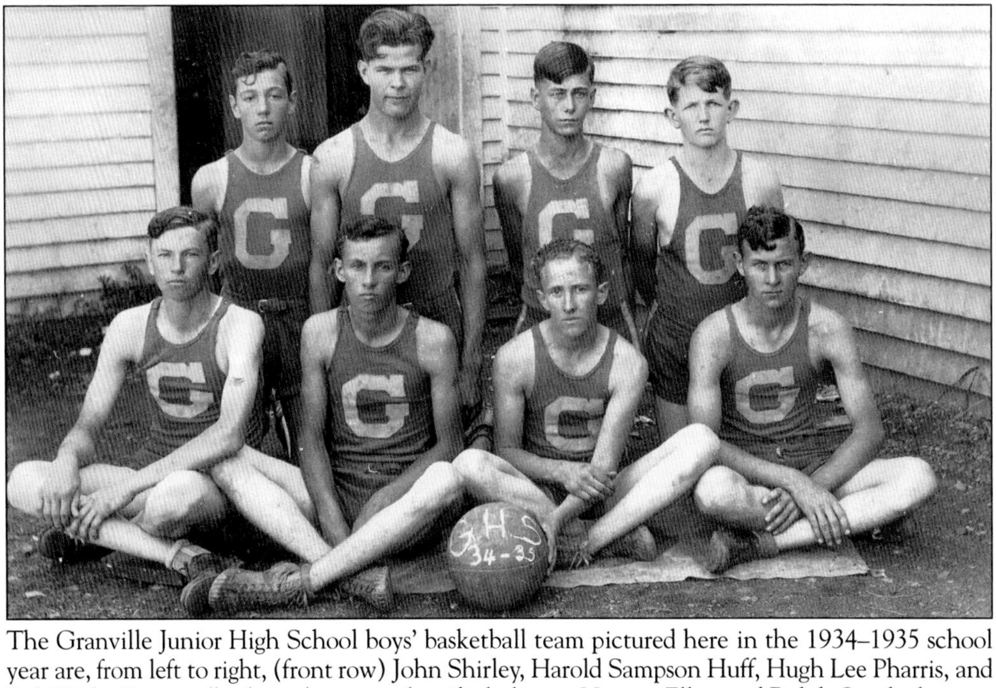

The Granville Junior High School boys' basketball team pictured here in the 1934–1935 school year are, from left to right, (front row) John Shirley, Harold Sampson Huff, Hugh Lee Pharris, and Bob Taylor Brown; (back row) two unidentified players, Vernon Eller, and Ralph Spurlock.

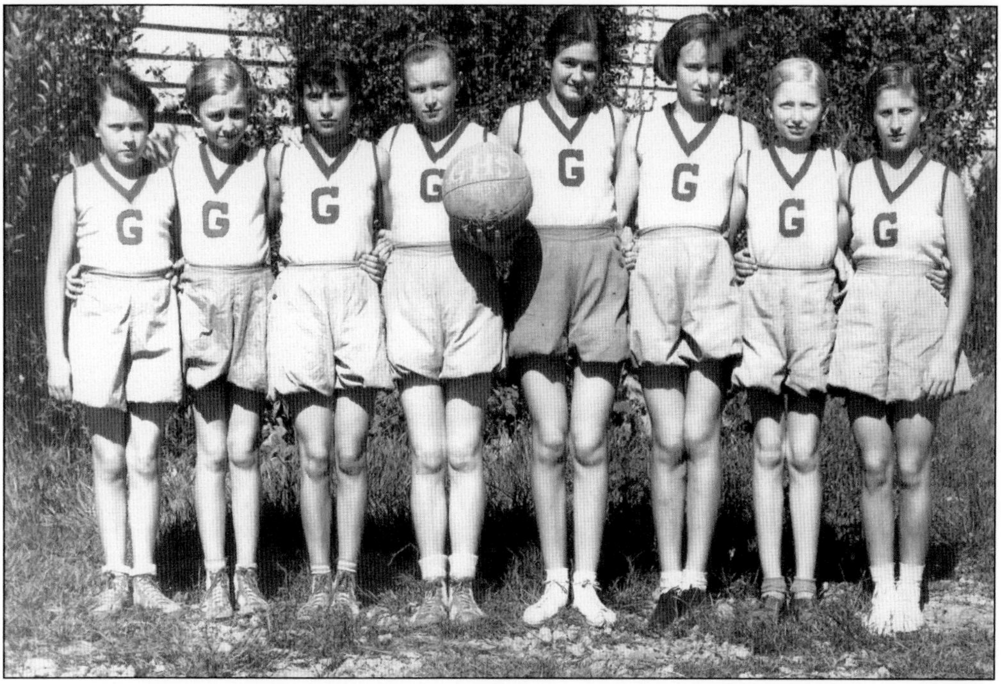

The younger girls' team of basketball players from Granville, pictured in 1935, is, from left to right, Minnie Lena Clemons, Myrtle Lois Clemons, Geraldine Daniel, Helen Burgess, Ila King Ditty, unidentified, Marie Chaffin, and Florine Daniel.

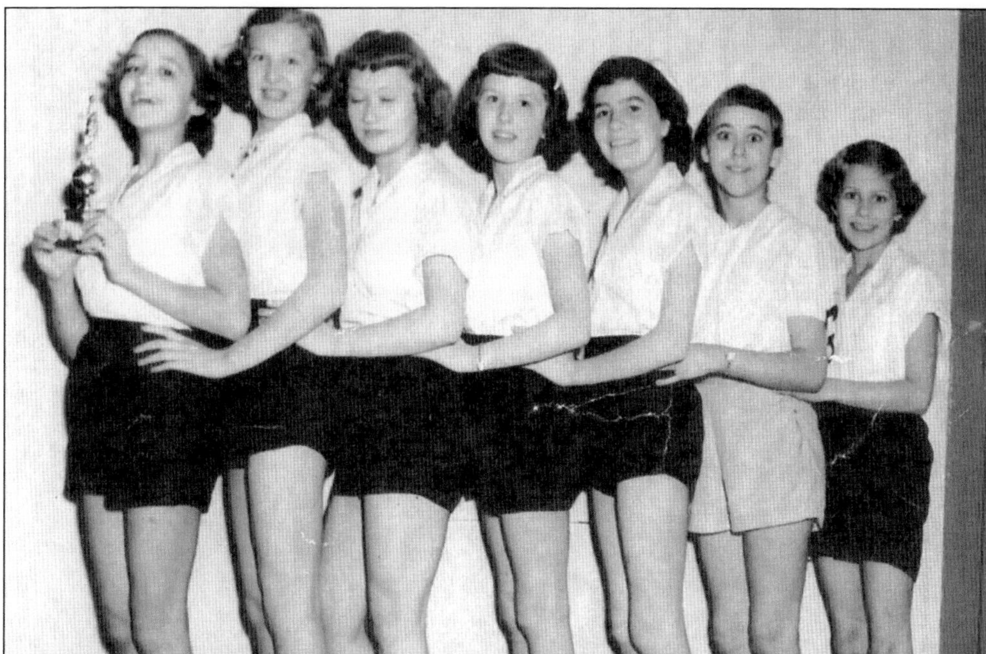

The Granville Elementary School girls' basketball team won the Jackson County Championship in 1953. Pictured, from left to right, are Jeanette H. Ragland, Katherine Kirby, Peggy Duke, Jeanetta Ragland, Fay Halfacre, Molena Collier, and Peggy Ragland.

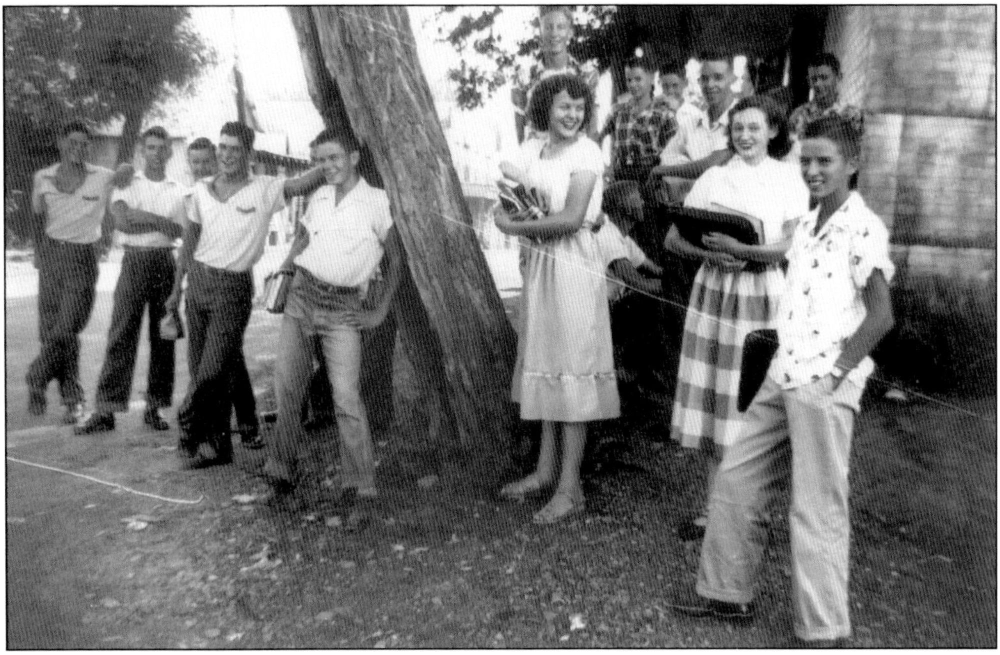

In the early 1950s, the Jackson County school bus would pick up children, dropping the high-school children in town to wait while the bus continued to pick up more children. Once the local route was complete, the bus would deliver the elementary children to the Granville School and come back for the high-school students seen here, who would be bussed on to Gainesboro.

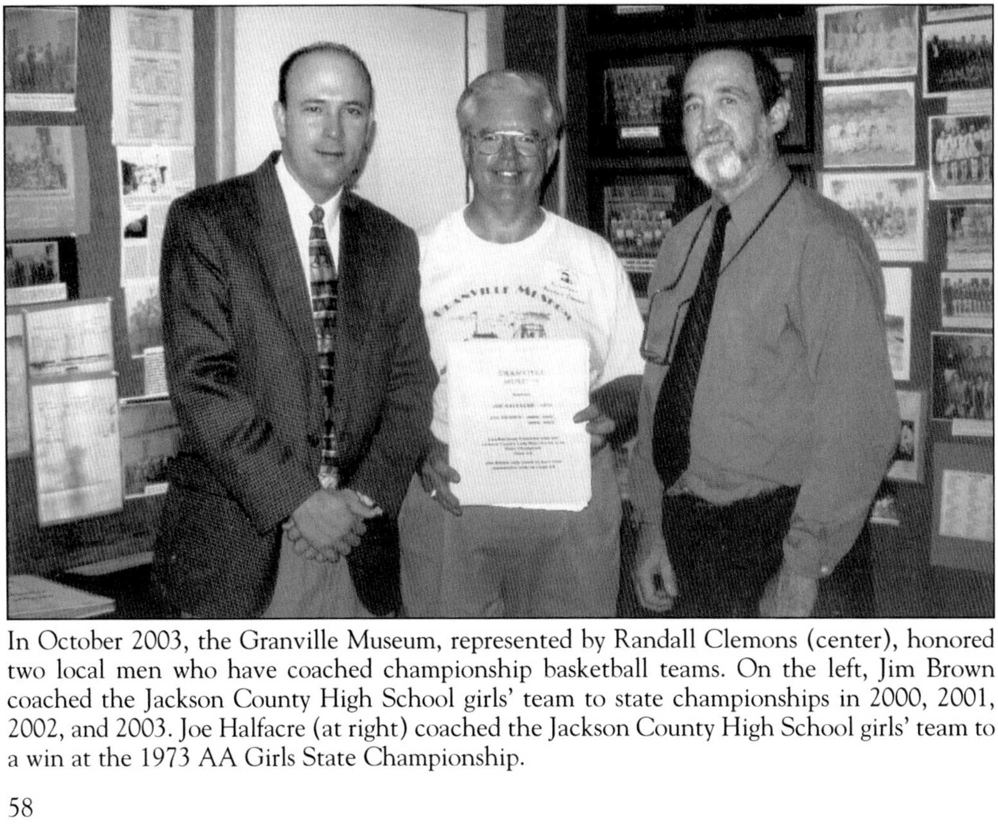

In October 2003, the Granville Museum, represented by Randall Clemons (center), honored two local men who have coached championship basketball teams. On the left, Jim Brown coached the Jackson County High School girls' team to state championships in 2000, 2001, 2002, and 2003. Joe Halfacre (at right) coached the Jackson County High School girls' team to a win at the 1973 AA Girls State Championship.

Five

FIGHTING FOR FREEDOM

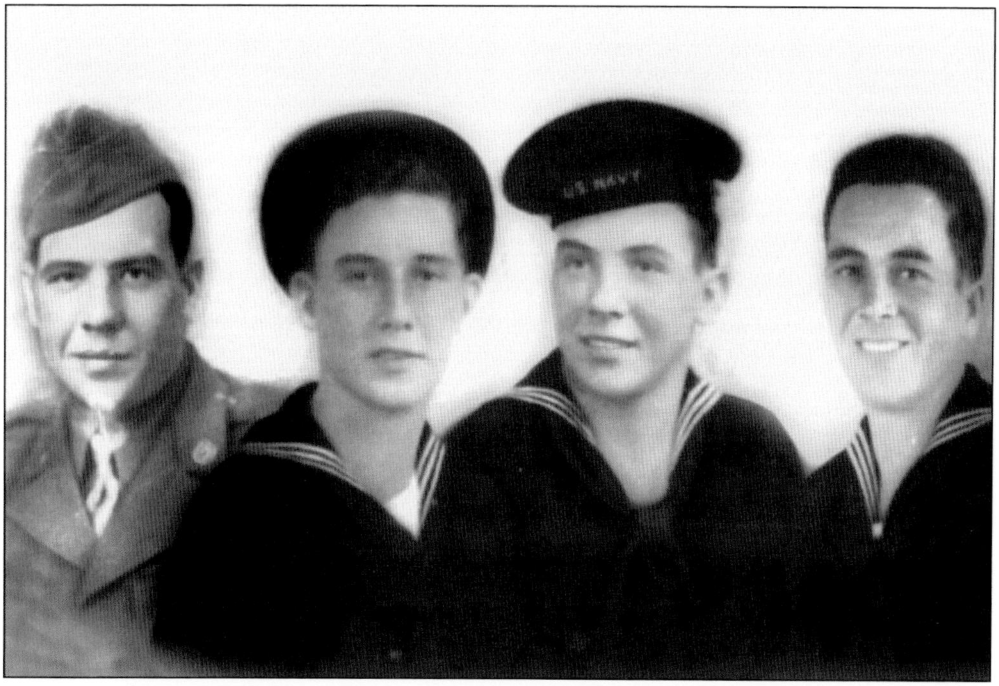

Lee Roy and Fannie Roberts Carter watched four of their sons enter the military during World War II. After Mac, far left, was drafted, the three other brothers, Alton, J.N., and Farmer, enlisted in the navy. All returned safely and lived out their lives in Granville and the surrounding area.

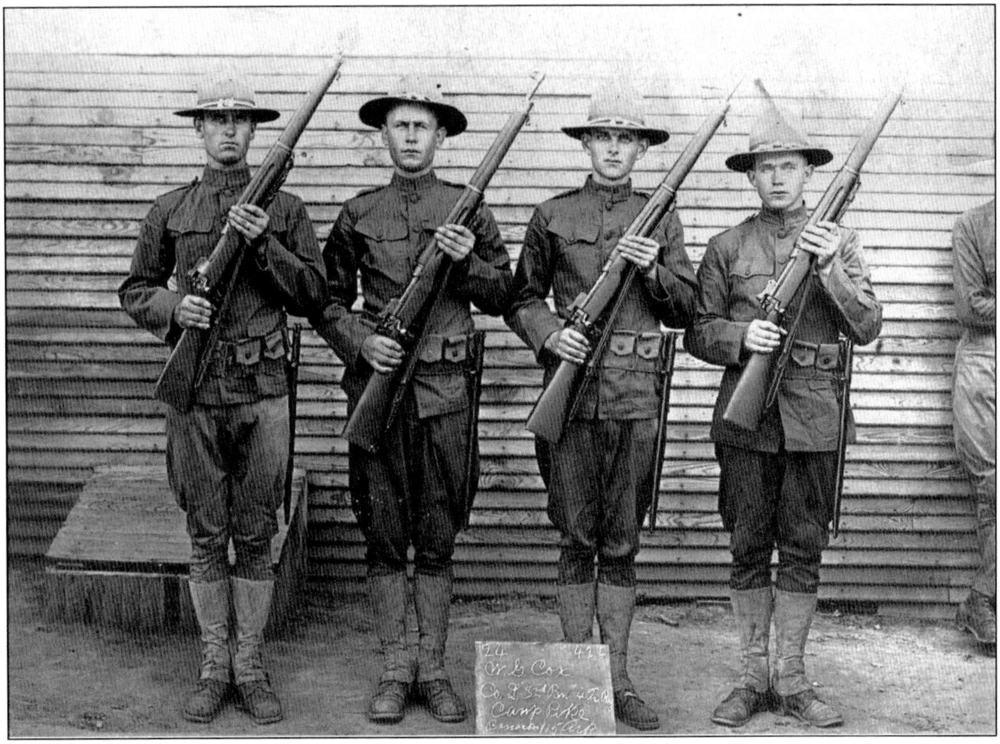

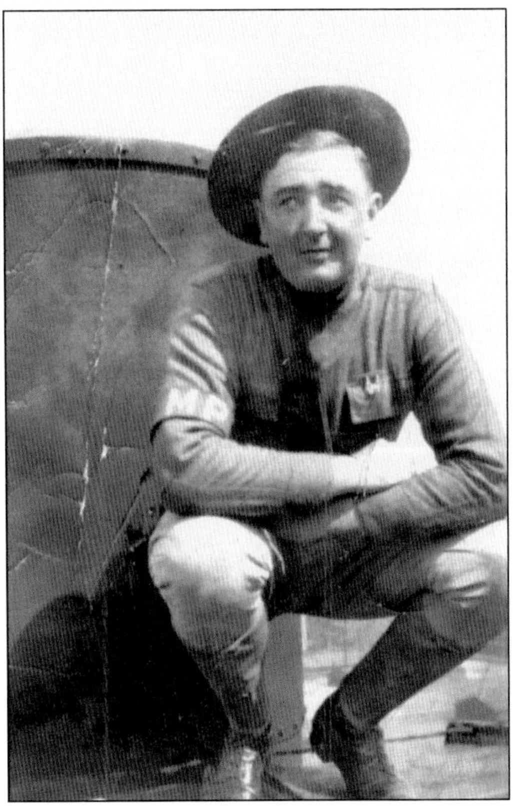

Tennessee is nicknamed the "Volunteer State" due to the number of residents who enlisted in the service during World War I and World War II. This group of Tennessee soldiers during World War I included Granville native Smith Stidham, third from the left. One local man, Ferd A. Stout, was killed in World War I.

Guy Grisham, pictured here, served in World War I along with the following local residents: Clifton S. Apple, Floyd Carter, Haskell Carter, Henry Howard Case, Robert Dawes, Jim Dowell, Charlie Duke, James A. Fields, Peyton Hardcastle, Robert Hardcastle, Guy Maddux, Oscar A. Maggart, Wesley Mayberry, Wade Minnear, Harry Page, Horace Page, Peyton Pharris, Hugh Philpot, Will Philpot, Alonzo Stidham, Smith Stidham, Arthur Spurlock, Frank Spurlock, John Watts, Charlie Williamson, Robert Williamson, and Cecil Willoughby.

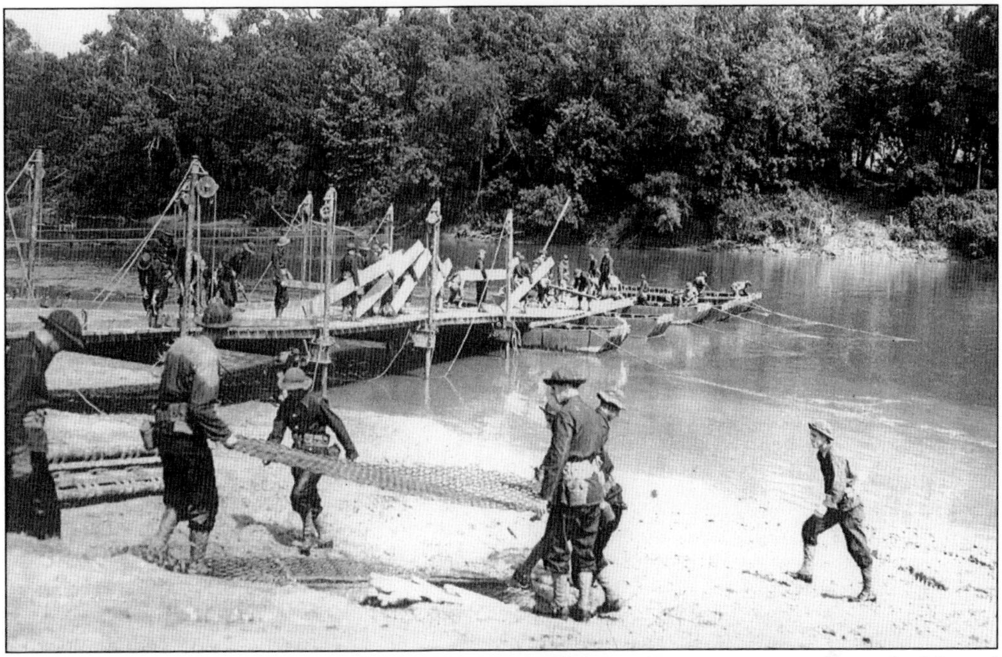

During World War II, the Granville area was a popular spot for training maneuvers by United States Army engineering divisions. They built pontoon bridges like the one pictured above, lived in tent cities, ate C rations, dropped "bombs" consisting of five-pound bags of flour, and trained for battle. The local camps were located on the Rena Fox and the Dowell farms on the edge of Granville.

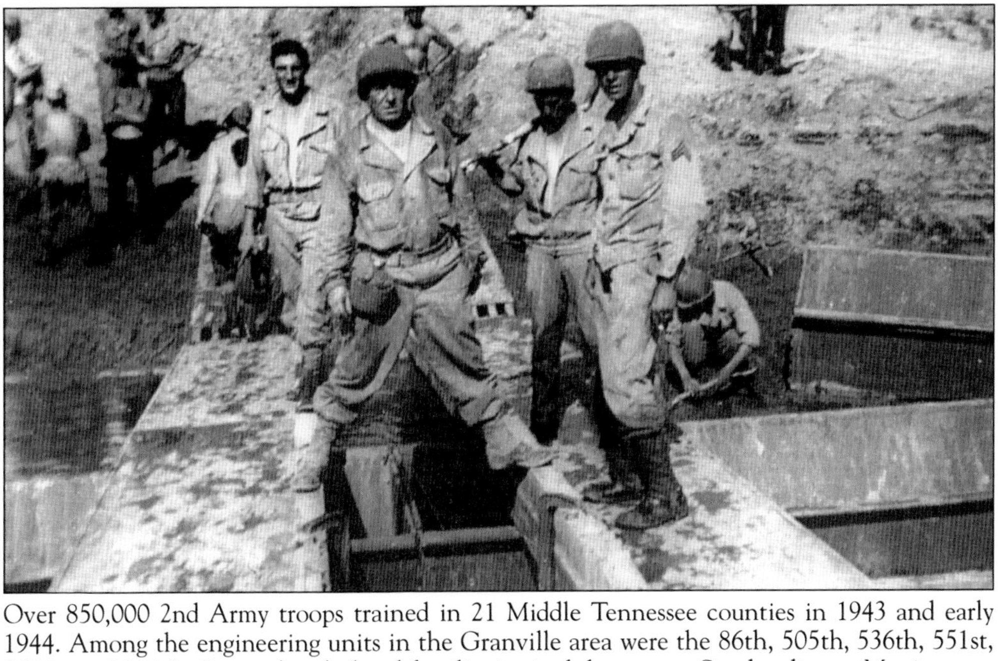

Over 850,000 2nd Army troops trained in 21 Middle Tennessee counties in 1943 and early 1944. Among the engineering units in the Granville area were the 86th, 505th, 536th, 551st, 557th, and 994th. On weekends, local families invited the men to Sunday dinner. Movies were shown outdoors near the camps or in the Granville Junior High School auditorium. The local terrain was representative of the actual combat fields.

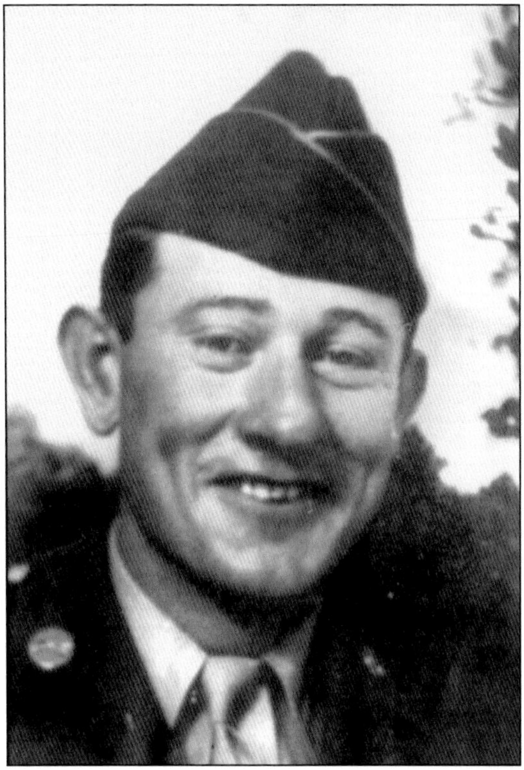

Four Mathis brothers, sons of George Washington and Martha Mathis, enlisted in World War II. Joe, pictured here—for whom the local American Legion post was named—was killed in action on April 10, 1944. Raymond returned "shell shocked" with the mind of a child; Garlin "Junior" suffered from frozen feet and hands and spent six months in a hospital. Herman Lee "Jack" was the only son who was enlisted but saw no action.

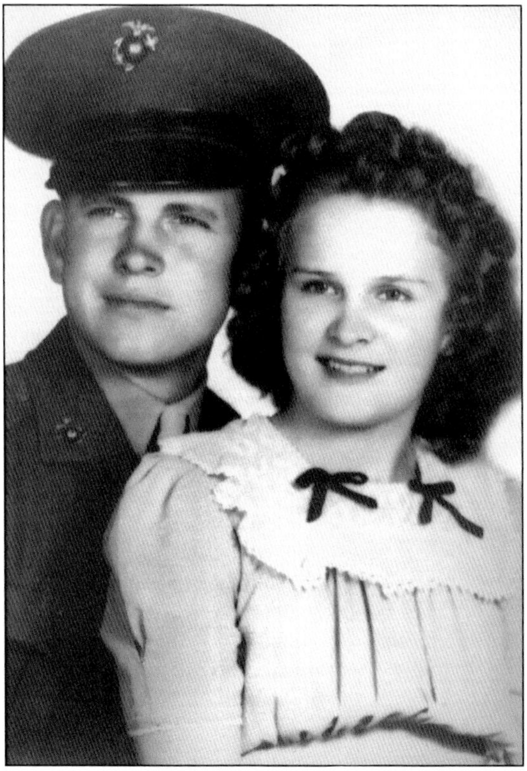

Another casualty of World War II was Robert Grisham, pictured here with his wife, Marie Scott Grisham. He was awarded a posthumous Purple Heart. Robert was a young Marine who lost his life in the Pacific just weeks after marrying his high-school sweetheart. Marie worked in Michigan as a "Rosie the Riveter" helping build planes for the war effort. She later married another veteran, Odell Braswell.

Vincent B. "Little Moe" DeNardo arrived in Granville on July 4, 1943, with the 551st Engineering Battalion from Camp Gordon, Georgia. He became friends with the Guy Grisham and Arthur Fields families and returned for many visits from 1949 through 1970. Moe was honored at the Veteran's Appreciation Day here in 2001. His photographs of this community, which appear throughout this volume, are invaluable in the preservation of our history.

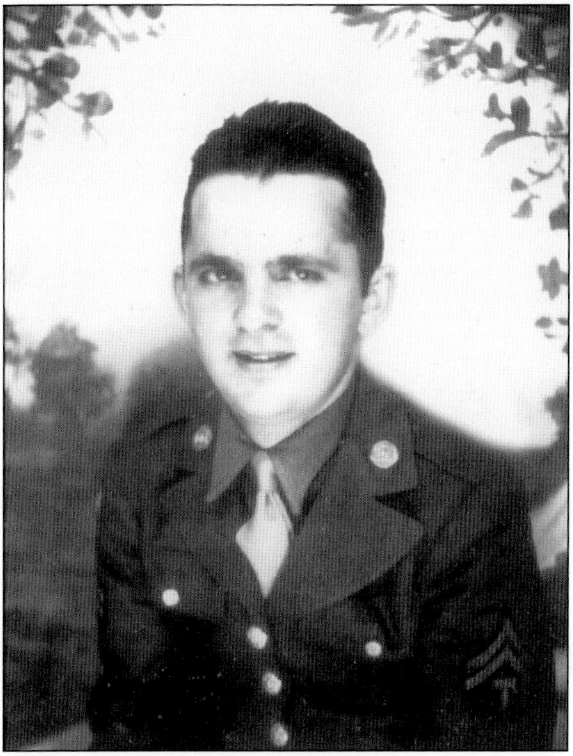

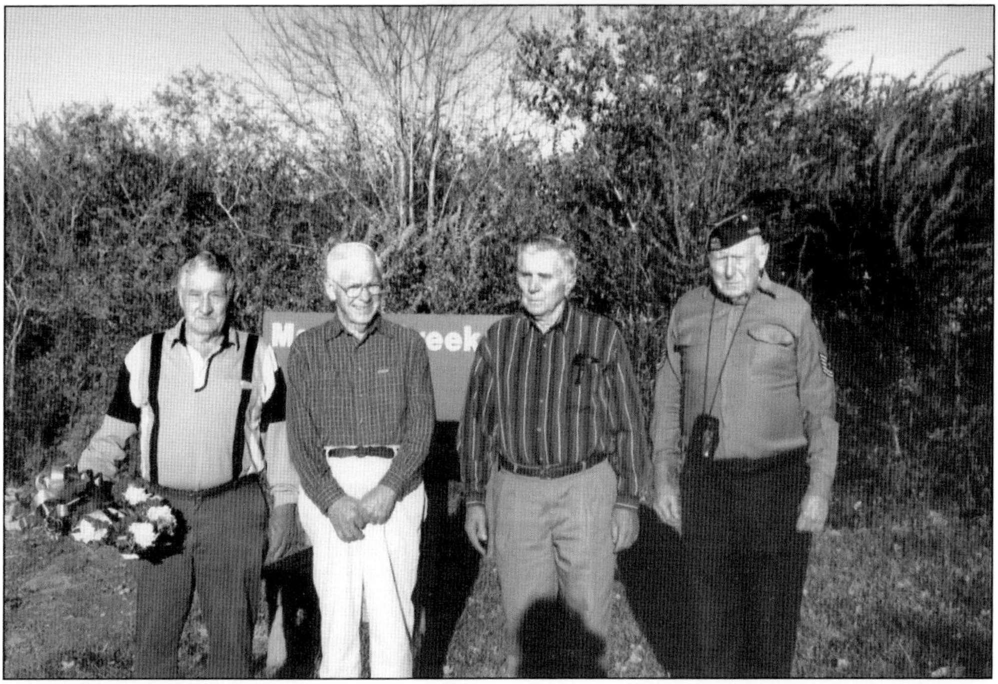

The Granville Museum honored World War II veterans on November 4, 2001, at the Granville Veterans Park. Granville had 94 men who served in this war. Pictured above at the service are, from left to right, veterans Alton Carter, Albert Ragland, Arnold Reynolds, and James Fletcher.

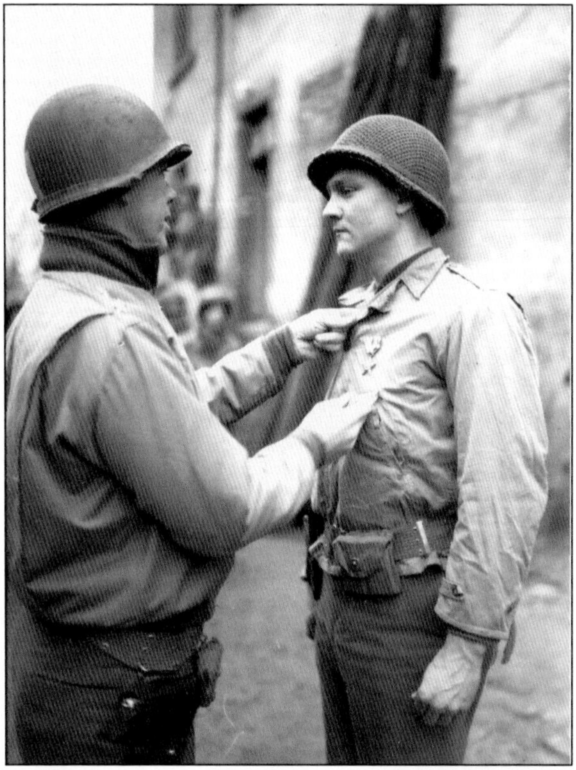

During World War II, Granville native Lonnie James Stout was presented the Silver Star by Maj. Gen. James A. van Fleet for his gallantry in action near Gavisse, France. He crossed the flooded Moselle River five times in a storm boat to install wire cables, establishing vital communications that greatly aided the 90th Infantry Division's missions. Many local soldiers returned home decorated with medals.

Bob Taylor Brown, shown here on the right with his friend Lawrence Redshaw, was inducted into the army in World War II and spent five continuous years in the South Pacific without leave. He engaged in battle on the front line in many Japanese conflicts. After returning home, he served as county clerk for many years.

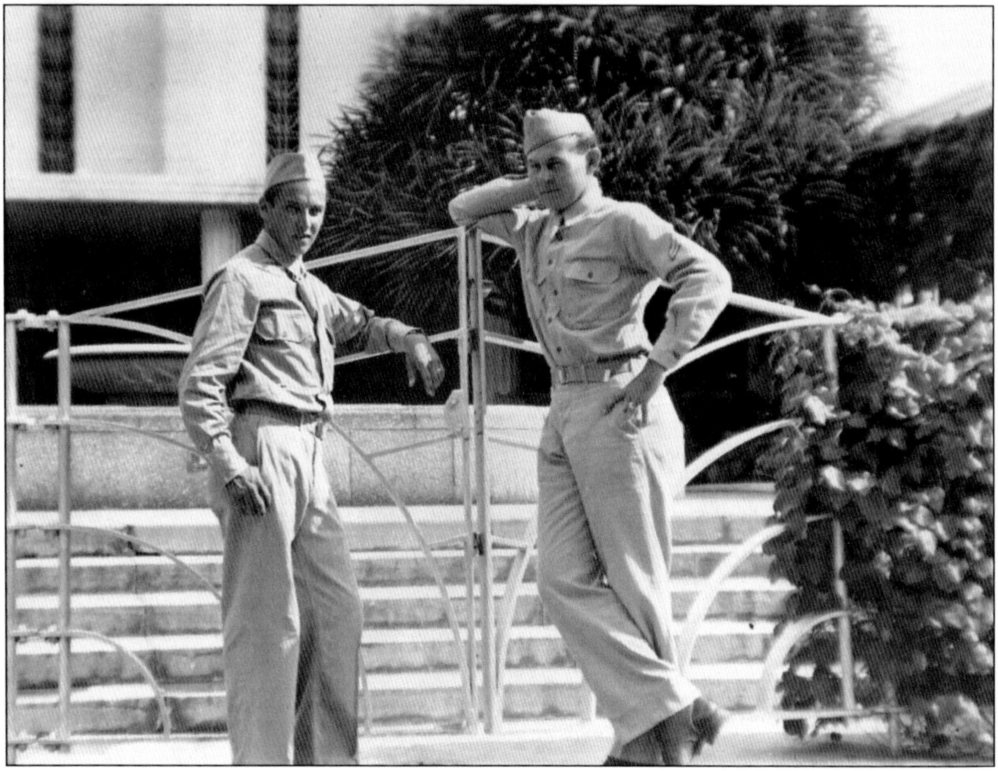

Eldridge Philpot was drafted into service at the beginning of the Korean War. He spent 28 months as a prisoner of war in North Korea. After repatriation, he was debriefed and spent time in medical care before returning home in 1953. He received a hero's welcome, with many in the community driving 40 miles to meet him and escort him home in appreciation for his service.

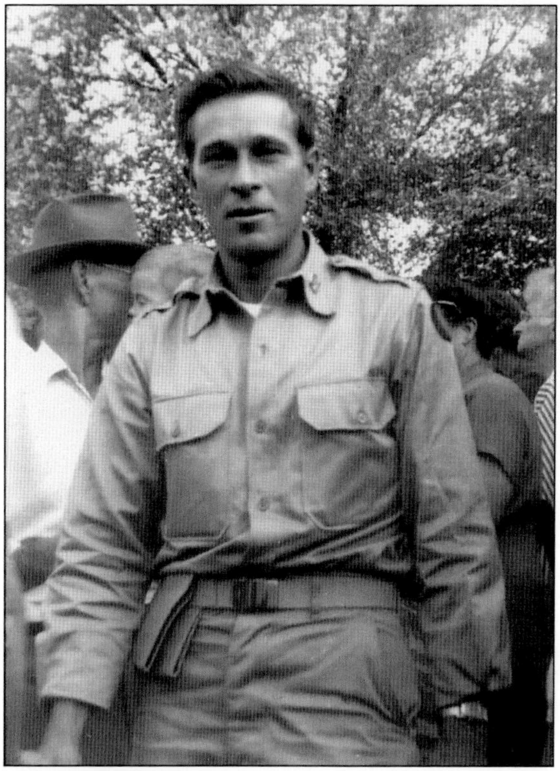

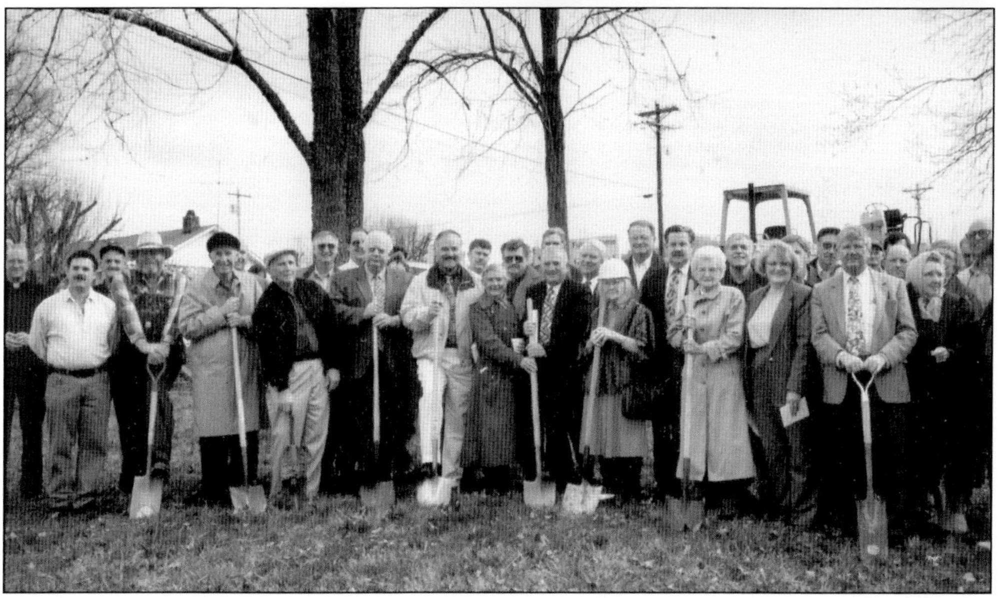

In February 1999, a park was created on Army Corps of Engineers land leased to the Granville Community Club. Present at the groundbreaking are, from left to right, (front row) County Commissioner Don Chimoy, Preacher Anderson, Ray Leftwich, Arnold Reynolds, two unidentified citizens, Gainesboro mayor Dutch Warren, Sen. Tommy Burks, Dona Mae Lee, School Superintendent Gary Lee, Minnie Ada Holleman, Ann Turner, County Manager Frank Williams, and Myrtle Reynolds.

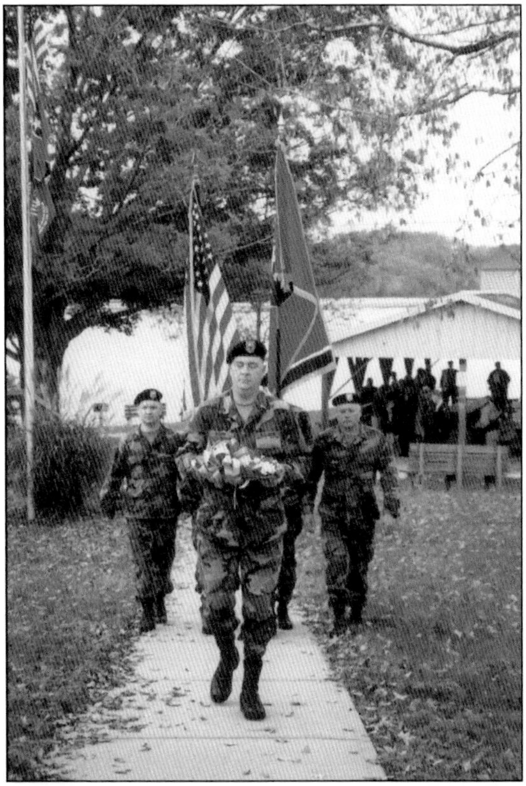

In 2001, a veterans' memorial service was held at the Granville Veterans Park. Chris Neeley played taps to close the ceremony. The color guard, pictured here, tossed a wreath into the lake in memory of those who served. Since World War II, 48 local men and women have served our country in Korea, Vietnam, and the Persian Gulf. Local residents are still active in Iraq and various parts of the world.

"We hear your fighting man has just returned on the Queen Elizabeth." This line opens the photo offer sent to families whose World War II soldiers returned from the European theater of war on the *Queen Elizabeth*, shown docking in New York Harbor on July 20, 1945. Pvt. Garlin J. Mathis's family purchased this picture documenting his return to the United States for $1.25 from the Press Association, Inc.

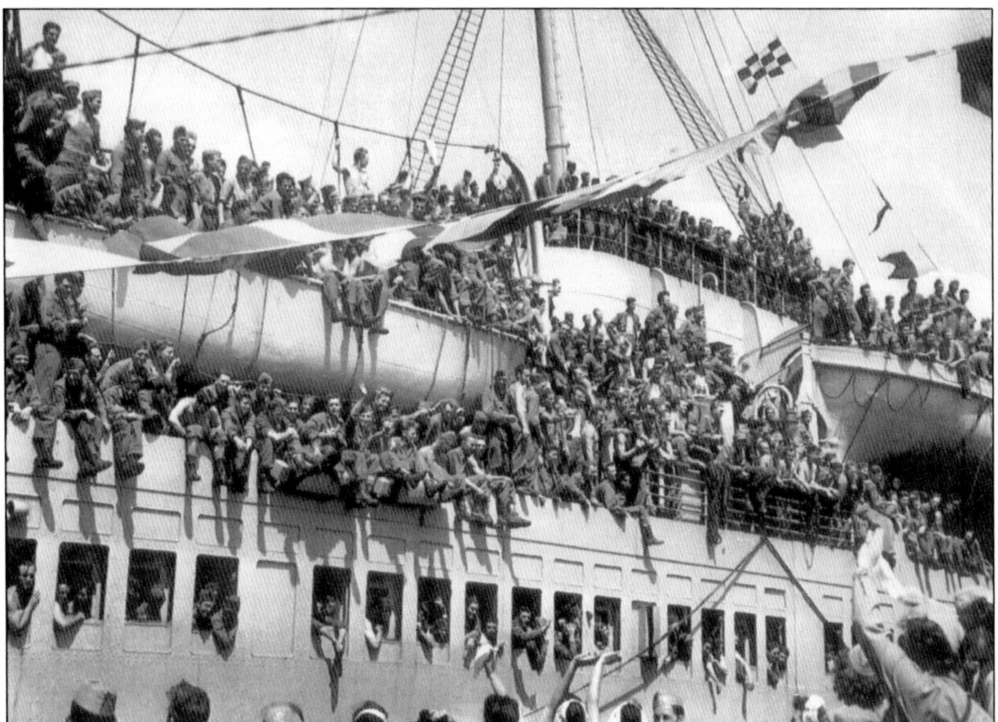

Six

MAIN STREET AND FRONT PORCHES

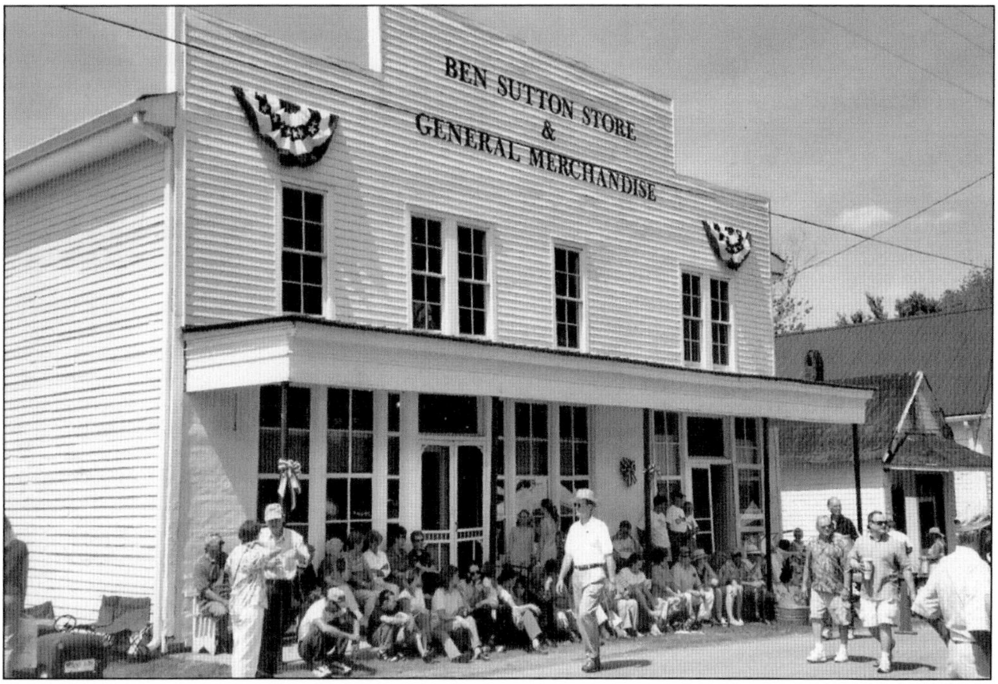

Granville comes alive with people enjoying a visit to yesteryear during the Heritage Day Celebration held on the Saturday before Memorial Day each year. The Ben Sutton Store, with original fixtures, is a step back in time, with its lunch counter, hand-dipped ice cream, and general merchandise.

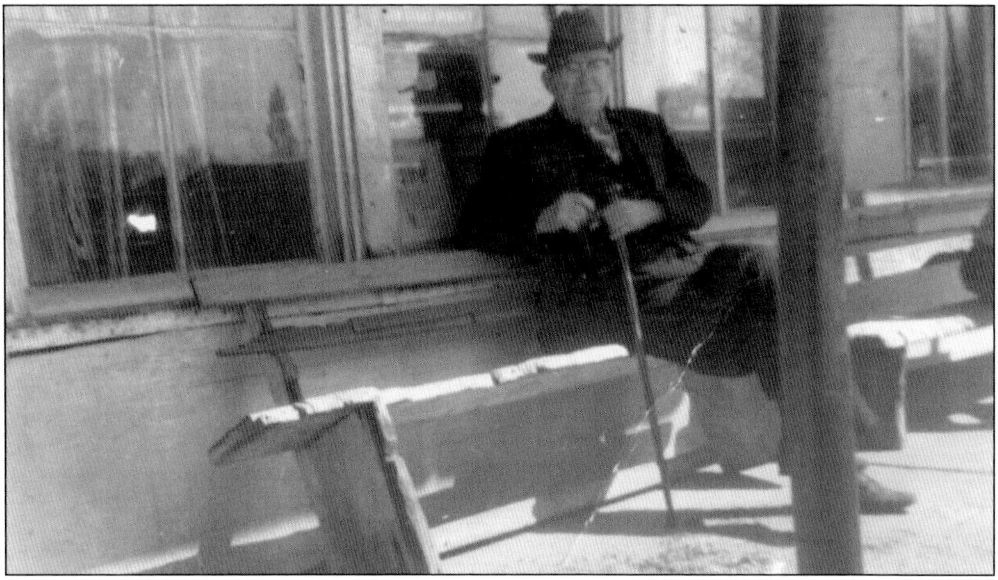

Ben Sutton, pictured in 1967, operated the T.B. Sutton store until it closed in the early 1970s. Originally opened in the 1800s as Hargis and Son General Merchandise, it was known as B.F. Cooper's in the early 1900s before becoming Sutton's. After a short period of operation by John Clemons, the store remained closed until purchased, remodeled, and re-opened by Harold and Beverly Sutton on May 26, 2001.

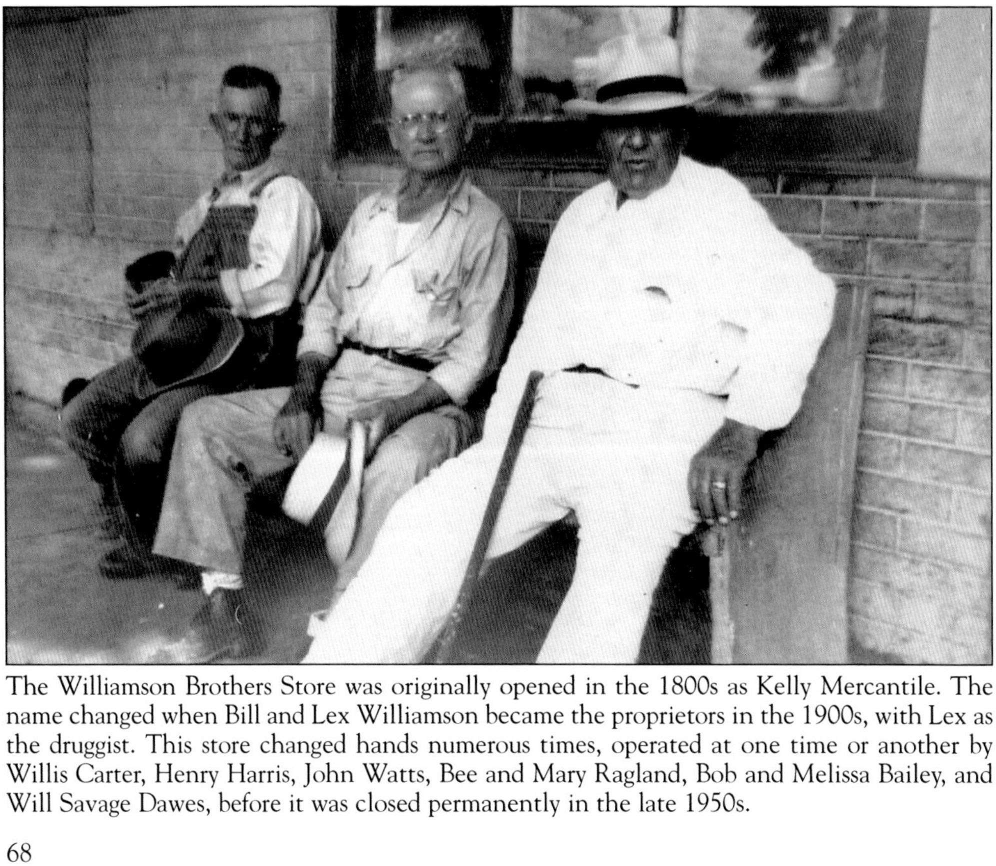

The Williamson Brothers Store was originally opened in the 1800s as Kelly Mercantile. The name changed when Bill and Lex Williamson became the proprietors in the 1900s, with Lex as the druggist. This store changed hands numerous times, operated at one time or another by Willis Carter, Henry Harris, John Watts, Bee and Mary Ragland, Bob and Melissa Bailey, and Will Savage Dawes, before it was closed permanently in the late 1950s.

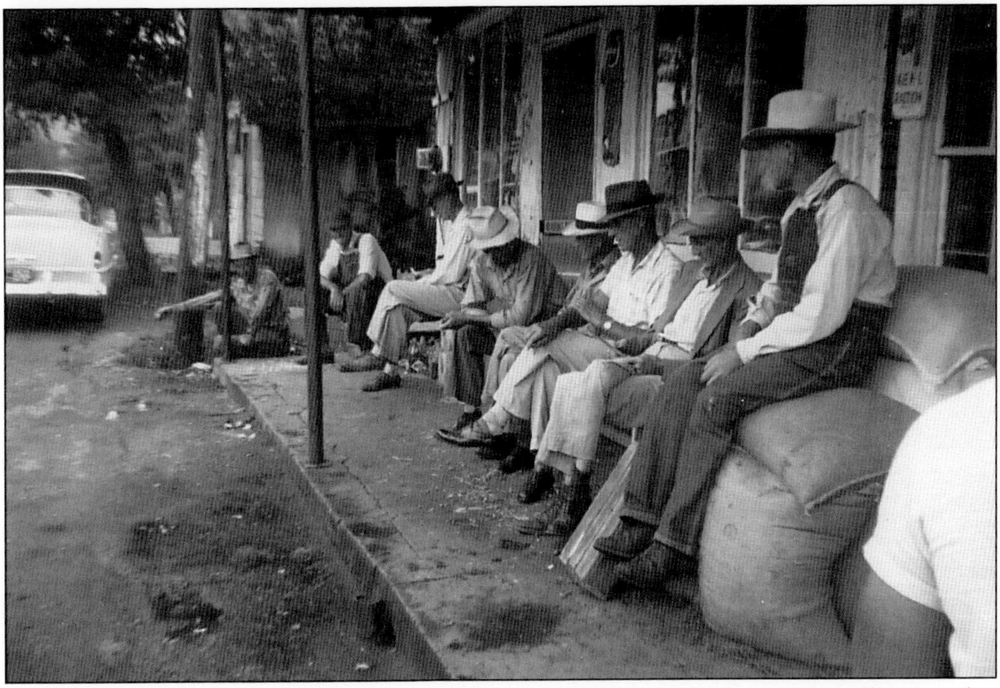

The Jim King General Store was opened in the early 1900s and was known for selling wooden caskets. In 1936, Hooper Brown and Cordell Ragland bought the store, though Ragland sold his share relatively soon. Brown operated the store until 1960, specializing in the Remington line of guns as well as feed sold from the side room addition. Bob and Melissa Bailey later re-opened the store.

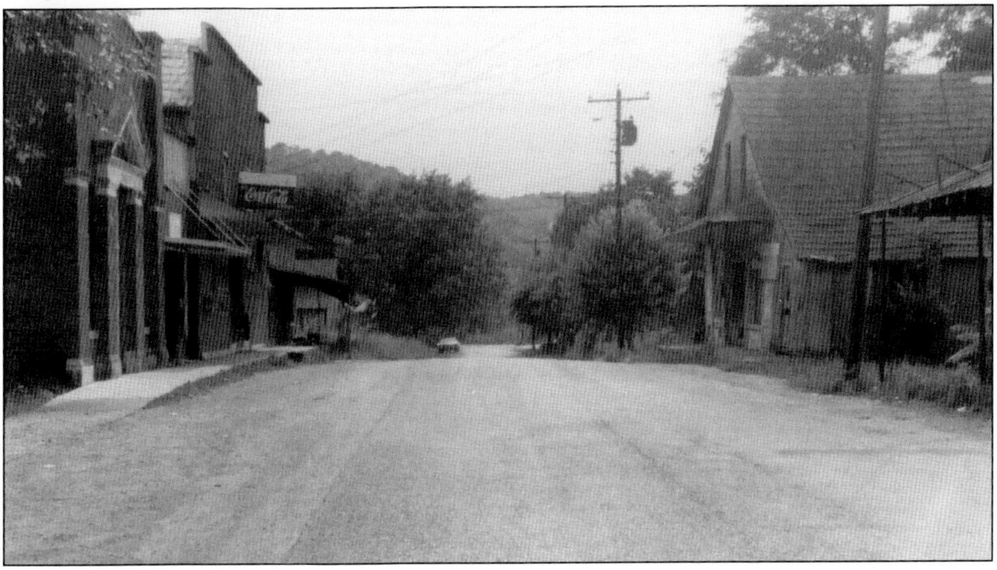

On the right in this picture stands a store building opened in the 1920s by Davis Huff and son-in-law Raymond Haile. The business changed hands many times. The other owners in chronological order were Carl Huff and Berry Shirley, Oscar Grisham, Berry Shirley and Joseph Carver, Carl Huff, Frank Carroll Robinson, and finally Willard Stanton. The store closed in the late 1950s.

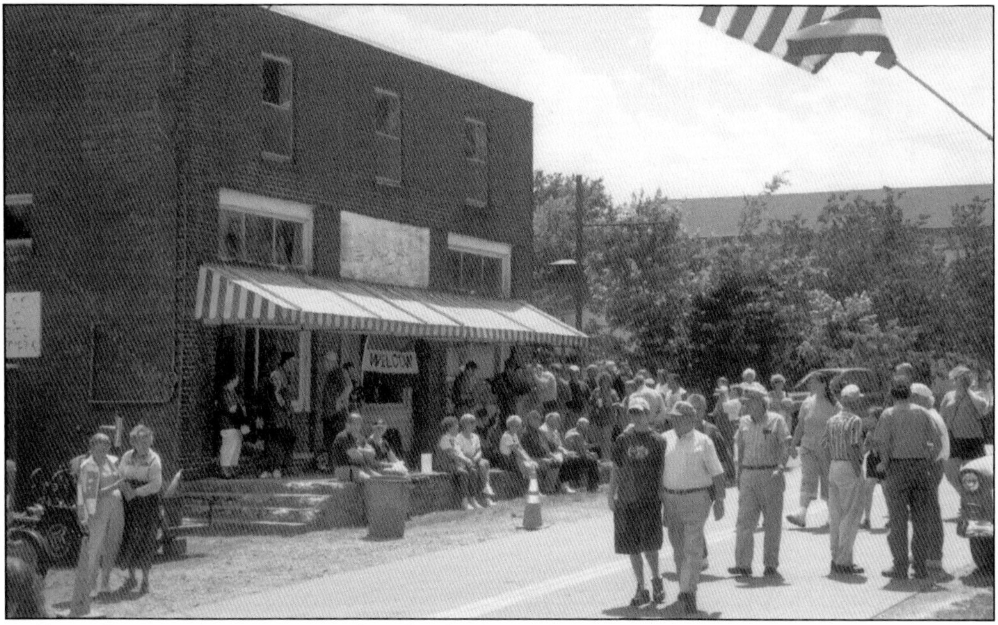

Still standing on Clover Street today, this brick building known as the Mercantile was operated by Thurman T. Dowell, Walter Cooper, and Bill Cornwell of the Granville Merchandise Company. After the store closed, Dowell operated a funeral home at this location from 1929 to 1949. John Clemons and Hope Philpot later opened stores here. The last business to reside in this building was a video store and auction barn, which closed in the 1980s.

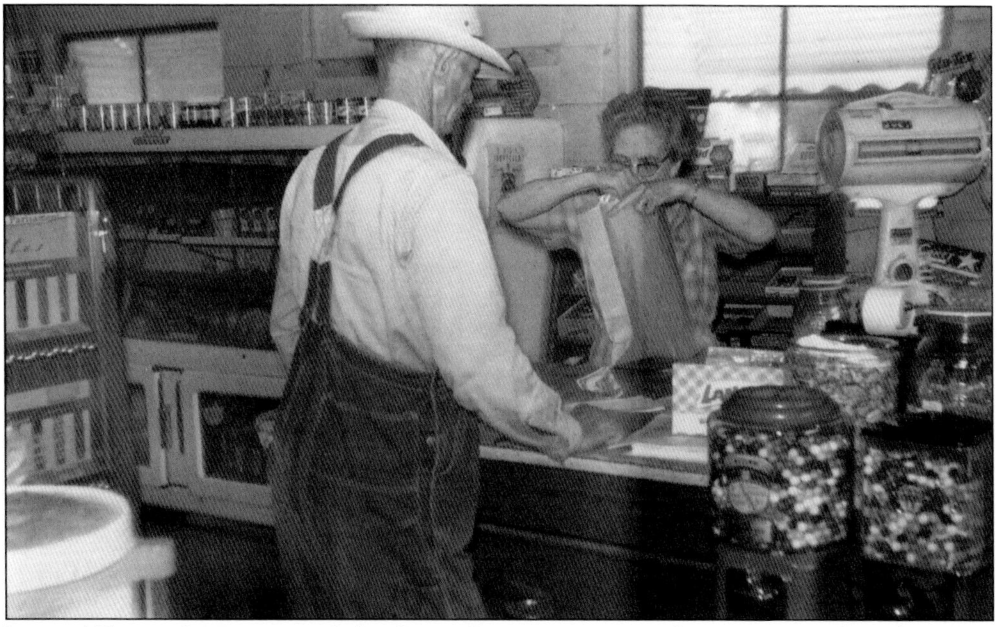

Lee and Fannie Carter operated the Carter Store, a grocery and creamery, on their farm near the Granville School. Their son, Farmer, operated a garage and appliance store across from where Veterans Park is located today. In 1944, Farmer enlisted in World War II, and the Carters moved their store to his garage location. In 1957, they built the West End Market with help from their sons Alton and Malcolm. That store closed in the late 1960s.

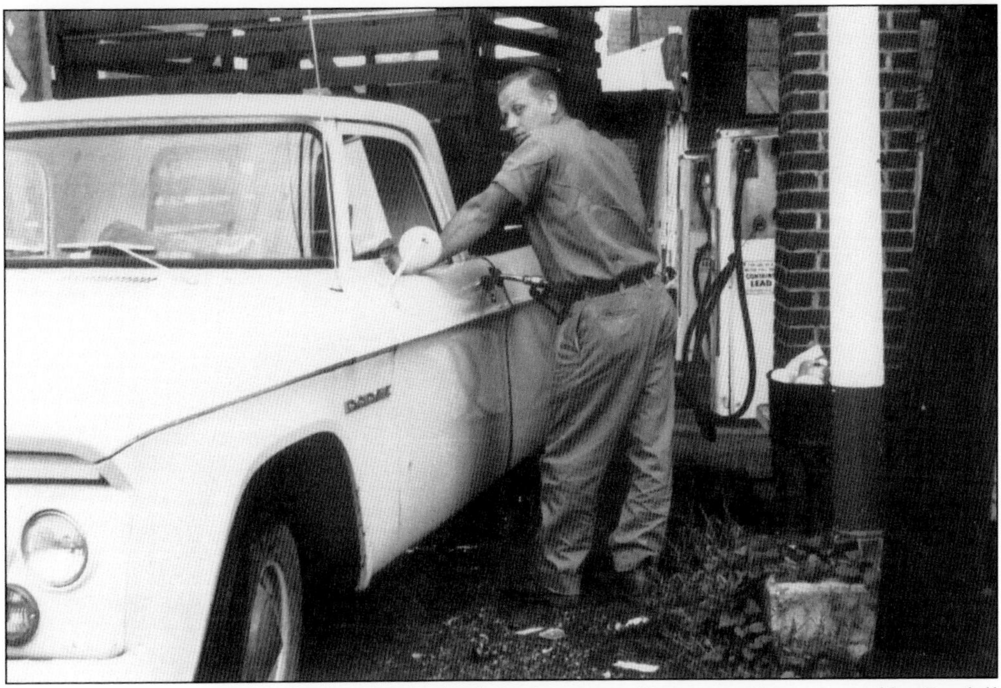

This service station and garage, originally built by Arrington Ditty, was also operated by Cordell Ragland, Ralph Halfacre, Gerd McCrary, Chuck Guess, and David Montgomery. In 1953, Jonas Ragland purchased the property from Montgomery and operated it until March 1968 at this location.

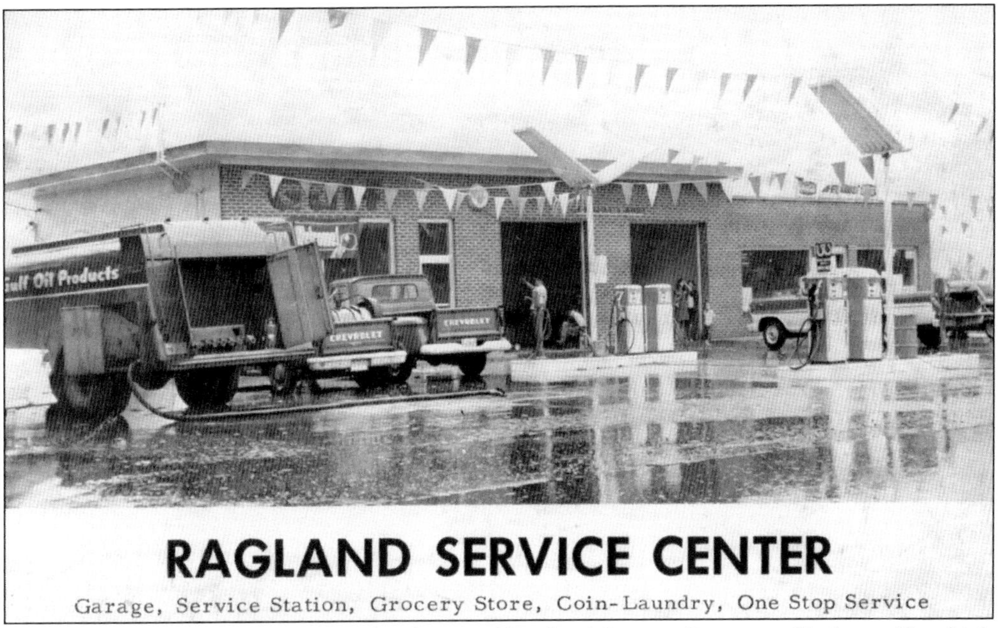

In March 1968, Jonas and Ann Ragland opened Ragland Service Center on Highway 53, which offered "one stop service" with a grocery store, service station, garage, and coin-operated laundry. The Raglands closed down shop in 1993. Harold and Tammy Cherry and Eugene and Tonya Hamlet are currently operating the grocery store and gas pumps.

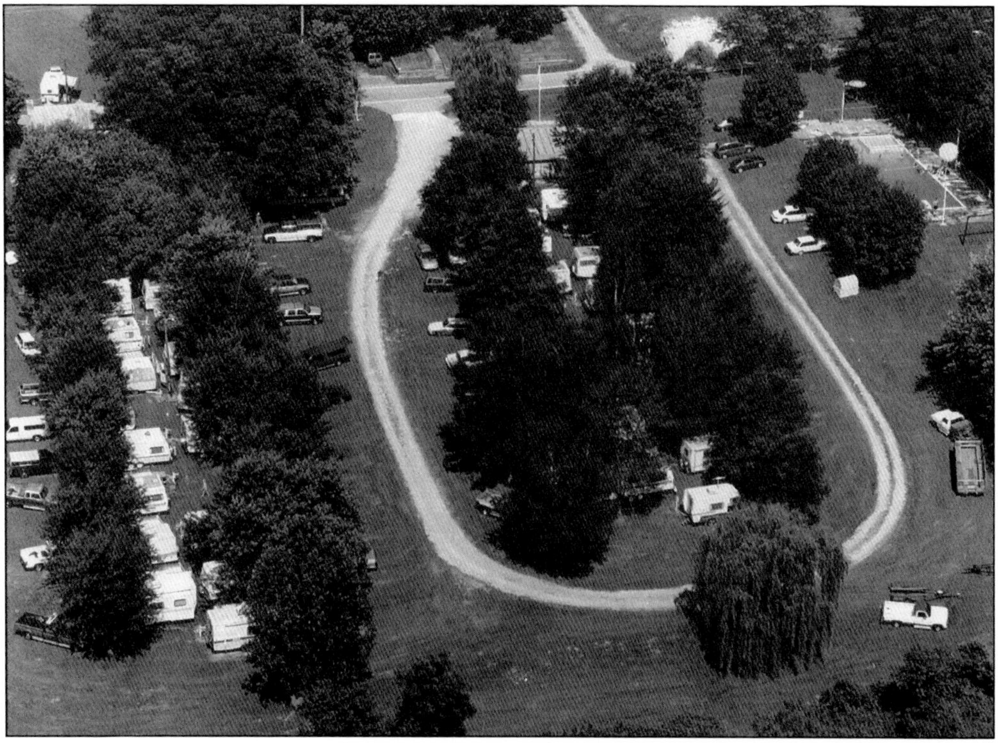

Jonas and Ann Ragland opened Ragland Campground in August 1975. This public campground included a swimming pool and electric and water hookups. Campers came from all across the United States to camp here, as it was known for Badeye's country music. The Raglands owned it until October 1998. The campground is open today as Maple Grove Campground, owned by Gerald and Pat Myers.

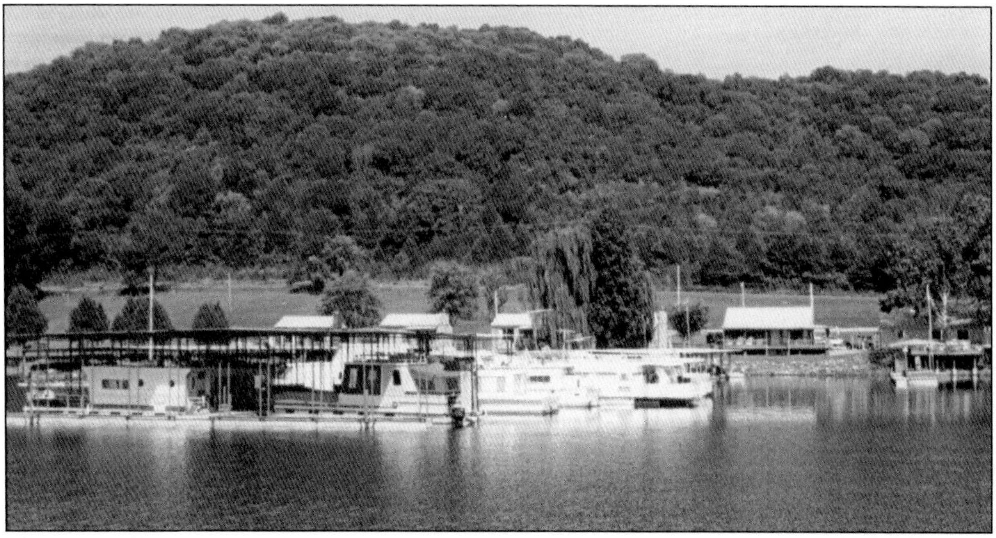

The Granville Marina and Resort was opened in the mid-1970s by Sue and Doug Kell. The 38-acre recreation area offers cabins, campsites, a boat launch ramp, boat slips, and houseboats, with food available at the full-service restaurant. It is currently owned and operated by Johnny and Barbara Taylor.

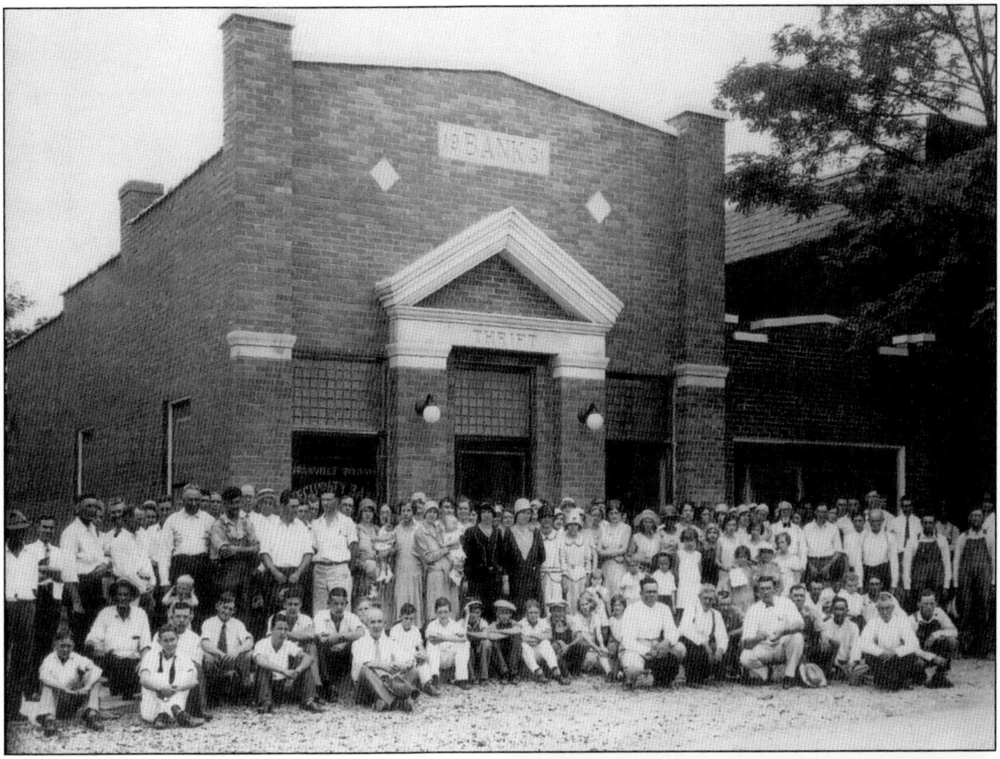

The opening of the Security Bank and Trust on July 1, 1931, was cause for a grand celebration in Granville. The community turned out to share the excitement for the new building where the Bank of Granville, which was chartered on April 7, 1905, and closed on March 27, 1931, had once stood. The directors were W.F. Sadler, H.M. Haile, and Harry L. Page. Frank Gailreath was the head teller.

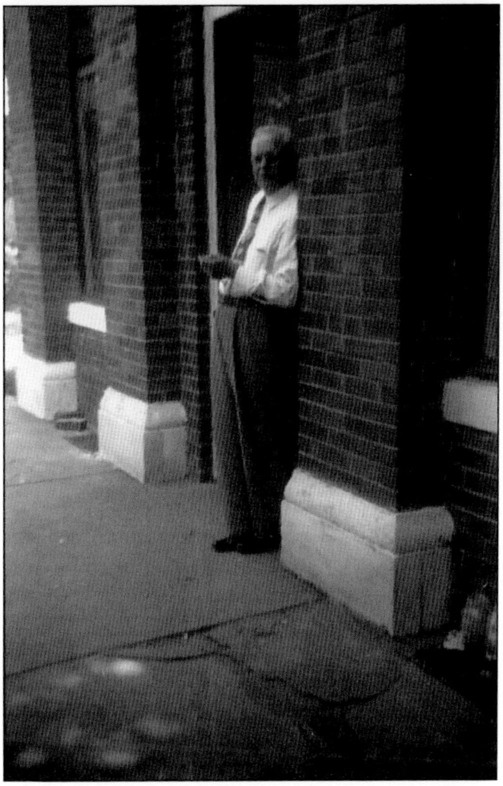

Security Bank and Trust became a branch of the Jackson County Bank in 1934. Arthur Willoughby was the manager and vice president. He worked for both previous banks as well. Other bankers serving the Granville community included J. Clark Jackson, Charles C. Brown, Berry Shirley, Arnold Reynolds, Katherine Willoughby Stanton, and Mildred Haile Carter.

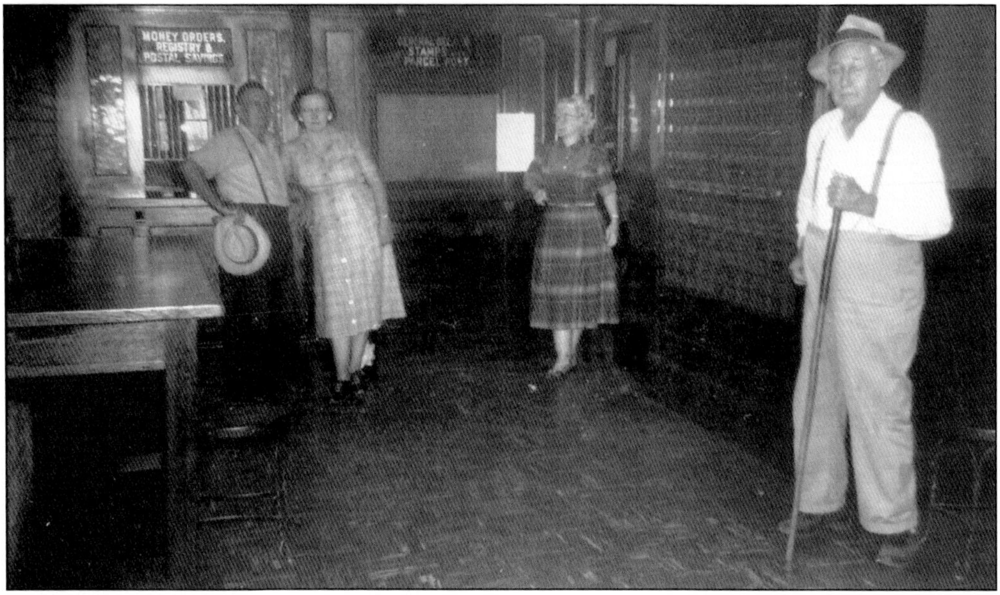

Shown from left to right in this photograph are Will H. (Bill) Cornwell, mail carrier; Lois Carter McKinley, clerk; Anna Ruth Hargis Huff, postmaster; and Morgan Duke, customer. Huff served as the postmaster from September 30, 1952, until January 31, 1969. Dr. Luther M. Freeman had the position from 1928 until 1952. Cornwell was postmaster for five years prior to becoming a mail carrier from 1928 until 1954.

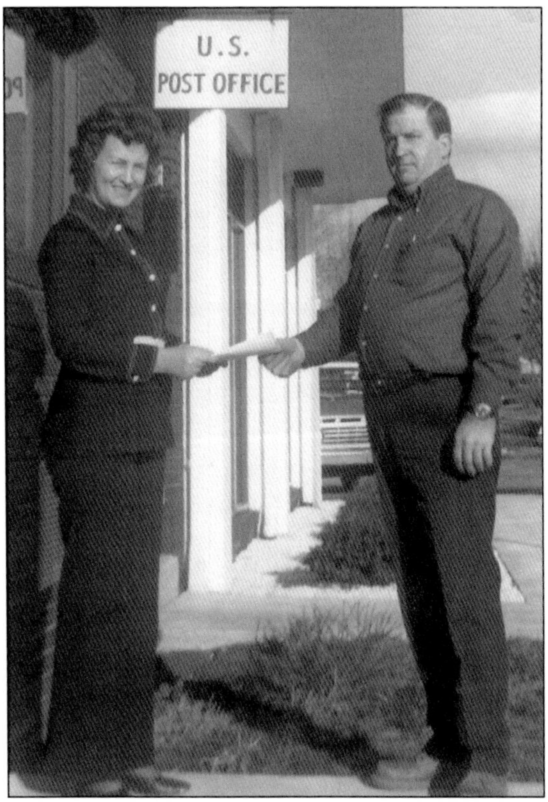

In this 1977 picture, Postmaster Elise R. Halfacre Huff and mail carrier Lloyd Halfacre are shown in front of the Granville Post Office, which was behind the Jackson County Bank on Granville Highway from 1972 until 1985. Elise Huff is the second longest-serving postmaster here, serving from 1969 until 1988. Lloyd Halfacre is the longest-serving Granville mail carrier, serving from 1955 to 1990.

In 1905, Dr. Luther M. Freeman graduated from the University of Tennessee Medical School in Nashville. He came to Granville on horseback in 1906 to set up his practice. He married local girl Ethel Maddux and settled into the community. Dr. Freeman practiced medicine until shortly before his death at the age of 94. He performed dual roles in the community, as he was also Granville's longest-serving postmaster.

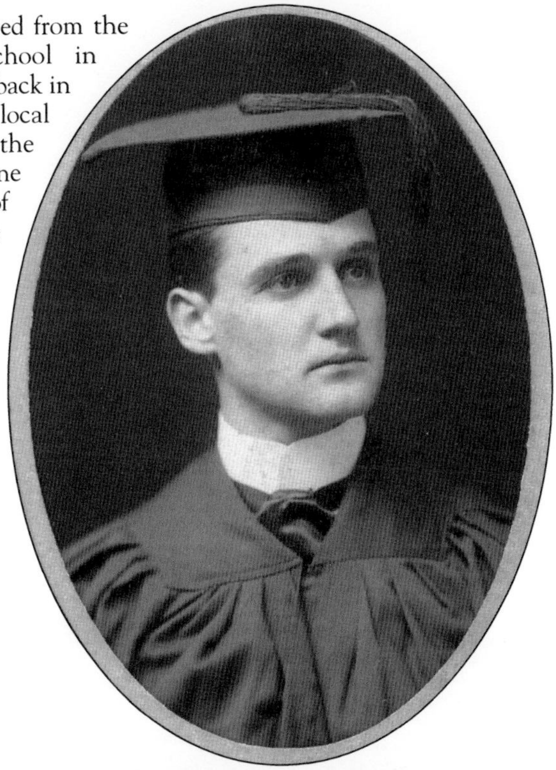

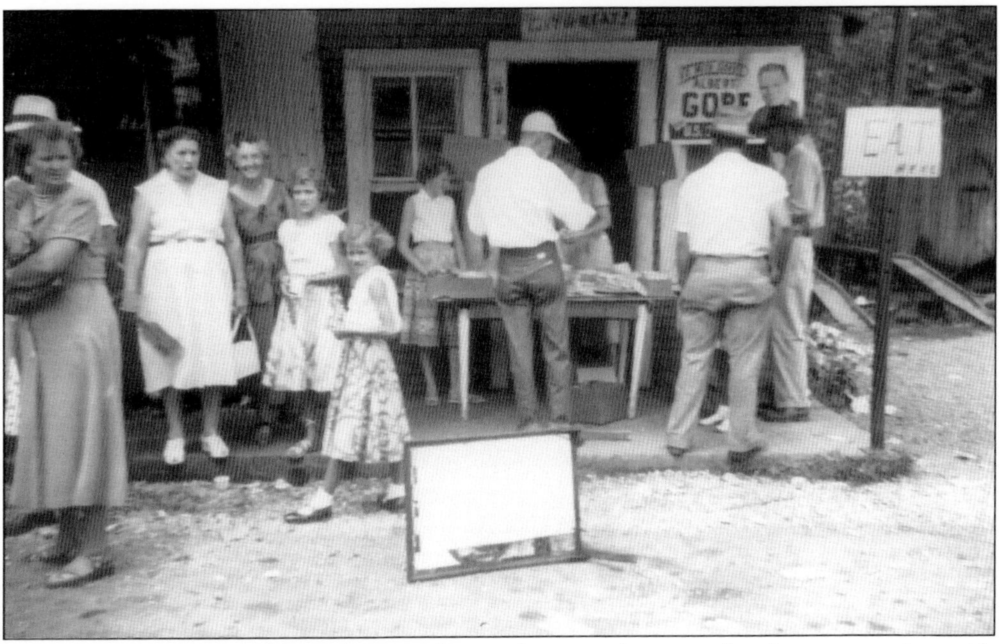

Early elections were held outdoors and were big social events for the community, with "commercial" ice cream, lemonade, watermelon, and even a stage built for entertainment. Candidate Albert Gore Sr., who won election to the Senate, was born in Granville, just across the river.

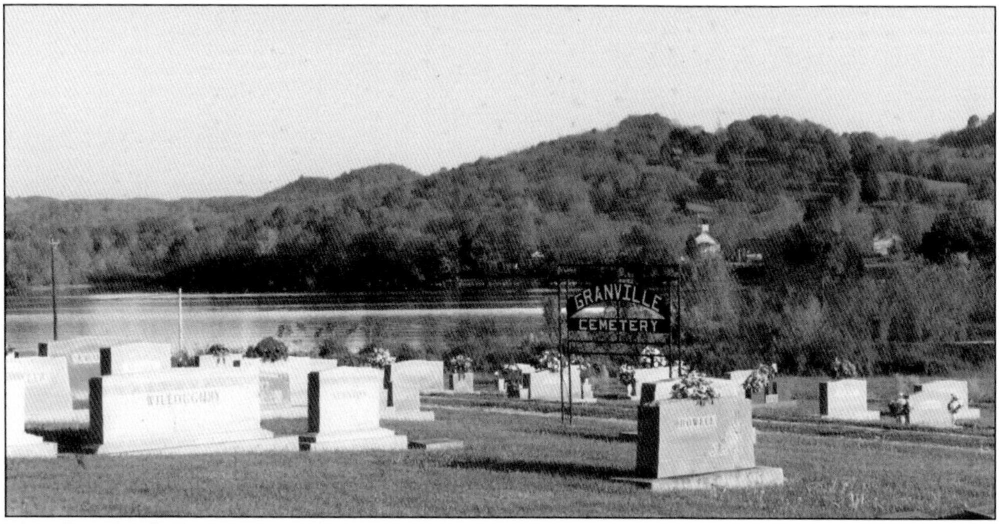

The first land donation to the Granville Cemetery Association came from the family of R.H. Dowell in 1927. Other land has been added through the years to make up the present cemetery. The first trustees were R.L. Hargis, B.P. Shirley, H.S. Holleman, T.T. Dowell, T.D. Hargis, and J.F. Williamson. The cemetery association was reorganized in 1978 and chartered perpetual care in 1985.

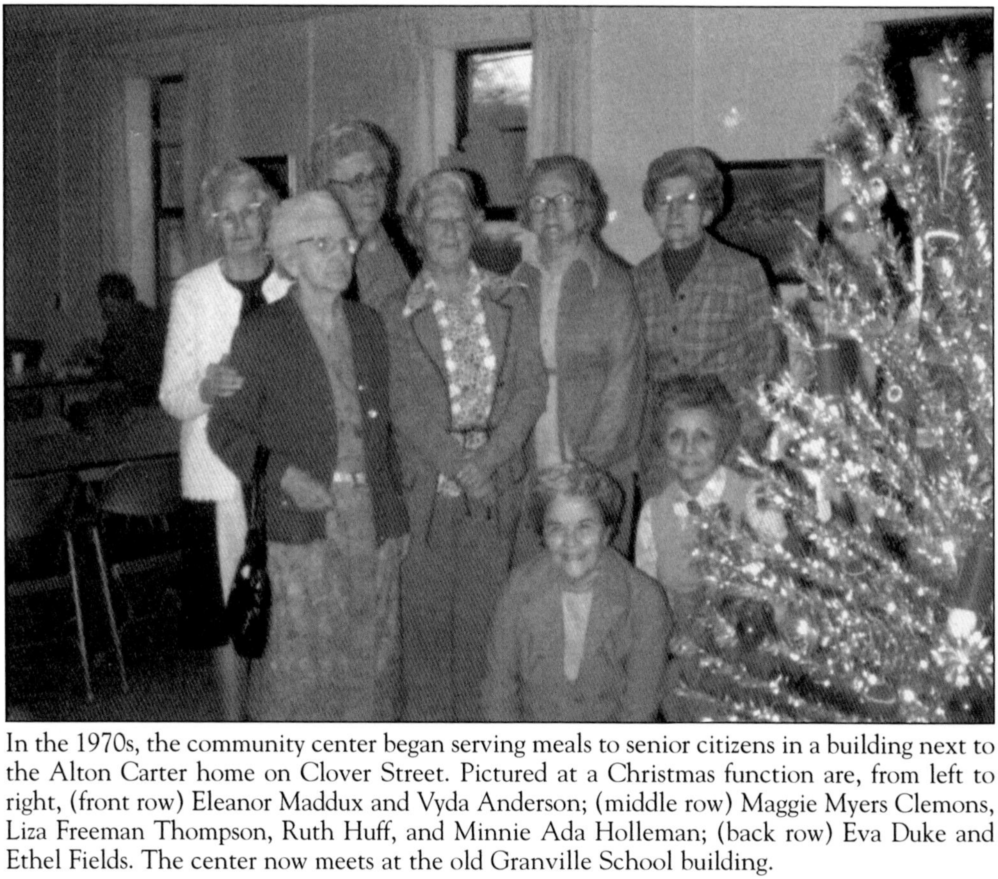

In the 1970s, the community center began serving meals to senior citizens in a building next to the Alton Carter home on Clover Street. Pictured at a Christmas function are, from left to right, (front row) Eleanor Maddux and Vyda Anderson; (middle row) Maggie Myers Clemons, Liza Freeman Thompson, Ruth Huff, and Minnie Ada Holleman; (back row) Eva Duke and Ethel Fields. The center now meets at the old Granville School building.

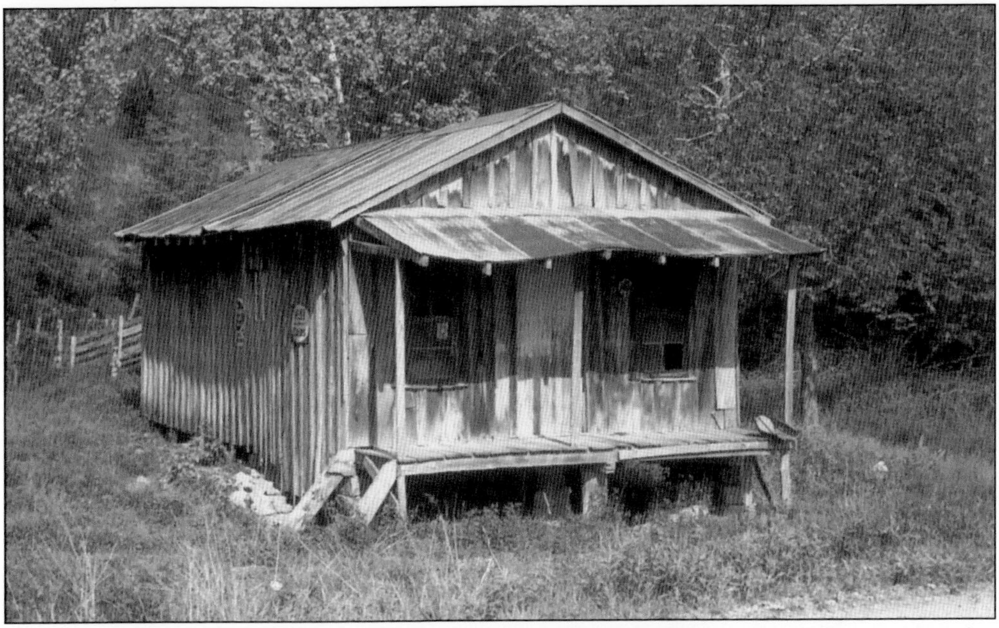

The Corinth community had a general store opened by Sam Duke in the 1920s. In 1940, his son, Allison Duke, and wife, Audra, took over operations. In 1947, Lenard Jack Woodard purchased the business. In 1949, it changed hands again when Harrison H. and Carl H. Woodard purchased it. It was sold again in 1953 to Jim and Ruby Givens and closed permanently in the late 1950s.

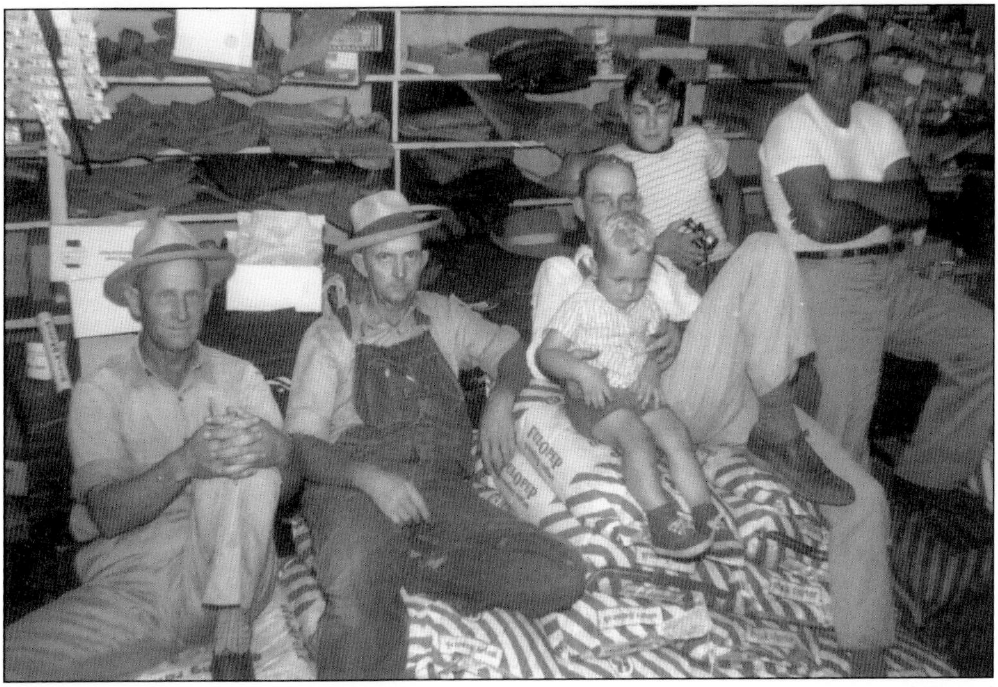

In this photo, from left to right, Lester Ragland, Douglas Holleman, John Clemons with David Eller in his lap, Jerry Eller, and Clyde Eller, are seated on a stack of feed sacks in Hooper Brown's store. The store carried a variety of household items, farm supplies, and clothing.

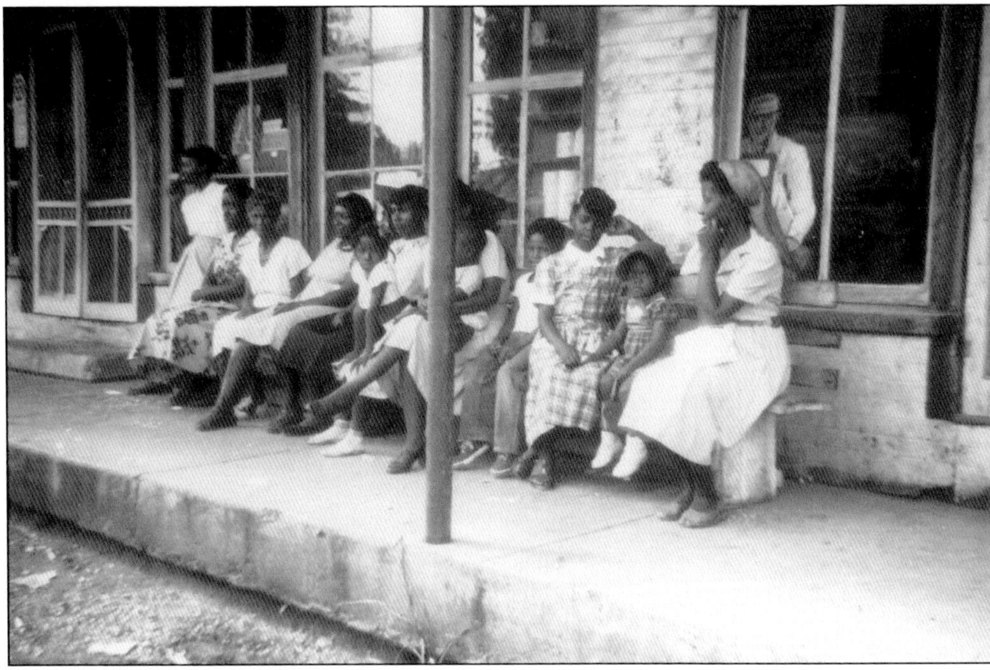

Families would come to town on Saturday to socialize as well as take care of their errands. This group was relaxing and visiting on the porch of the Ben Sutton Store in the 1950s.

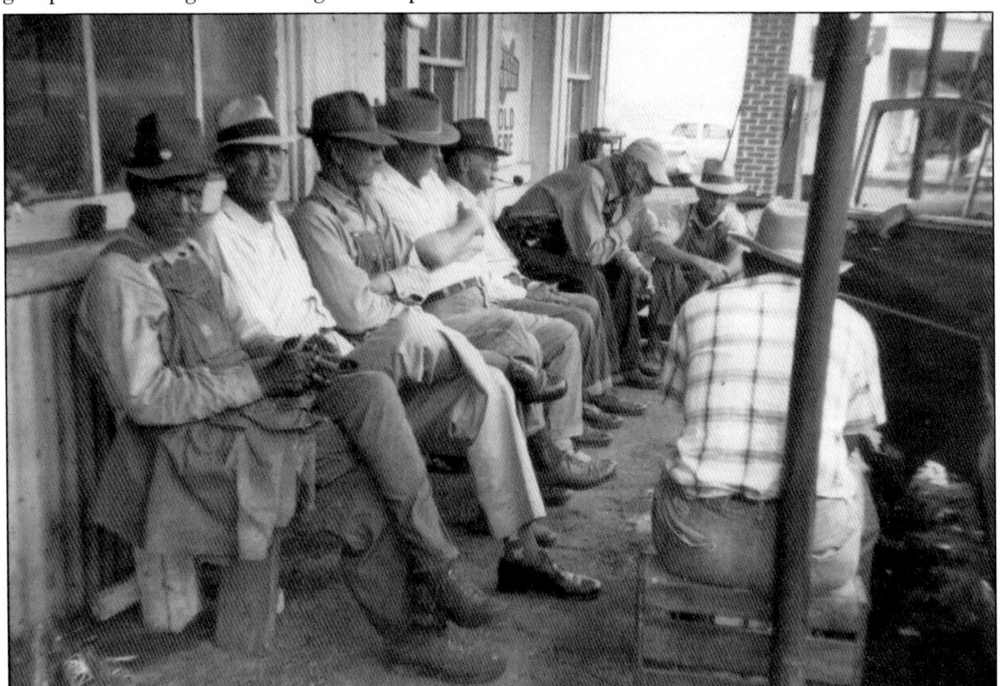

Men gathered on the front porches of the Granville stores to trade stories, whittle, and solve the world's problems. Pictured in front of the Hooper Brown Store, from left to right, are Anthony Myers, Pack Fields, Howard Lee, unidentified, Howard Flatt, unidentified, Douglas Holleman, and (with back to camera) unidentified.

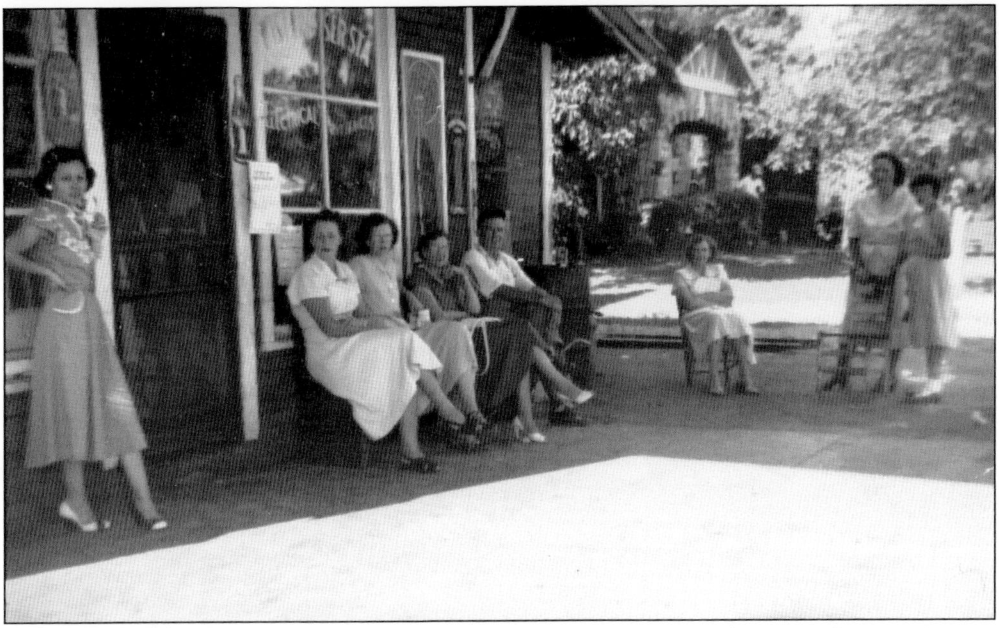

The ladies also gathered to trade news while in town. In front of Farmer Carter's Service Station, this group consists of, from left to right, Vyda Anderson, Nell Harris, Clara Harris, two unidentified, Reba Harris, Gayle Harris, and unidentified.

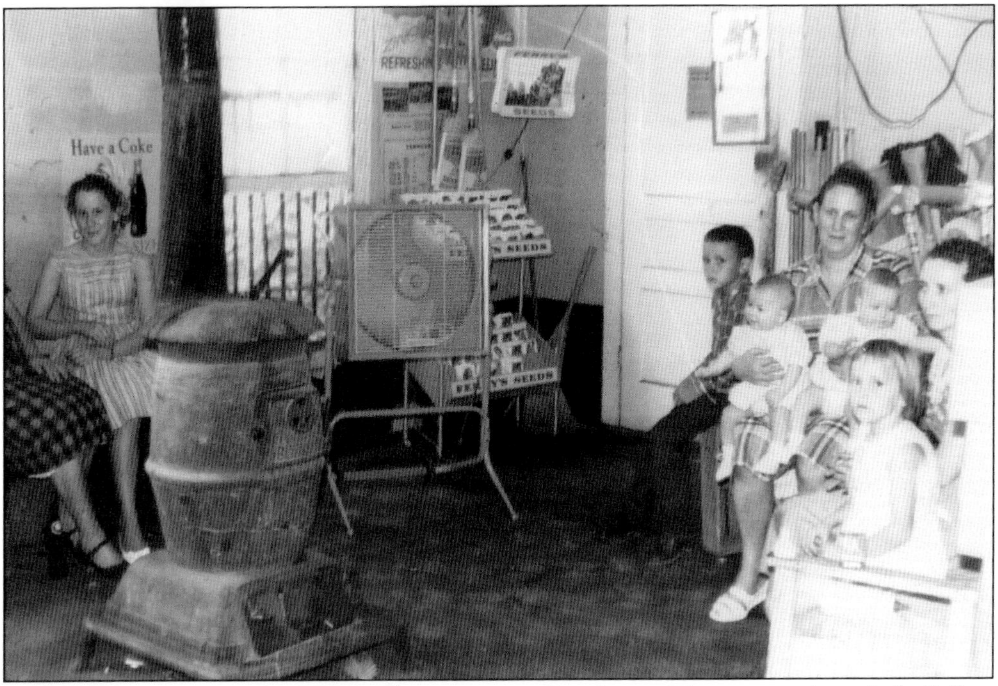

Hooper Brown's store welcomed families to sit a spell and visit. This picture shows Judy Collier (at left) and Louise Collier (at right), holding twins Peggy and Patty, and Stanley, Dimple and Shirley Huff. Without modern central heat and air, the wood stove in the center would be stoked up in winter for heating and the floor fan would be used in the warmer months for cooling.

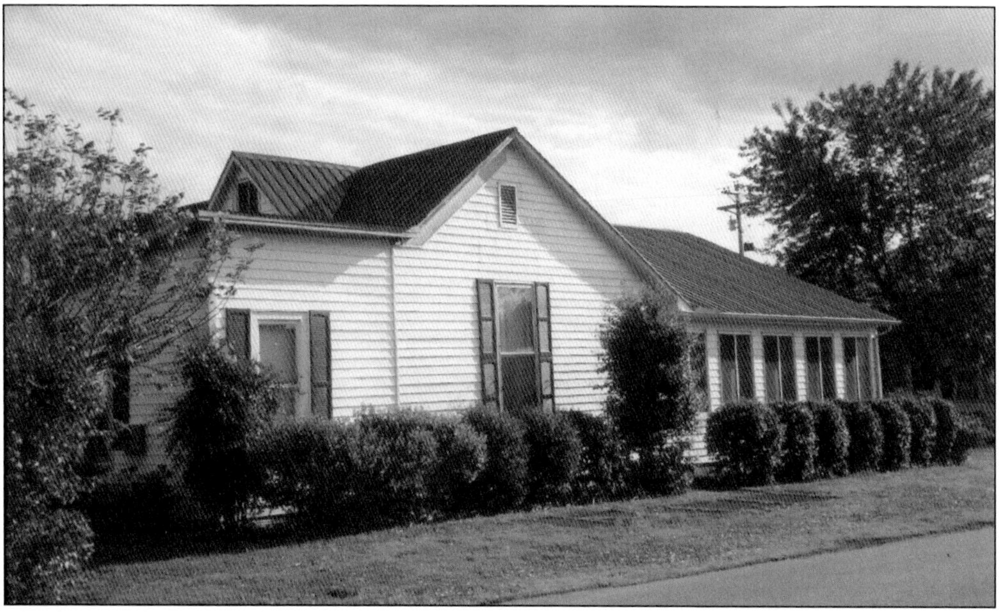

The home of Alton and Mildred Carter is the oldest home in Granville. Built prior to the Civil War, a general in the Confederate Army is said to have stayed in this home. The front east corner room was the second Granville Post Office, and the old Granville Delivery Stable was also located on the property. Previous owners of the property were the Williamsons and the Suttons.

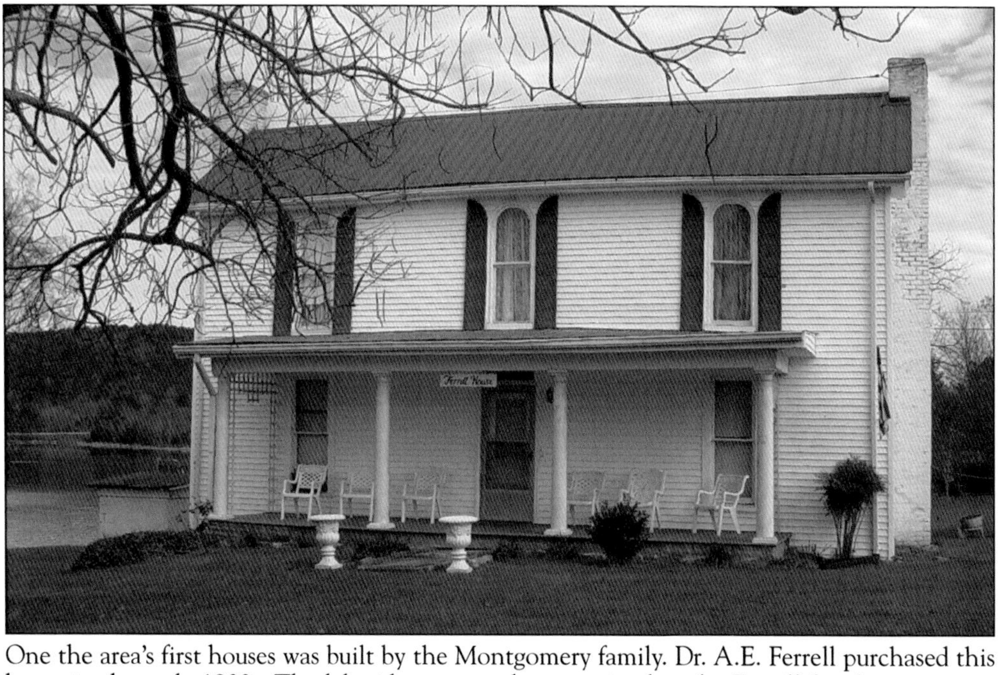

One the area's first houses was built by the Montgomery family. Dr. A.E. Ferrell purchased this home in the early 1900s. The lakeside property has remained in the Ferrell family ever since. Dr. Ferrell's daughter, Mary Nell, and her husband, John Watts, raised their family here. Their son, Dr. Glenn Watts, worked hard to preserve the home. The home, pictured above as it looks today, is currently owned by the grandchildren of Mary Nell and John Watts.

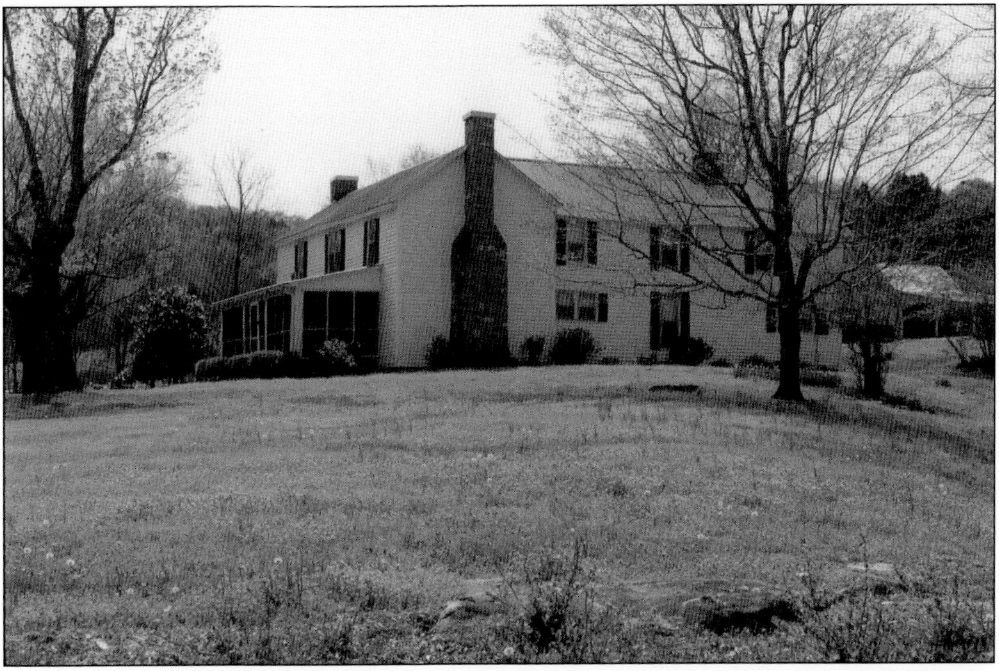

This beech log home, later remodeled, and its farm make up one Granville property held by the same family for its entire history. Thomas Jefferson and Maggie Burton Maddux inherited this farm through their family lines, the Stanton and the Montgomery families. The farm was acquired by the Montgomerys as a land grant from Sam Houston over 200 years ago.

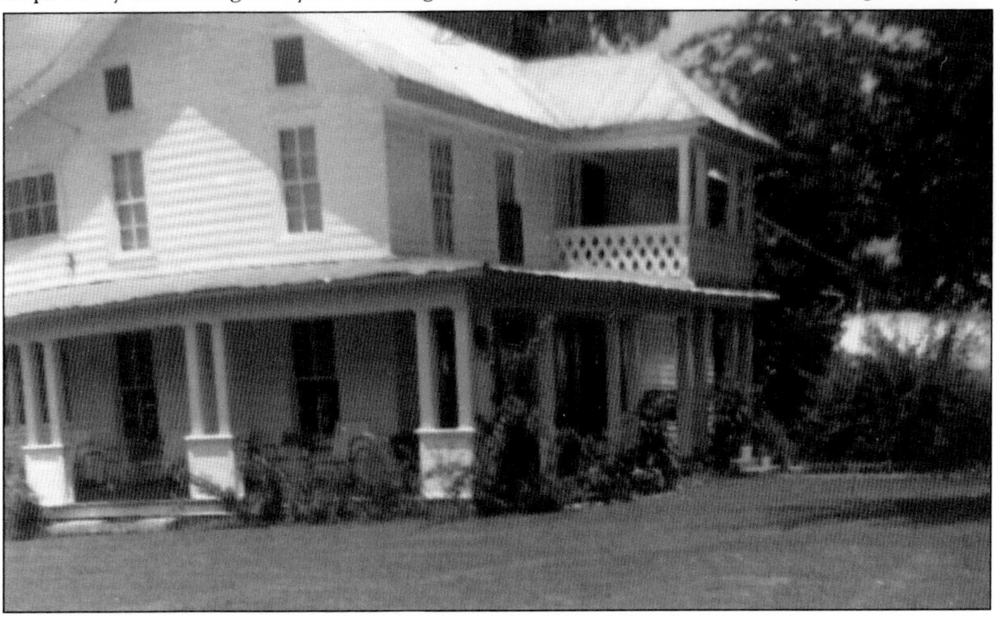

This home was built for F.A. Kelly, the owner of Kelly Mercantile, in the 1800s. In the 1920s, the house was purchased by Claudess Williamson and later became the home of W.C. "Bill" Williamson until 1947. The home and porch were remodeled during the ownership of Benton and Dora Carter Halfacre and again after the purchase of the home by Ward and Peggy Ragland Mallory in 2001.

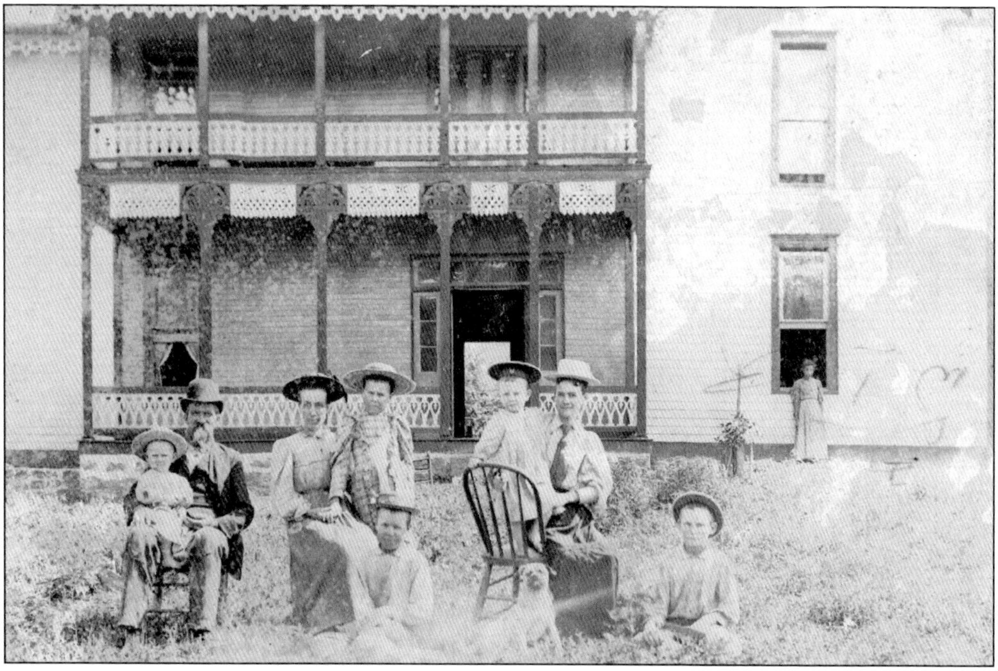

Originally built in 1890, this home was purchased and rebuilt by Samuel S. Carver in 1892. This 1896 picture shows, from left to right, family members (front row) Joseph R. Carver and Haden Clark; (back row) Samuel Carver holding Berry Shirley, Amanda West Carver, Florence Carver, Zerelda Carver Russell holding Donald Russell, and unidentified. Samuel Carver's great-grandson, Joe Moore, and his wife, Ann, live in the home today.

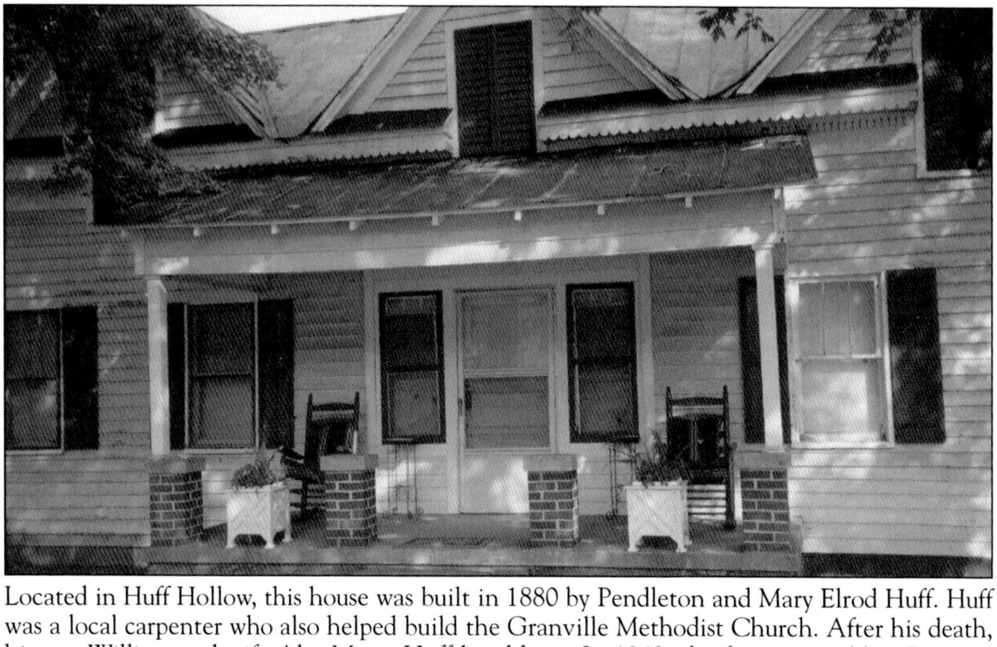

Located in Huff Hollow, this house was built in 1880 by Pendleton and Mary Elrod Huff. Huff was a local carpenter who also helped build the Granville Methodist Church. After his death, his son William and wife Alta Myers Huff lived here. In 1942, the farm was sold to Bee and Mary Clark Ragland and is currently owned and being restored by their daughter, Jeanette, and her husband, Jack Dalton.

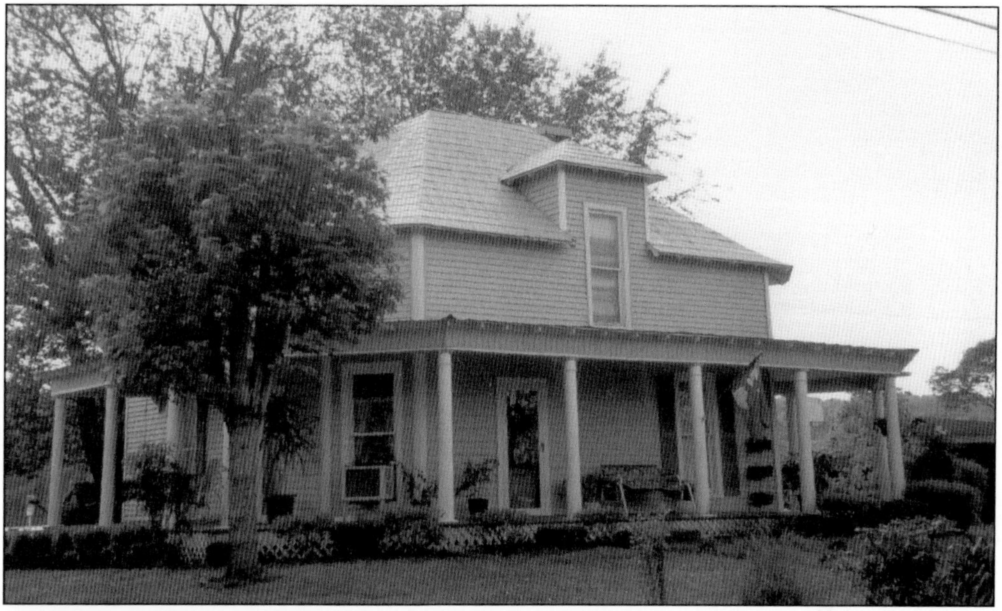

The Granville home pictured here was built in the early 1900s by Arthur Fox and later owned by Sid and Helen Sutton. Alonzo and Minnie Tittle Huff lived there from 1941 until 1944 and then sold the property to J. Howard and Avo Jones Daniels, who lived in it until 1965. After purchasing the property from Virgil Halfacre, Glenn Fitzpatrick completely remodeled the home. The current owners are Jim and Vanessa Williams.

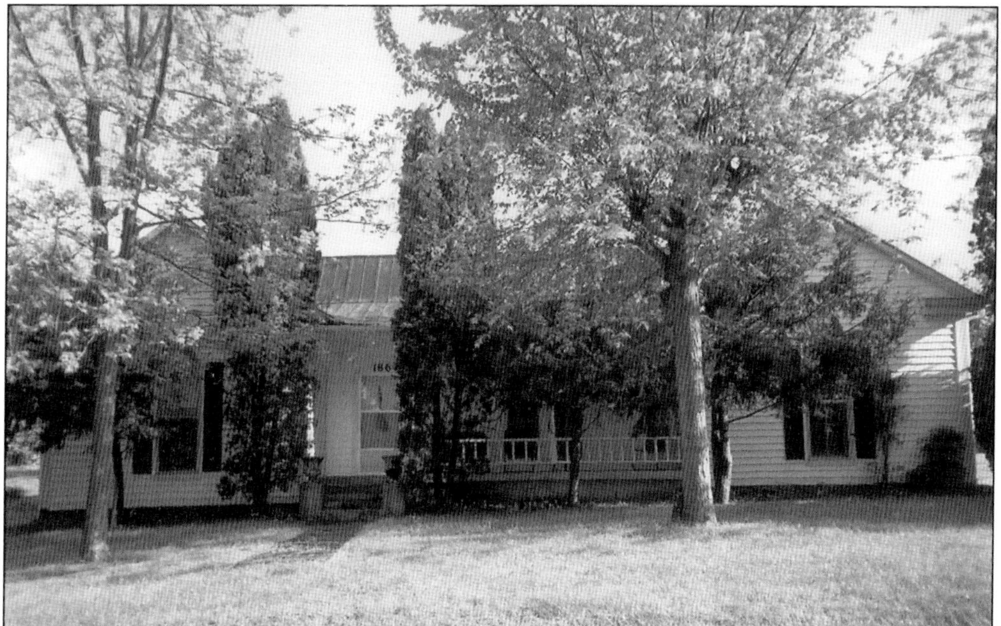

This home, located on Clover Street across from the Granville Methodist Church, was built by Dr. B.L. Simmons in the early 1900s. It was first sold to Orus Bascom and Nannie Agee Brown. Their daughter, Ethel, and her husband, Ben Sutton, moved into the home in 1949 and lived there until 1980, when the current owners, Loyd and Jewel Clark, purchased the property.

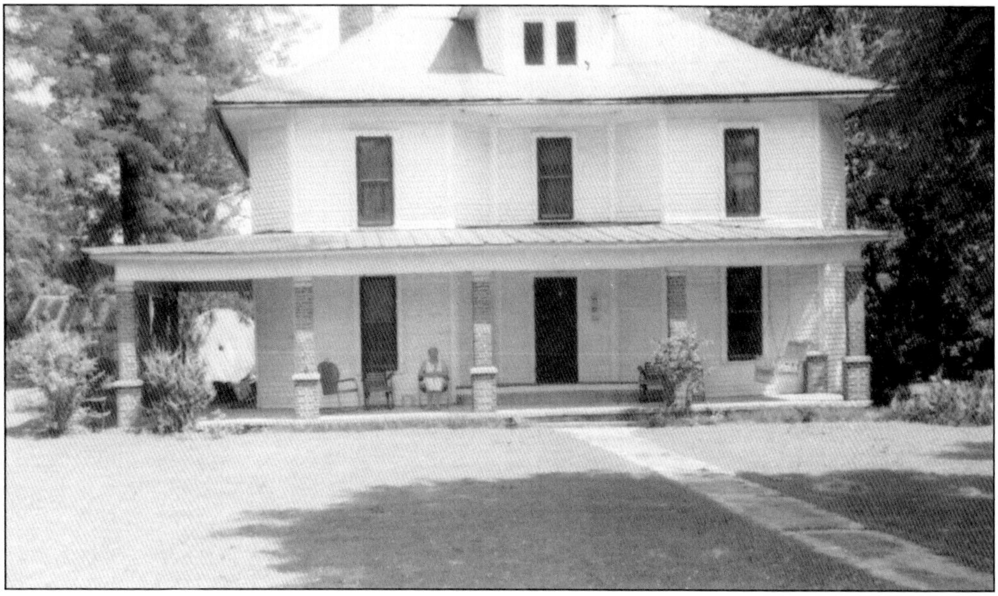

During the 1950s, Mrs. Snowie Fields, wife of Arthur Fields, is shown taking a break on the front porch of their home on Clover Street. This house, built by John Hargis, was the first house in Granville to have an indoor bathroom. It was moved to its present location next to the Methodist Church by Dois Fields after the lake came in. Henry and Missy Fincher currently own the house.

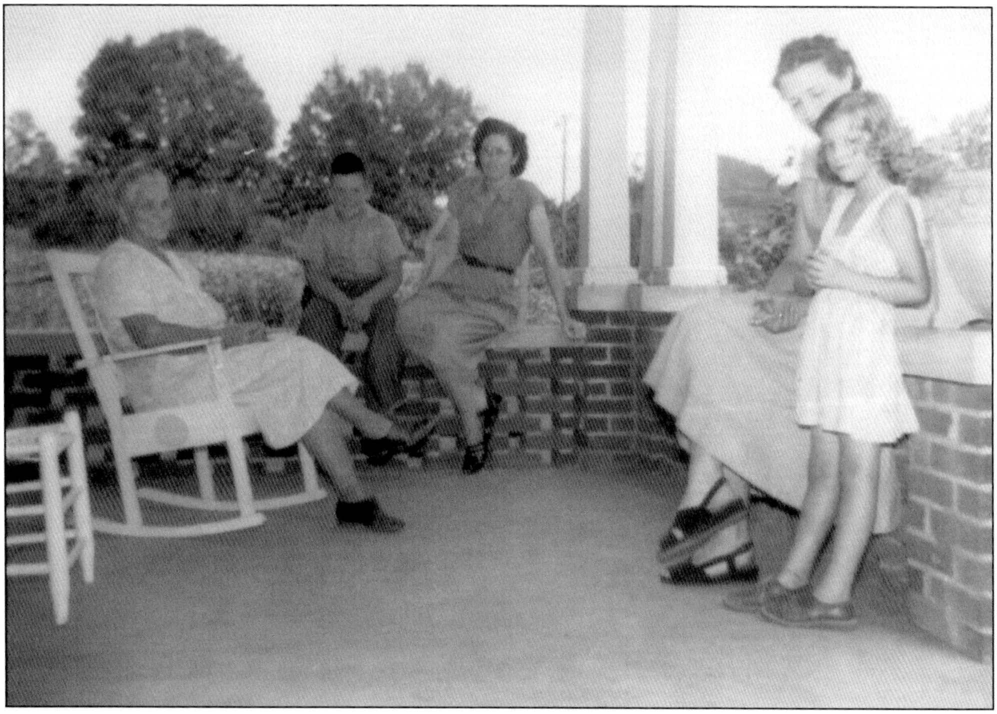

Front porches have been gathering places for families throughout the generations. The family members shown on the front porch of Earlie and Frances Harris enjoying a visit together are, from left to right, Frances, Junior, Clara, Nell, and Gayle Harris.

Seven

FAMILIES AND FACES

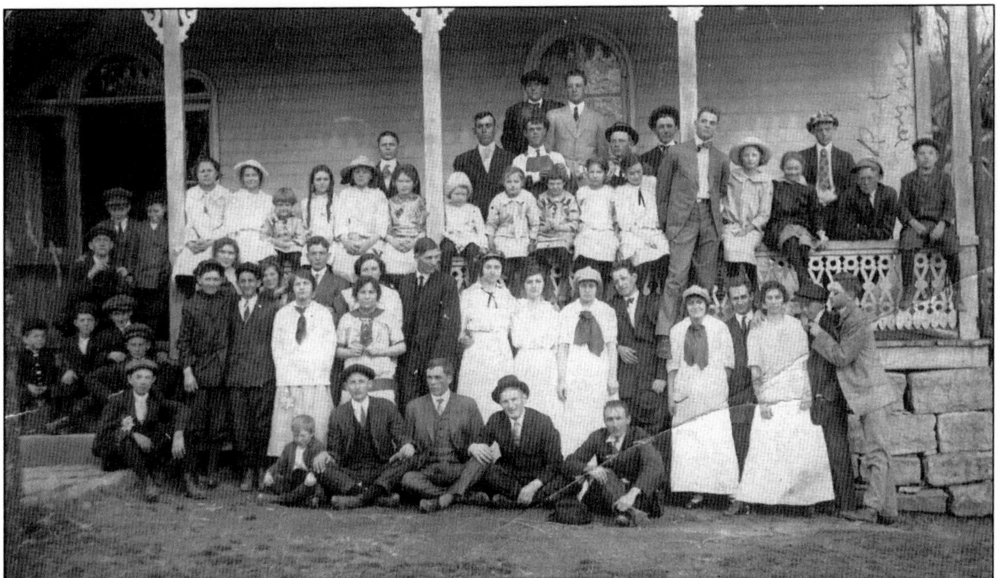

This 1915 photograph is of an Easter celebration that took place at the home of N.B. "Bone" Myers. Family surnames represented in addition to the Myers are Burton, Cooper, Cornwell, Duke, Eller, Elrod, Grisham, Hackett, Harris, Huff, Jones, Loman, McDonald, Page, Pharris, Richardson, Shirley, Smith, Sutton, and Williamson.

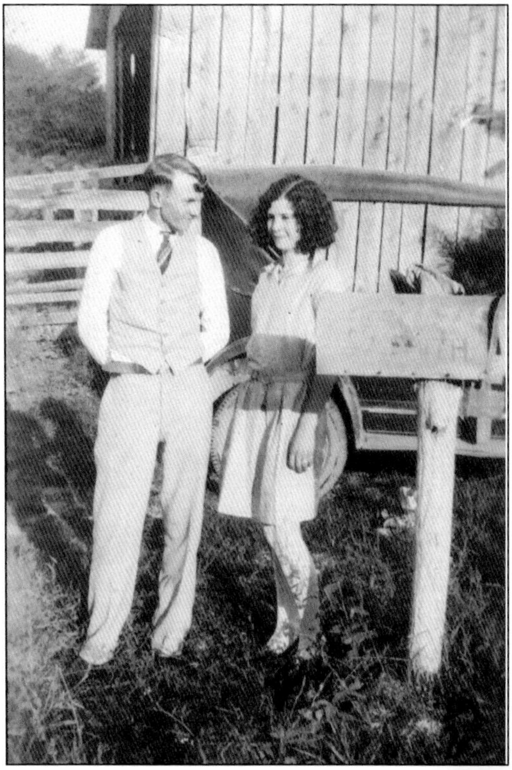

James "Hooper" and Neva "Ethel" Ragland Brown are pictured here in the early days of their marriage. They had three children—Billie Reginald, James Buddie, and Linda Diane Brown Draper. Hooper was a merchant in Granville for many years.

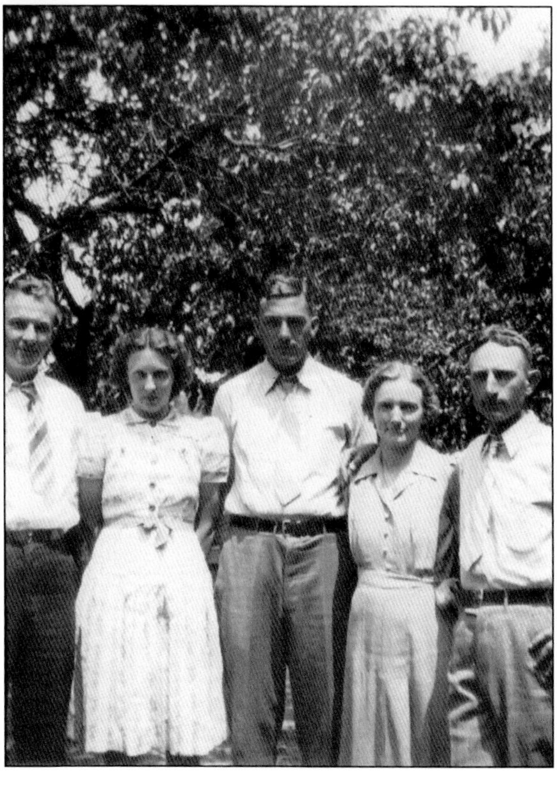

Pictured, from left to right, are Hooper Brown, Amanda Jane Brown Eller, Clyde Eller, Ruth Carter Brown, and John Marshall Brown. The Eller and Brown families were both farming families in Granville. The Ellers had two sons, Jerry and David. John and Ruth Brown's sons were Charles and Dale.

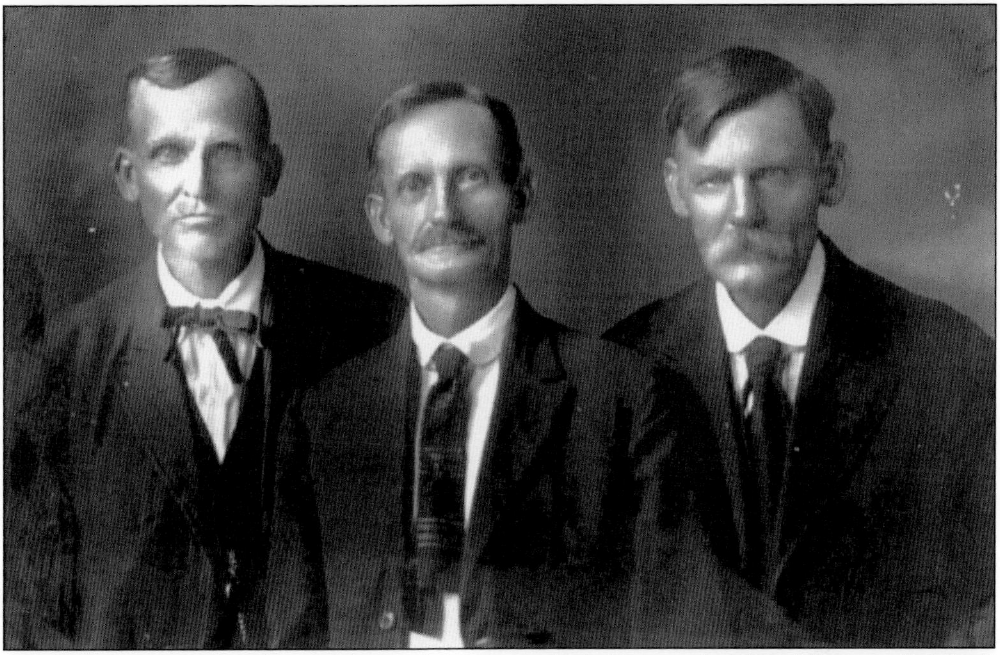

Pictured, from left to right, are three of the sons of Jubal Lee and Mildred Virginia "Middie" Holleman Burton—Jefferson Davis, Joseph P., and Henry Richard Burton.

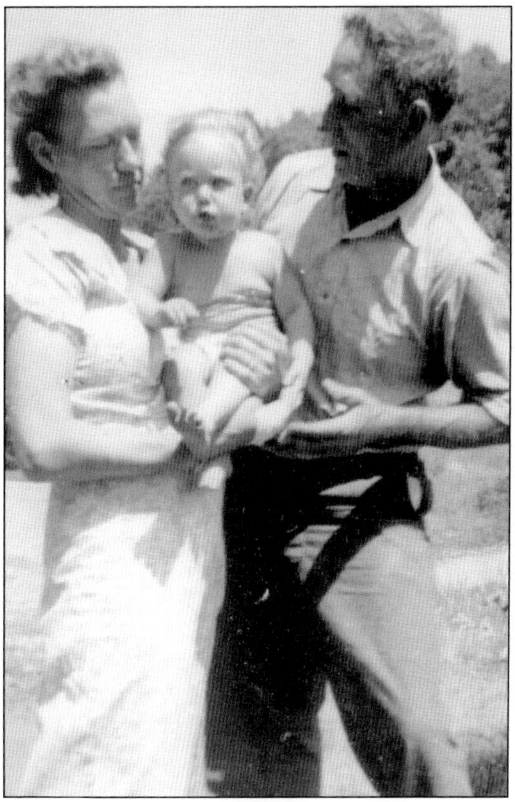

Mary Ruby Vantrease Byrne, baby Thomas Uriah "Tommy," and Henry "Bascom" Byrne pose together for this family snapshot taken in 1955. Tommy died in 1957 at the age of three.

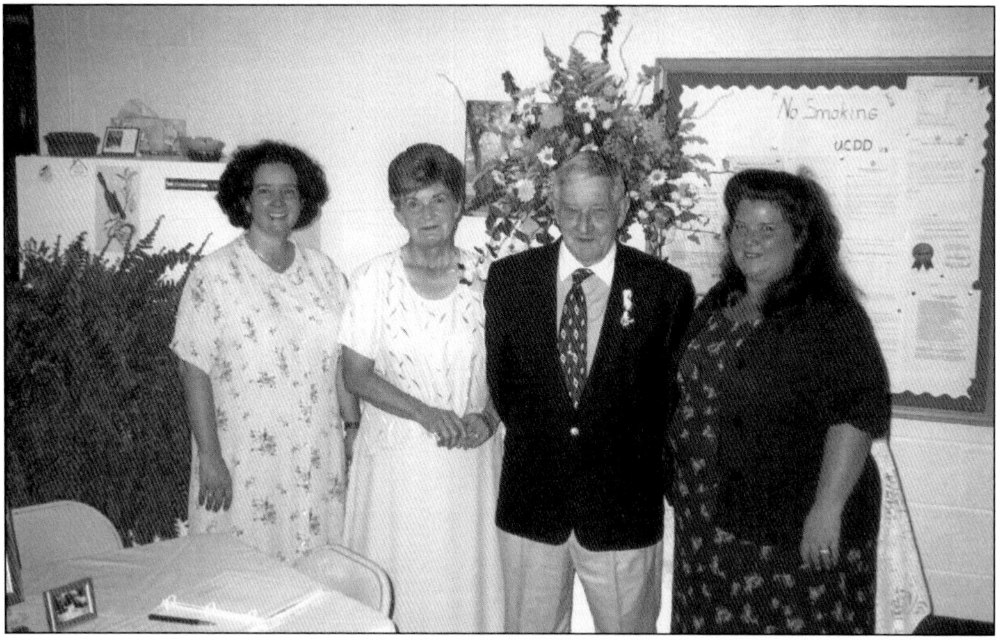

Alton and Mildred Haile Carter were married July 25, 1948, making their home in Granville. Here they are pictured celebrating their 50th wedding anniversary in 1998. Pictured with Mildred and Alton are their daughters, Carolyn, to the left, and Jeanie, to the right.

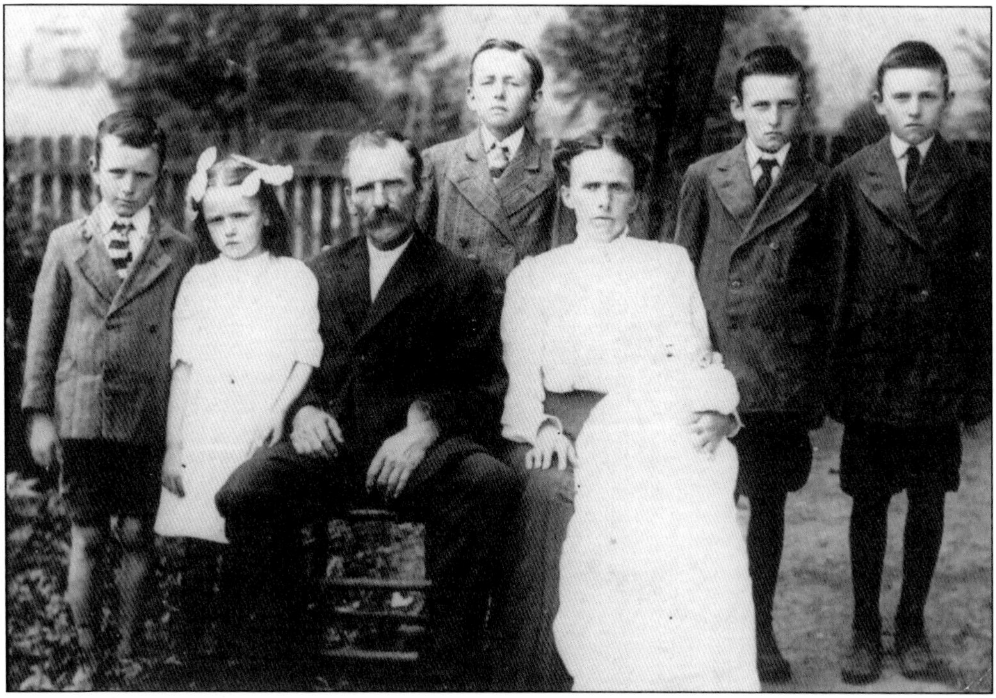
The Charlie Richard Carter family lived on Martin's Creek. Charlie, son of Robert and Jane Cannon Carter, married Ida Belle Kirby, daughter of Jessie M. and Nancy L. Davidson Kirby. Pictured here, from left to right, are Bob, Lois, Charlie, Bascom, Ida, baby Paul, and twins Willis and Will.

Ethel McKinley Carter, wife of Willis Carter, is pictured here with four generations. They are, from left to right, (front row) Thomas C. McKinley, Joyce Carter, and Willie Kinniard McKinley; (back row) Ethel McKinley Carter and Charles M. Carter. Willie McKinley lived to be one of Granville's oldest citizens, dying at the age of 95.

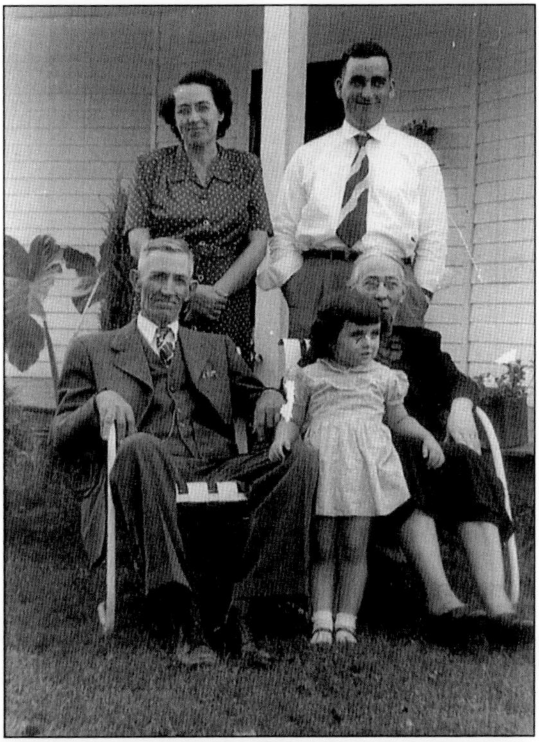

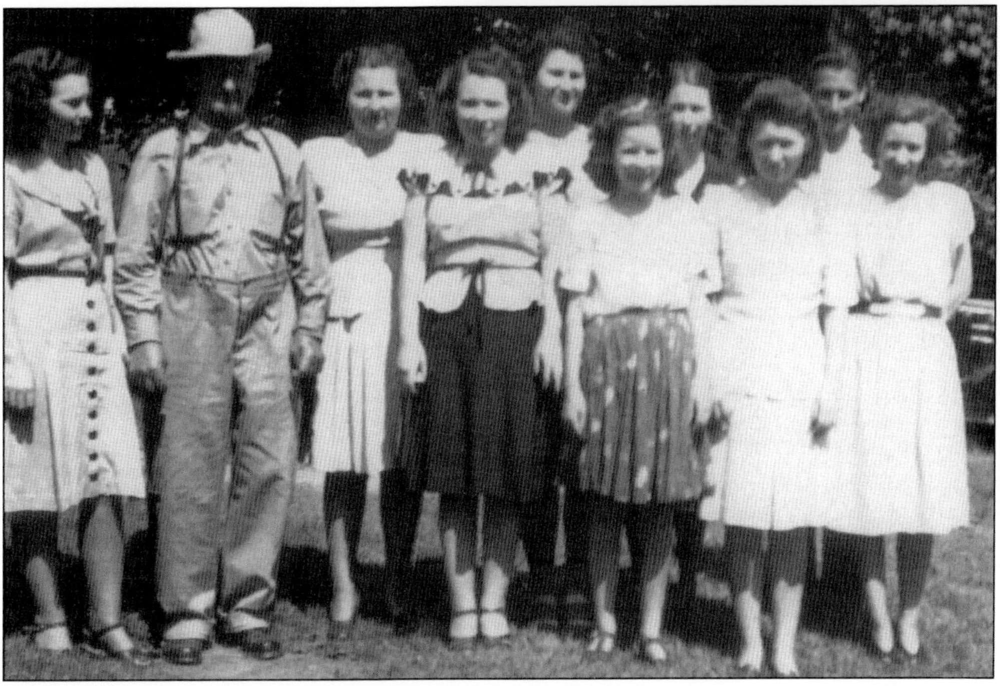

Henry and Alcie B. Ragland Carter raised their family in the Liberty community. Henry was the son of Robert and Jane Cannon Carter, and Alcie was the daughter of Savage and Julie Carter Ragland. This photo, taken after Alcie's death, includes, from left to right, Martha, Henry, Pearly, Magdalene, Bertha, Trixy, Ora, Carrie, Dow, and Bertie.

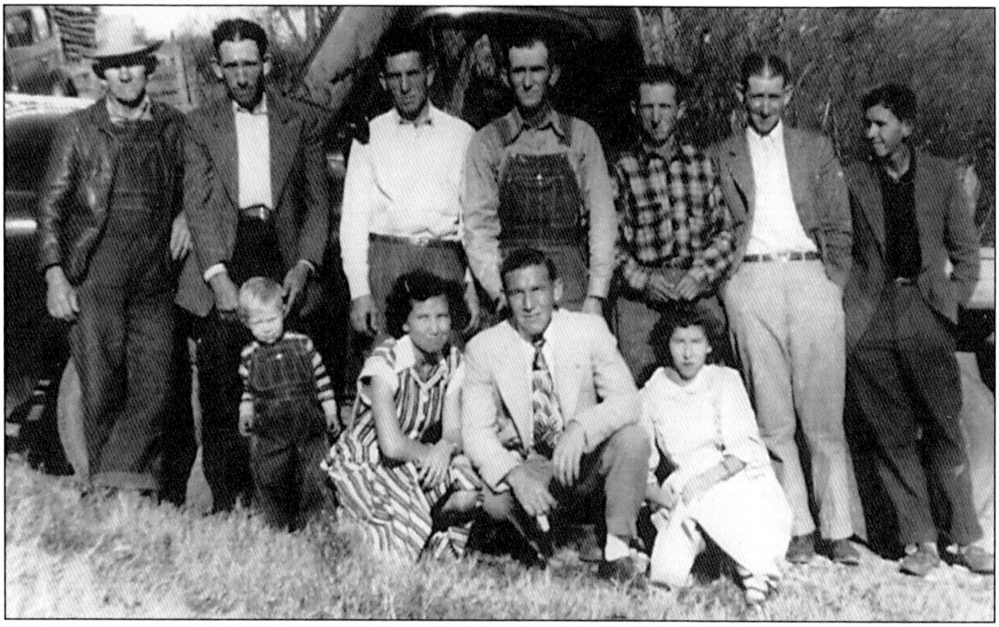

The John Tack Carter family posing for this photo are, from left to right, (front row) Ray Lee Carter, Mabel Ashley Carter Gillespie, John Ralph Carter, and Magdalene Carter; (back row) John Tack Carter, Ben Fox Carter, Charles Tolbert Carter, Haggard Carter, Willie Fred Carter, Thomas Edd Carter, and Eugene Carter.

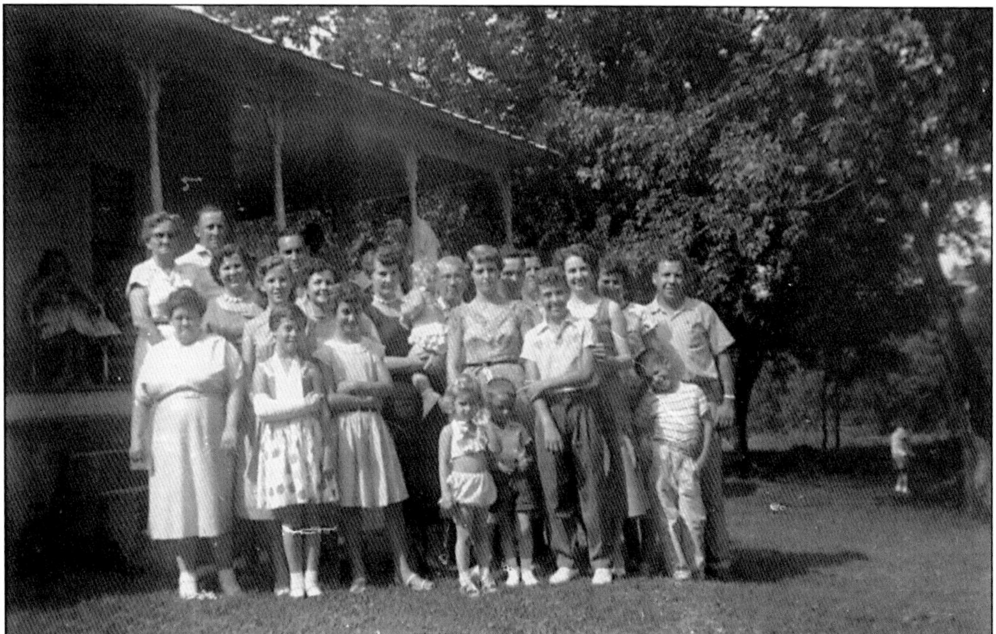

The Lee Roy and Fannie Roberts Carter Family Reunion in 1955 was held at the old Carter home, then occupied by Mack and Virginia Carter. Pictured, from left to right, are (front row) Emma, Jane Ellen, Gail, Mildred holding Jeanie, small children Carolyn and Bruce, Geraldine, Stites Ray, and Gary; (back row) Mrs. Fannie, Hugh Lee, Marie, Sandra Jo, Malcolm, Vyda, Lee, J.N., Farmer, Margaret, Virginia, and Mack.

Walter Lee and Willie Veteto Clark made their home in the heart of Granville for many years. This family photo shows, from left to right, Walter with Manda Lou in front of him, and Willie holding baby Charles Lee, with Loyd Taylor and James Roland standing in back.

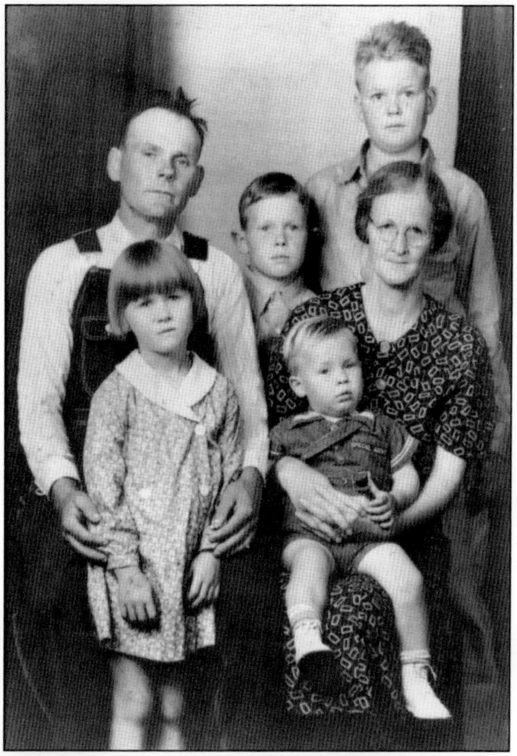

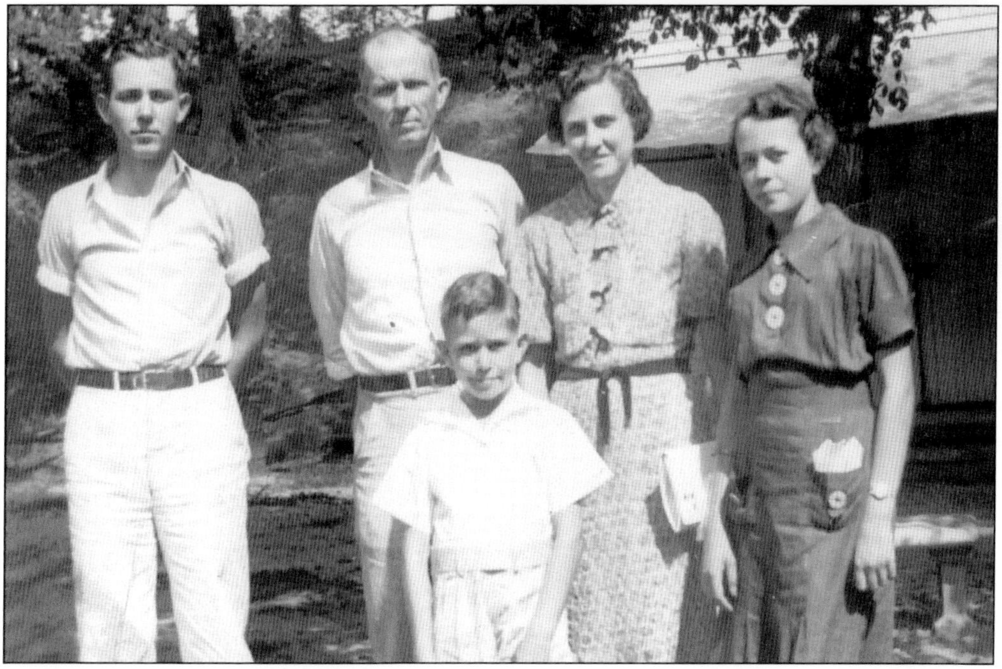

James Michael "Jimmy" (son of Moland and Selina Shumake Clemons) and Hallie Mai Huff Clemons raised their family on Indian Creek. Hallie Mai died at the age of 103, making her one of the oldest natives of Granville. Pictured, from left to right, are Jesse Lon, Jimmy, Hallie Mai, and Minnie Lena, with James Edward in the front.

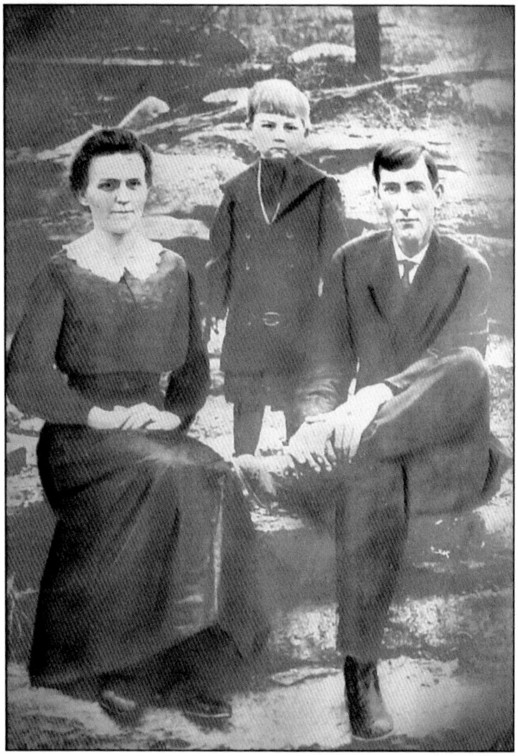

John Leslie and Leatha L. Brown Clemons are pictured here with their son, Comer. They lived on a farm above Liberty where their granddaughter, Suzanne Clemons Stafford, still lives. John ran a store in Granville for several years, where he was also a justice of the peace. They also had a daughter, Myrtle Lois.

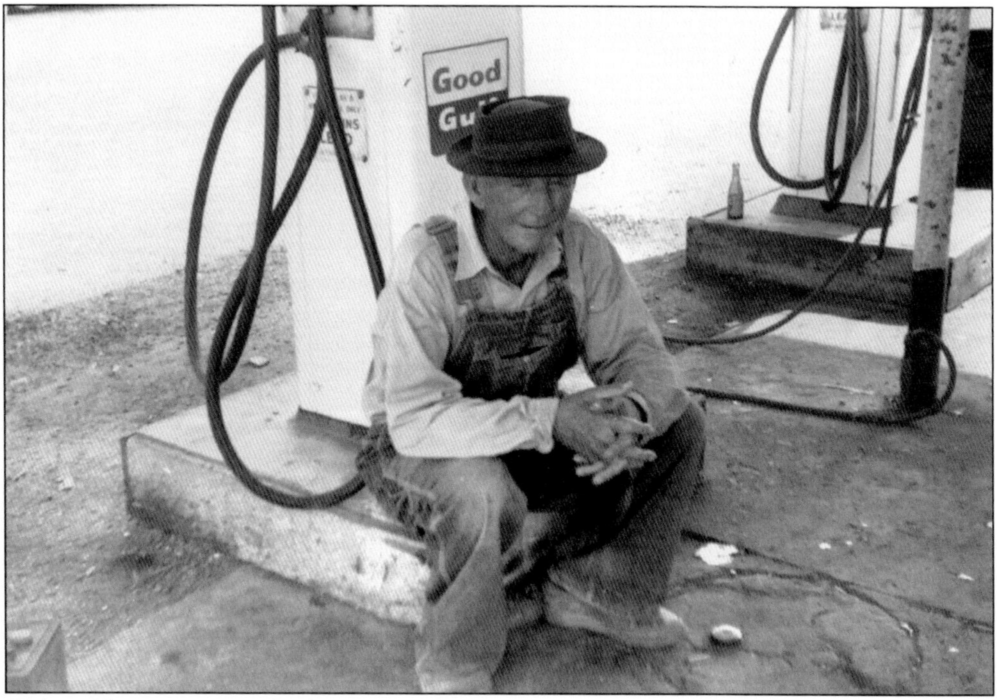

Walter Clemons, pictured relaxing at a local gas station, was a farmer, and he operated the Granville Ferry for a period of time. He was married to the former Flossie Ramsey, and they had six children: John Henry, Charles, Harold, Walter Jr., Ann, and Willa.

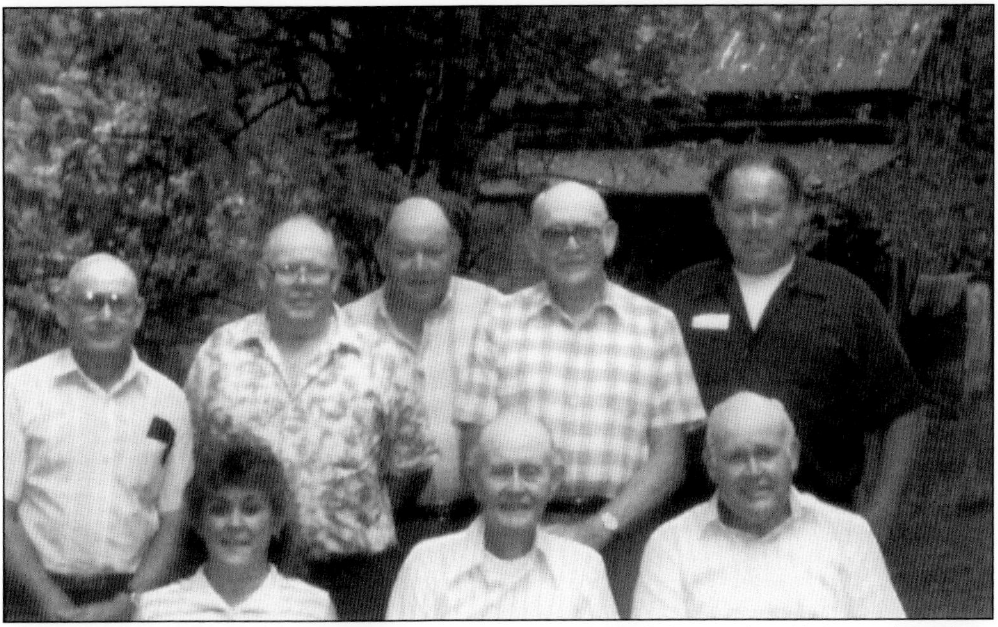

At the home place on Big Branch in this photo are, from left to right, (front row) Molena Collier Roberts, Buddy Haskel Collier, and Billy Richmond Collier; (back row) Larence Garland Collier, Bobby Lee Collier, Donald Clarence Collier, Luther Douglas Collier, and Doyle Braxton Collier.

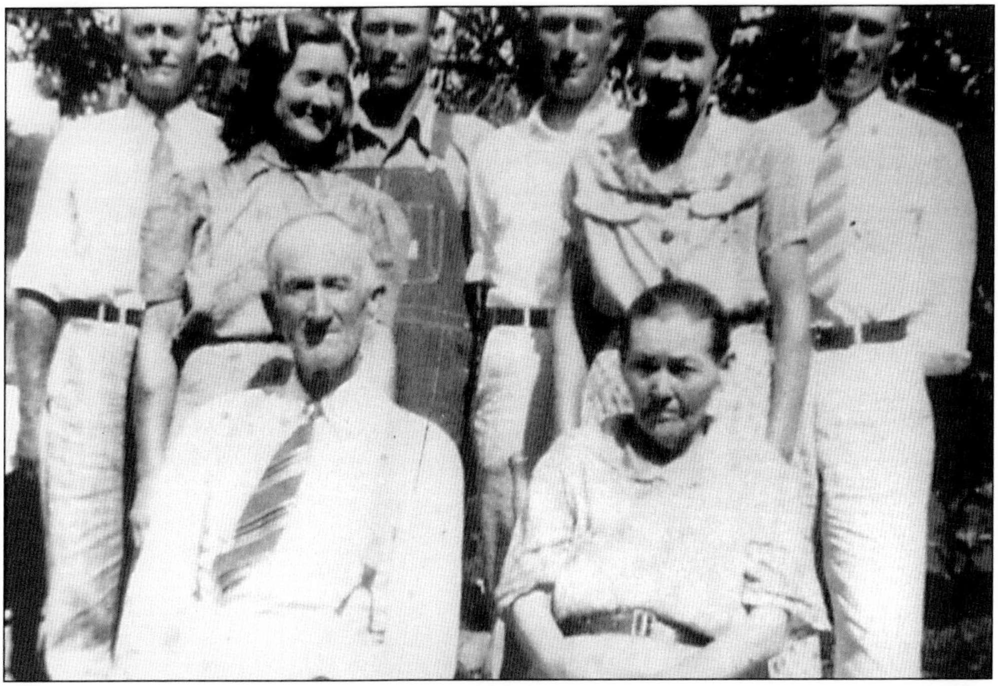

The John H. Collier family lived on Big Branch. Pictured, from left to right, are (seated) John H. Collier and Lela Ann Clark Collier; (standing) Buddy Haskel Collier, Daisy Collier Hargis, Harvey Collier, Luther Collier, Cora Alley Collier Guess, and Oscar Hickman Collier.

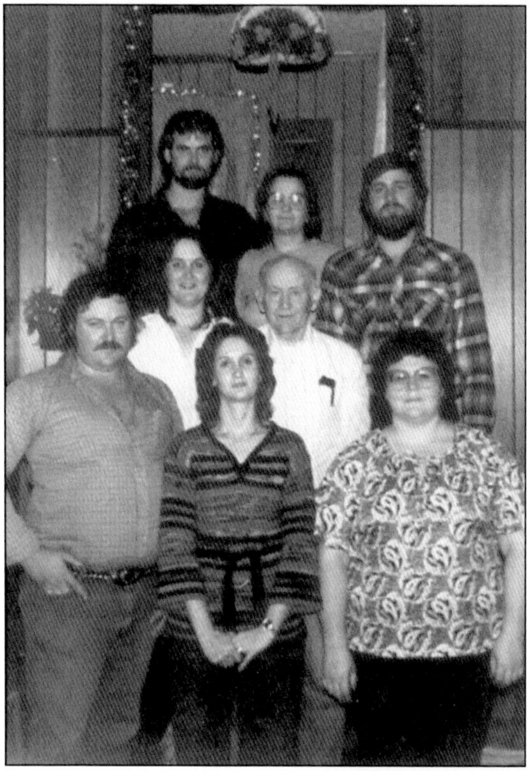

Luther Douglas Collier married Mary Jane Huff, daughter of Haskel Harvey and Vennie Esther Frizzell Huff. Pictured with Luther in this family photograph are, from left to right, his children, (front row) Luther Buddy, Bonnie Ruth, and Wandalean; (middle row) Elloise and Luther Douglas; (back row) Johnny Braxton, Mary Jane, and Jimmy Russell.

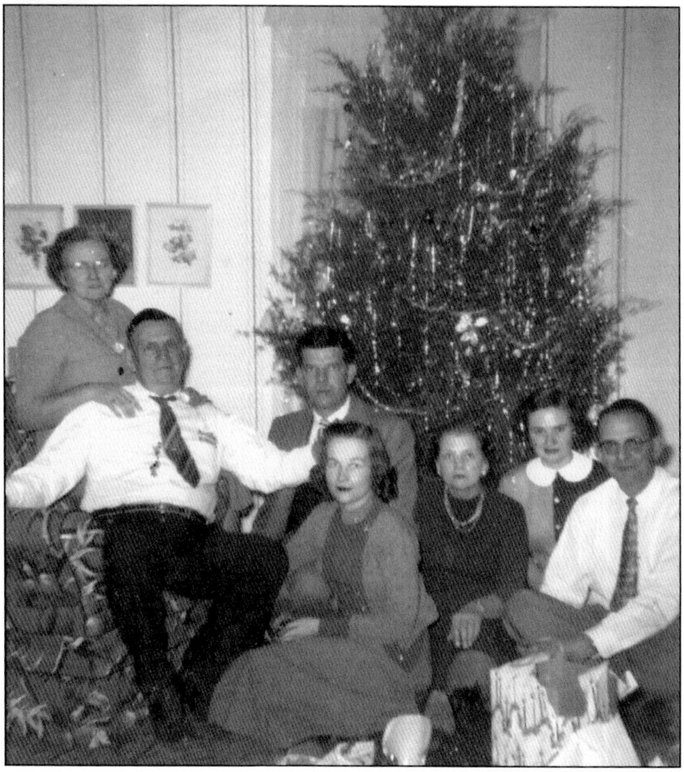

The Cornwell family lived where the Granville Veterans Park is located now. Bill was a mail carrier for 26 years. Pictured, from left to right, are Lois Carter Cornwell, Bill Cornwell, Miriam Cornwell, Bill Cornwell Jr., Ruby Williamson Cornwell, Judy Brown, and Carl Cornwell. These children, along with Lutrell, who is not pictured, belonged to Bill and his first wife, Ethel Maggart.

Roland H. Dowell, pictured here, was the son of John D. and Rebecca Barnes Dowell and was married to Emma Victoria Burton Dowell. They had two sons, Thurman and Walter, who remained lifelong residents of Granville. Walter and Thurman were both farmers in the area, with Thurman serving as a local undertaker also.

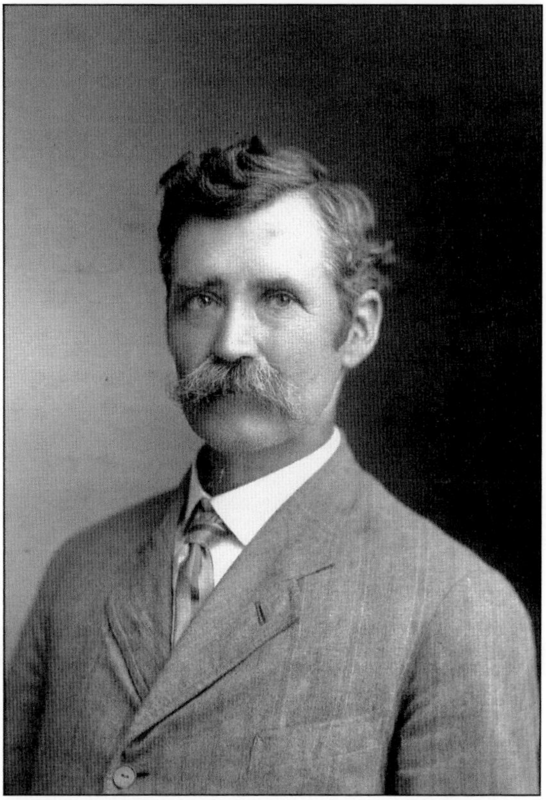

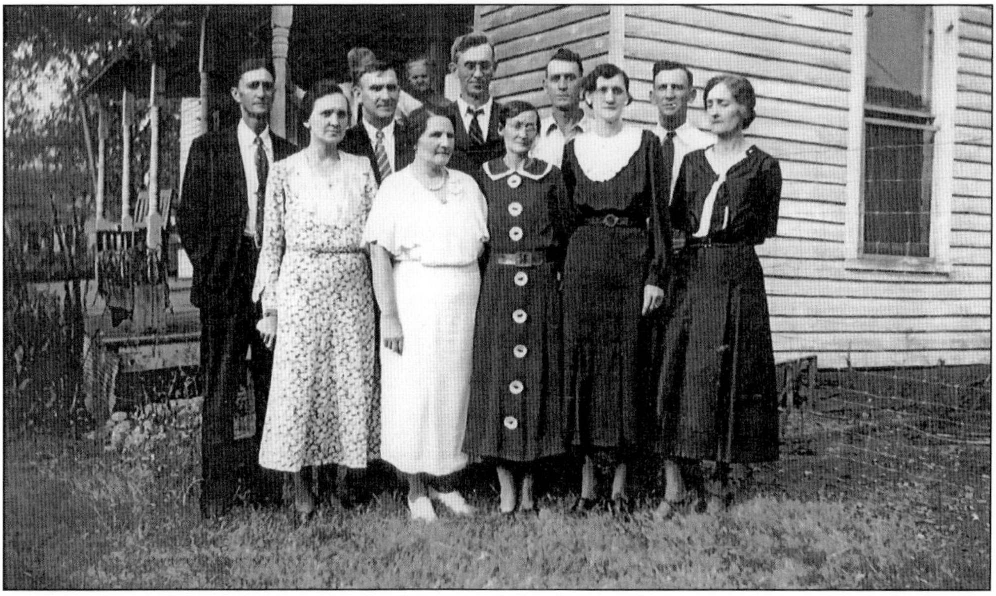

Here in front of their home, which also served the Granville community as the Duke Hotel, the Morgan and Elizabeth Duke family pose. From left to right are (front row) Vida Duke, Delia Duke, unidentified, Dorthenia Duke, and Leona Duke; (back row) Walter Vaughn, Charlie Duke, Will Duke, unidentified, and Sid Duke; (on porch) Morgan and Elizabeth Duke.

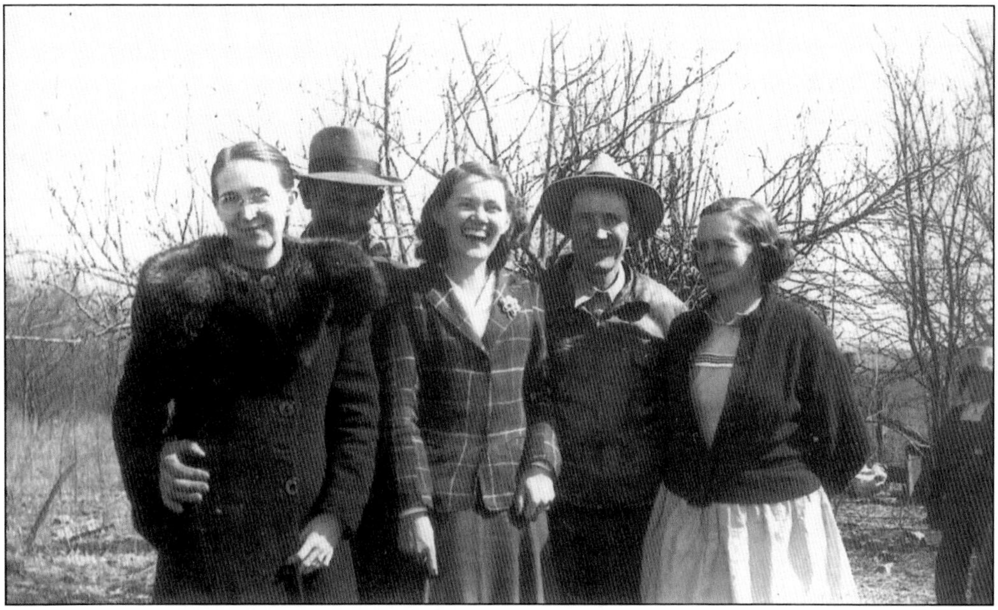

The Robert Lee and Lula Davis Duke children pictured here, from left to right, are Beulah Duke Ray, Ernest Duke, Lucyle Duke Kent, Frank Herbert Duke, and Edith Duke Clemons. Lillian and Robert Junior are not pictured.

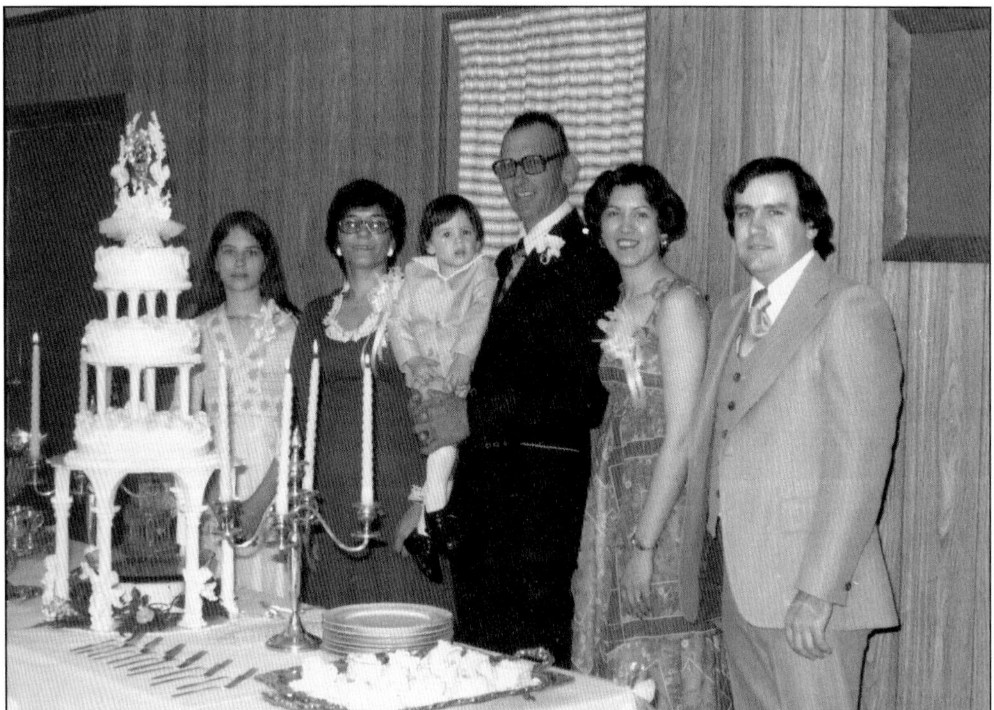

Dois and Kerry Fields celebrate their 25th wedding anniversary in this 1978 photo. Helping celebrate are, from left to right, Lisa Fields, Kerry Fields, Dois Fields holding Brian Loftis, Kay Fields Loftis, and Ronnie Loftis. Dois worked for Twin Lakes Telephone for many years. He died in a tractor accident in 1993.

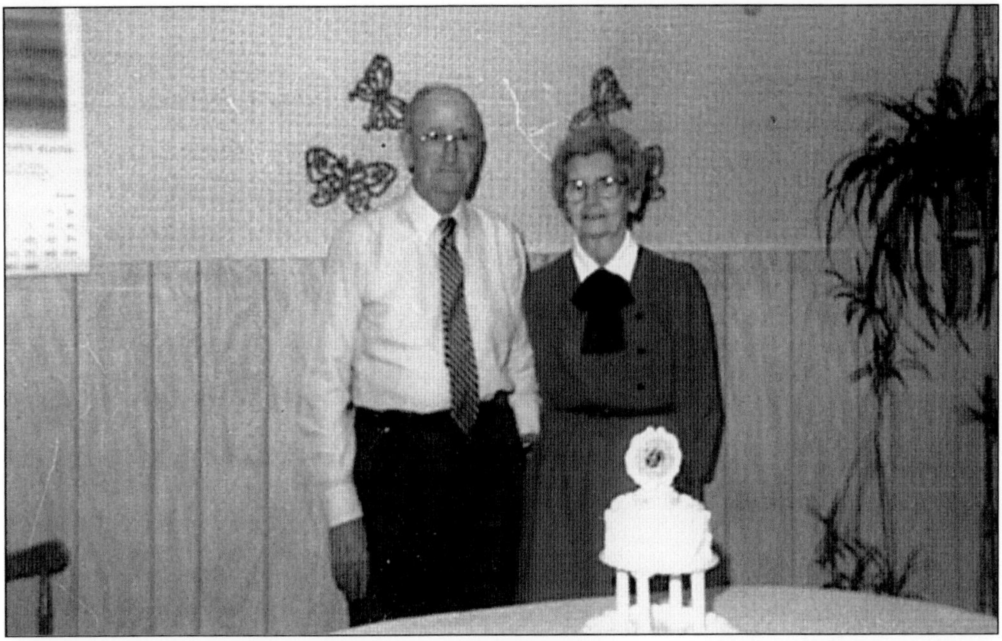

Paskel and Linnie McBroom Fields, shown here celebrating their 60th wedding anniversary, had two children, Helen Fields Reynolds and Dois Fields. Paskel was a farmer, a ferry operator, and a deputy sheriff for Jackson County. They lived in their Granville home, which was the former Cumberland Valley Preparatory School, for 40 years.

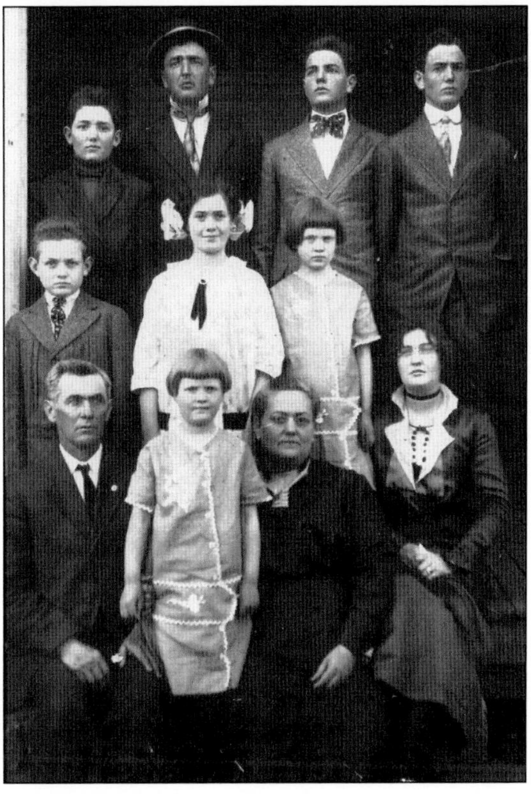

James Pryor Grisham married Cornelia Ann Tittle, daughter of George Washington and Mary Ann Watts Tittle. This 1915 family portrait includes, from left to right, (front row) James Pryor, Lillie, and Cornelia; (middle row) Charles Brown, Nell, Dymple, and Mollie (seated); (back row) George Taylor, Guy Thomas, James Tillman, and William Ernest.

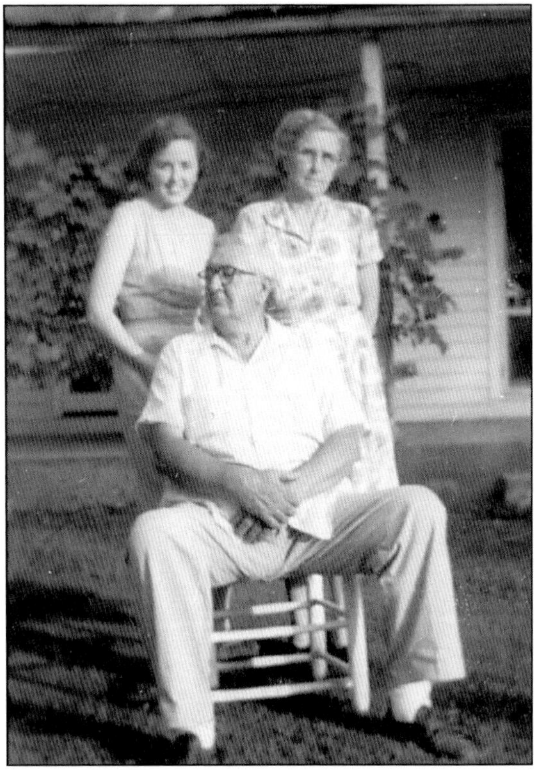

Seated in this photo is Guy Thomas Grisham, with his daughter, Anna Nell, and wife, Alice Lee Terry. Guy was a veteran and worked as a prison guard, while Alice was a cook at the Granville School. Anna Nell met and married a World War II soldier, Tony Toscano, who was here on maneuvers. They had one daughter, Susan Terry Toscano.

This photograph of Jennie and Oscar Grisham was taken in the early 1950s. Jennie Elizabeth, daughter of Robert and Helen Stafford Sutton, and Oscar A., son of Peyton and Floretta Montgomery Grisham, were married and made their home in Granville. Oscar was a local carpenter.

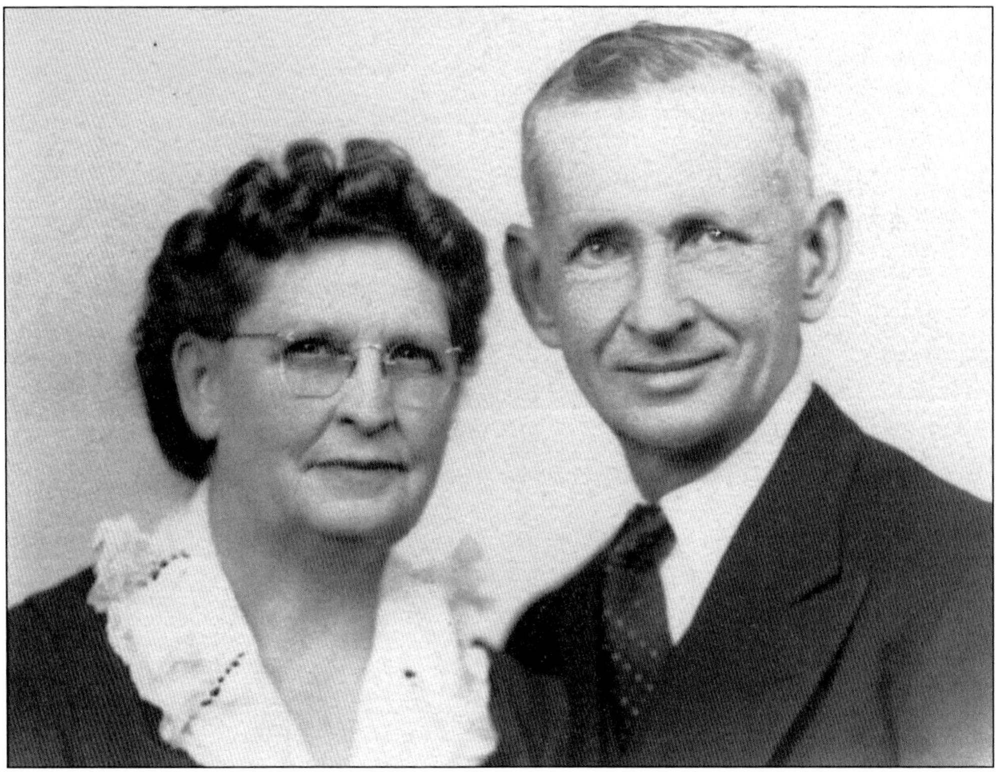

Russell and Bessie Allen Haile, pictured here, lived in the first house after leaving the Granville ferry on the other side of the river. They were the parents of four children: Evelyn, Avo, James, and Mildred.

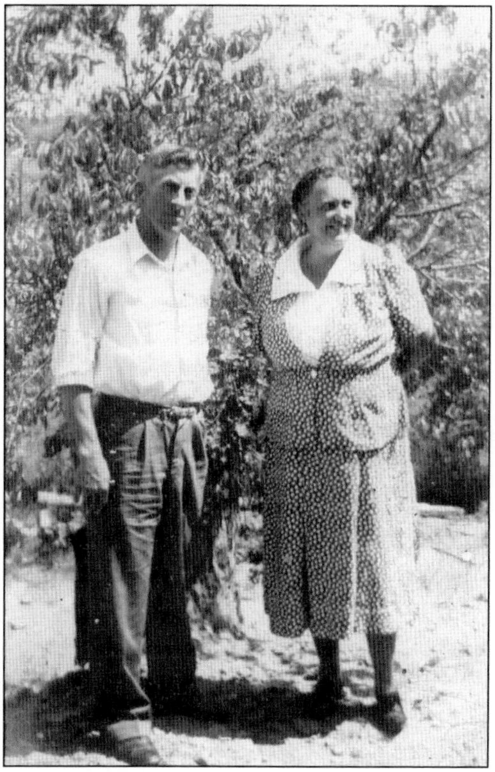

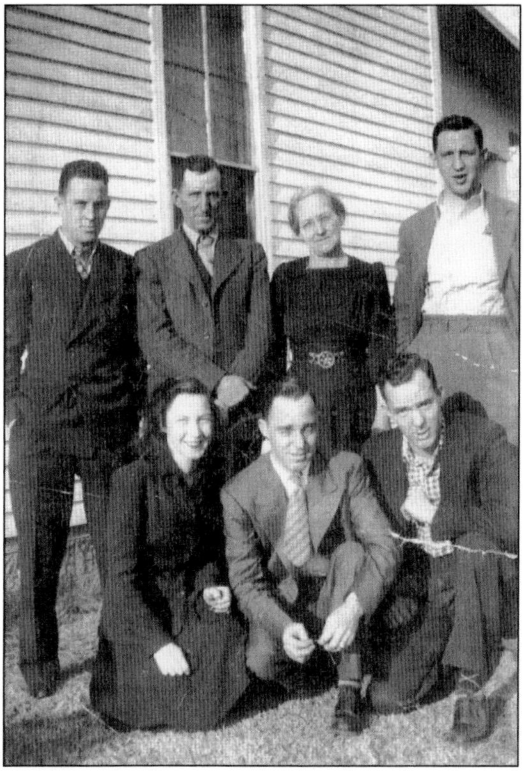

Bee and Georgia Ann Roberts Halfacre lived in this house in Holleman's Bend before moving to Granville. They are pictured with their children, from left to right, (front row) Ogeal, Ralph, and Donald; (back row) Edgar, Bee, Georgia, and Virgil. Bee was a member of the Jackson County Court for over 20 years. Donald and Virgil both served in World War II.

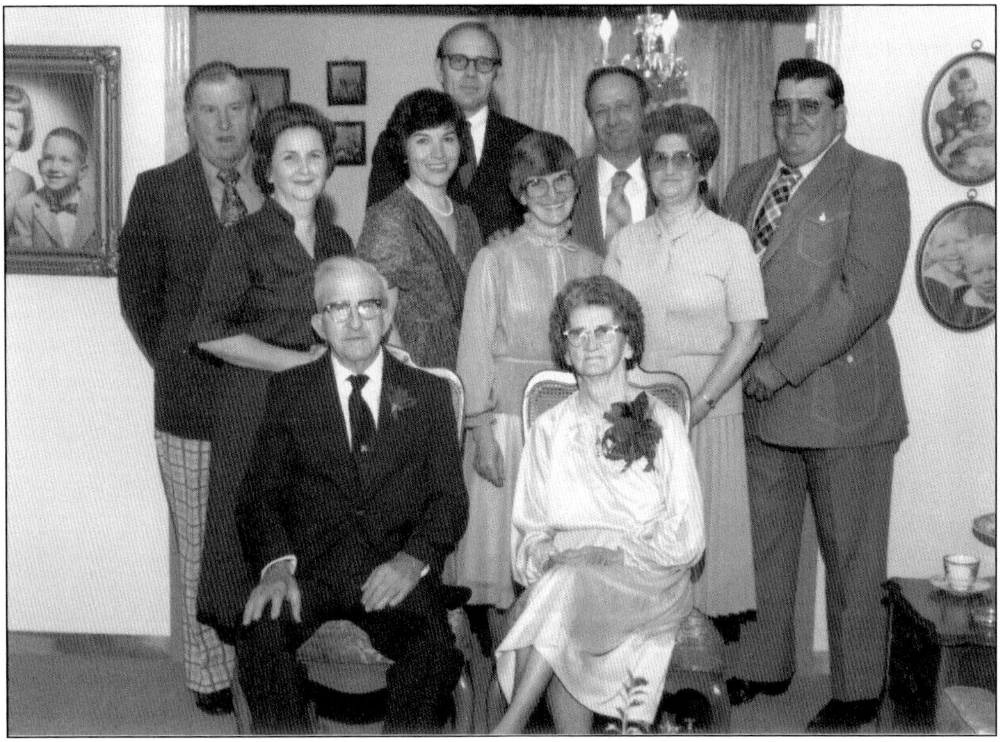

On December 25, 1979, Benton M. and Dora Mae Carter Halfacre celebrated their 60th wedding anniversary. They joined the community in 1934, when they moved from Putnam County to the Dr. Hugh Smith farm on Holleman's Bend. In 1947, they purchased the Bill Williamson house in Granville. Pictured here behind them, are, from left to right, Lloyd and Sue Halfacre, Faye and Travis Halford, Gerry and Jack Anderson, Pauline Brown, and Elb Halfacre.

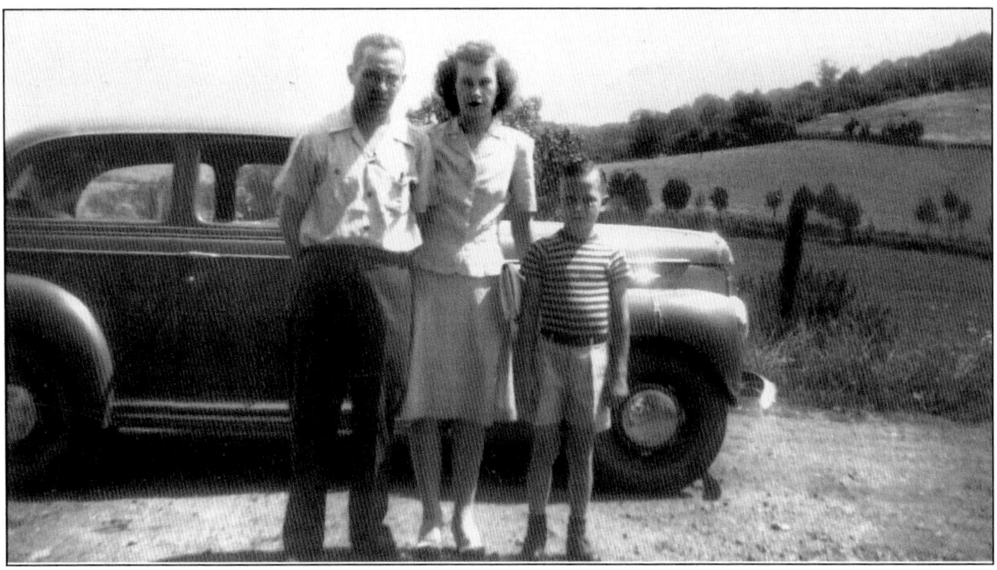

Edgar and Ada Myers Halfacre, pictured here with Edgar Jr., lived in the Holleman's Bend area until the lake came when they moved to Granville. Halfacre was a popular schoolteacher, coach, and principal in Granville as well as a farmer.

Ralph, son of B. Joseph and Georgia Roberts Halfacre, and Margie Brown Halfacre, daughter of Frank and Ella Scott Brown, owned the Chevrolet dealership in Gainesboro for many years. They had two daughters, Nancy and Betsy.

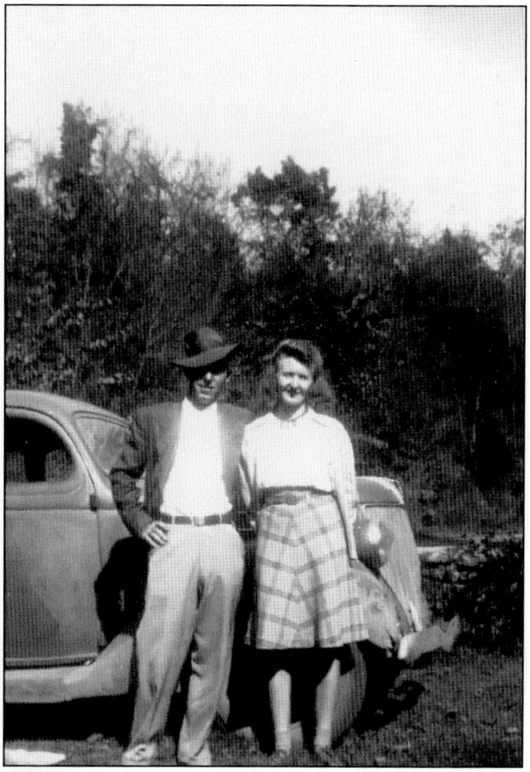

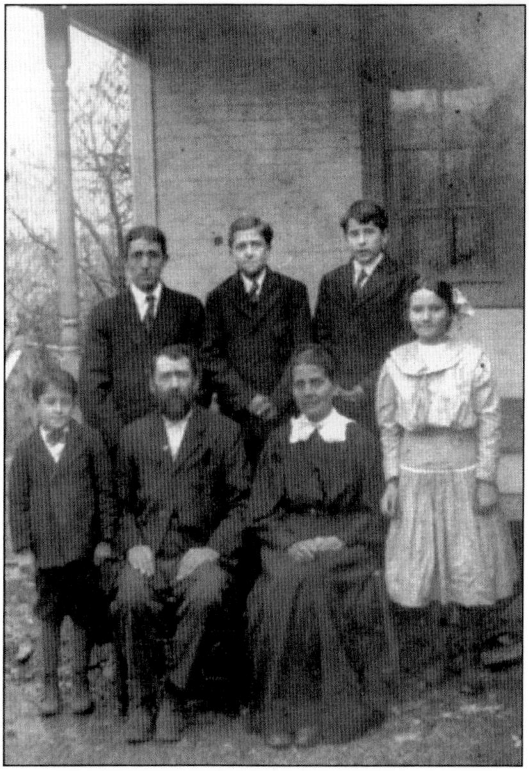

The Thomas Brooks and Lethia Frances Ortner Halfacre family members shown here are, from left to right, (front row) Benton M., Thomas Brooks, Alethia, and niece Flora Bandy; (back row) Joe B., Landon Logan, and Noah C. Halfacre.

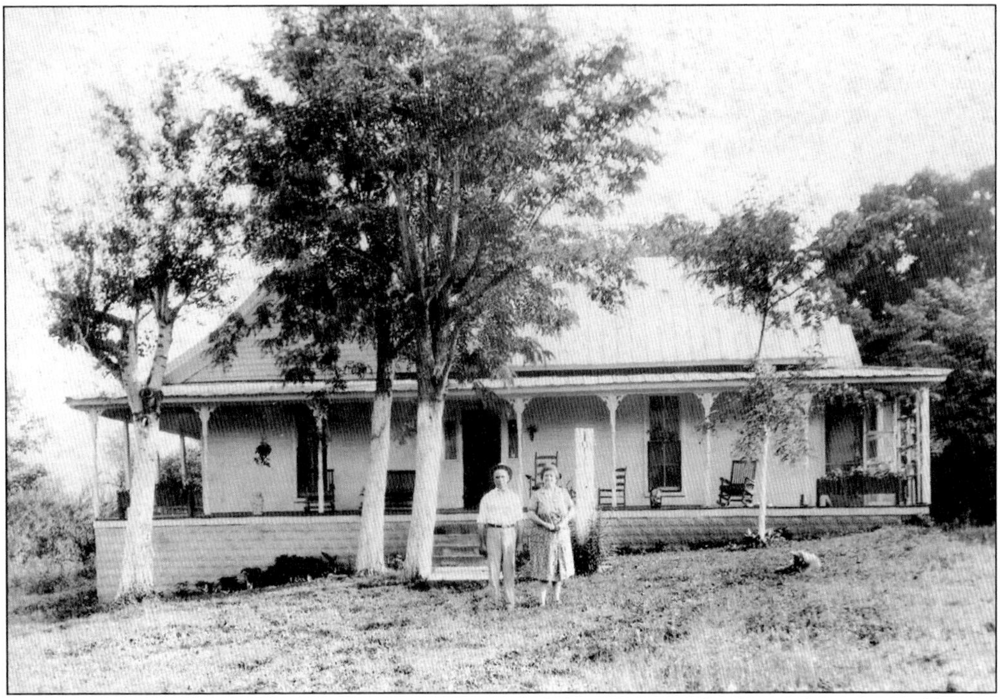

Bob and Otha Smith Hargis are pictured in front of their home, which was later owned by Lester and Louise Huff Ragland and Floyd and Reba Hargis Harris, on Highway 53. Otha taught school, while Bob was a farmer.

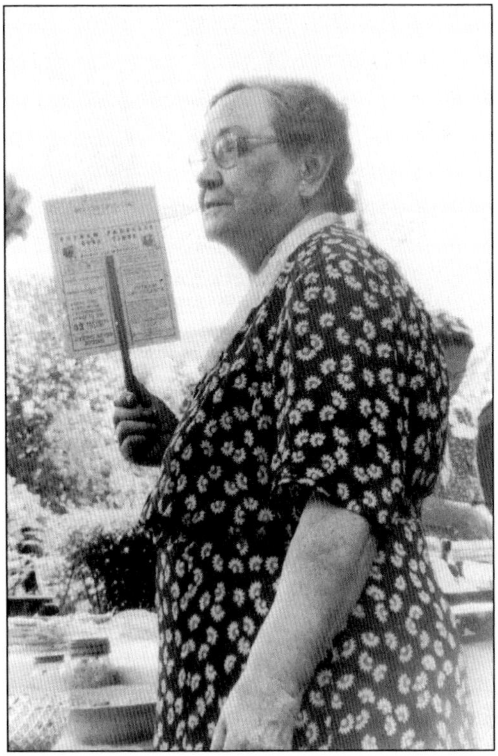

Shown in this photo, Hannah Lenore Holleman Ferrell Hargis, daughter of John W. and Anna Maxwell Richmond Holleman, was the wife of one of Granville's first doctors, Dr. Albert Ferrell. They were the parents of Mary Nell Ferrell Watts, who taught piano classes in the community. After Dr. Ferrell's death, Hannah married Abraham Bohannon "Bo" Hargis, and they had two sons, James Richmond and Edmond Hargis.

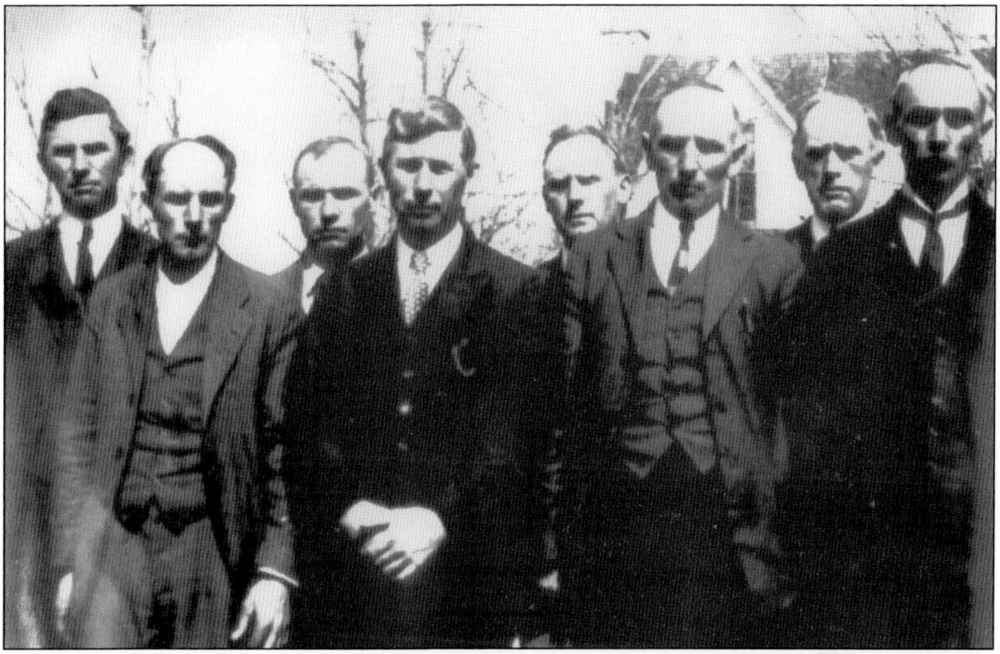

In this rare photograph taken on the day of their father's funeral, all eight sons of James H. and Elizabeth Martin Montgomery Hargis can be seen. They are, from left to right, (front row) James Martin "Jim," Dr. Frank Cooper, Abraham Bohannon, and Dr. William A.; (back row) Talmadge D., Robert Lewis "Bob," Hugh Smith, and John Hargis. Their father was a Civil War veteran.

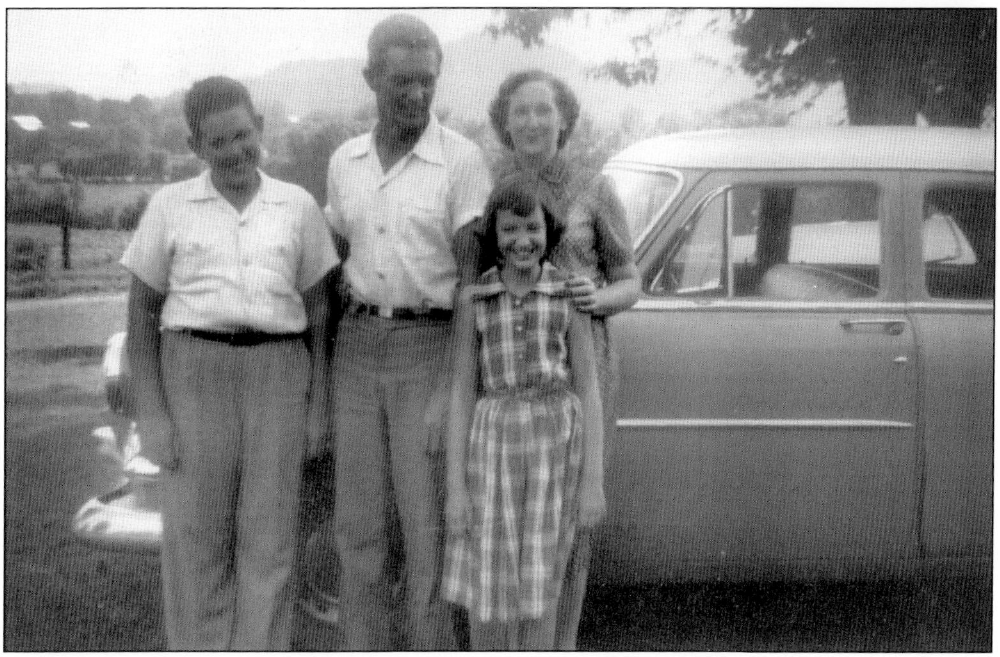

Floyd B., son of William Earlie and Frances Mayberry Harris, and Reba G. Harris, daughter of Shelby and Maggie Reynolds Hargis, are pictured with their children. From left to right are Floyd Jr., Floyd Sr., Reba, and Gayle. Floyd was one of the first employees at TRW, and he also farmed. Reba worked at the Carthage Shirt Factory for many years.

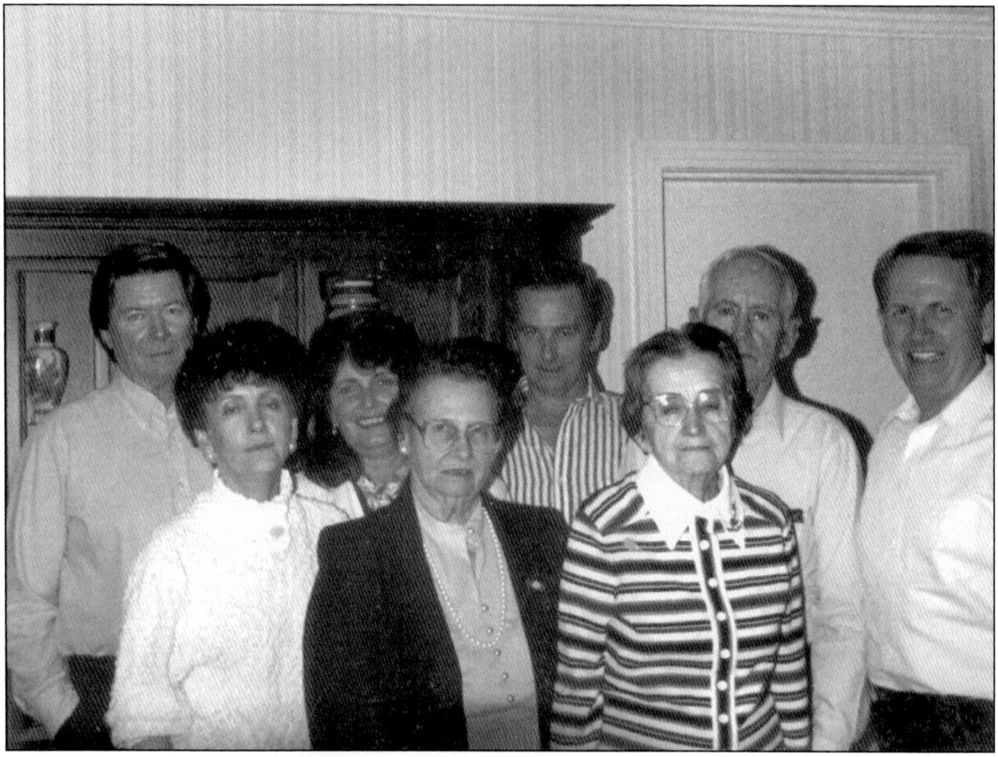

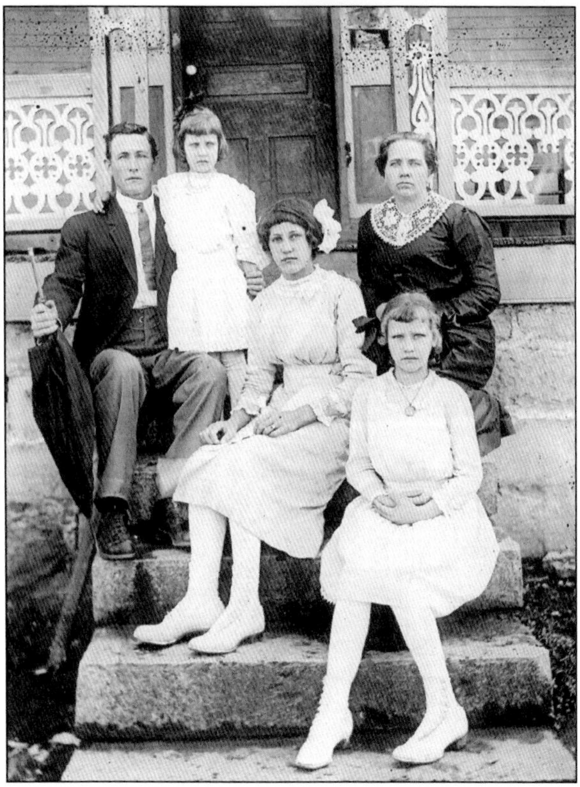

This family photo of William Henry, son of Charlie and Vista Apple Harris, and Pearly Carter Harris, features, from left to right (front row) Rachel, Pearly, and Ollie; (back row) Charles, Ruby, Hollis, Henry, and Royce Harris. Henry was a merchant in Granville and Liberty for many years. He farmed at Liberty from 1944 until his death in 2002.

The Alonzo H. Huff family photo shows, from left to right, Alonzo, Asbula, Hallie Mai, and Sina "Minnie" Tittle Huff, with Lina Sallie B. Huff in front. They lived in this house, which was on Indian Creek, until it burned. Alonzo was the son of Pendleton and Mary Elizabeth Elrod Huff, and Minnie was the daughter of William Tavener and Aleatha Tumutes Holleman Tittle.

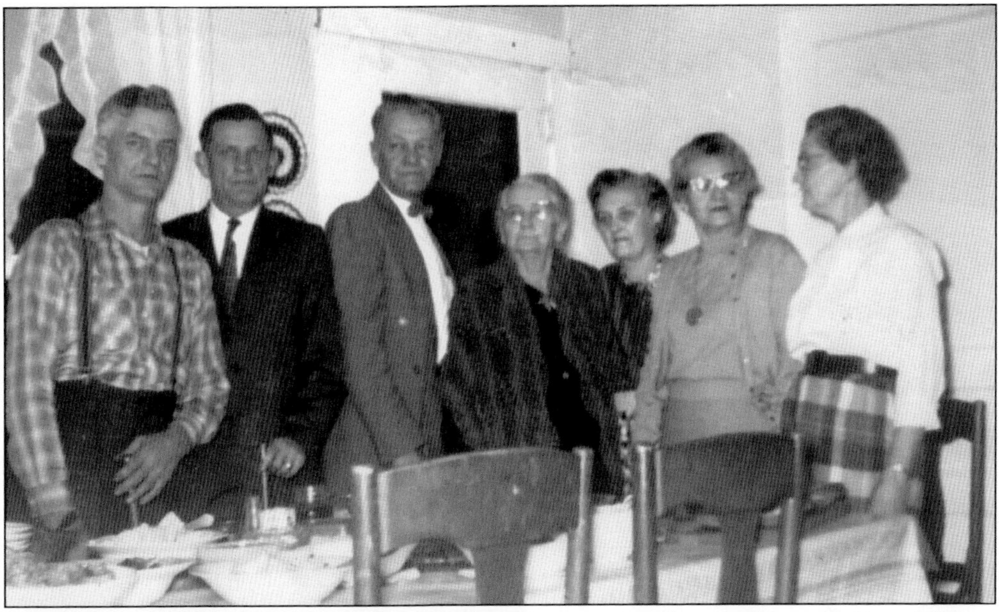

Alta Myers Huff, wife of William Albert Huff, is shown in this photo with some of her children. From left to right are Napolean Boneparte, Joseph Shaker, Robert Henry, Alta, Mary Nan, Bonnie Evagelina, and Grady Dimple.

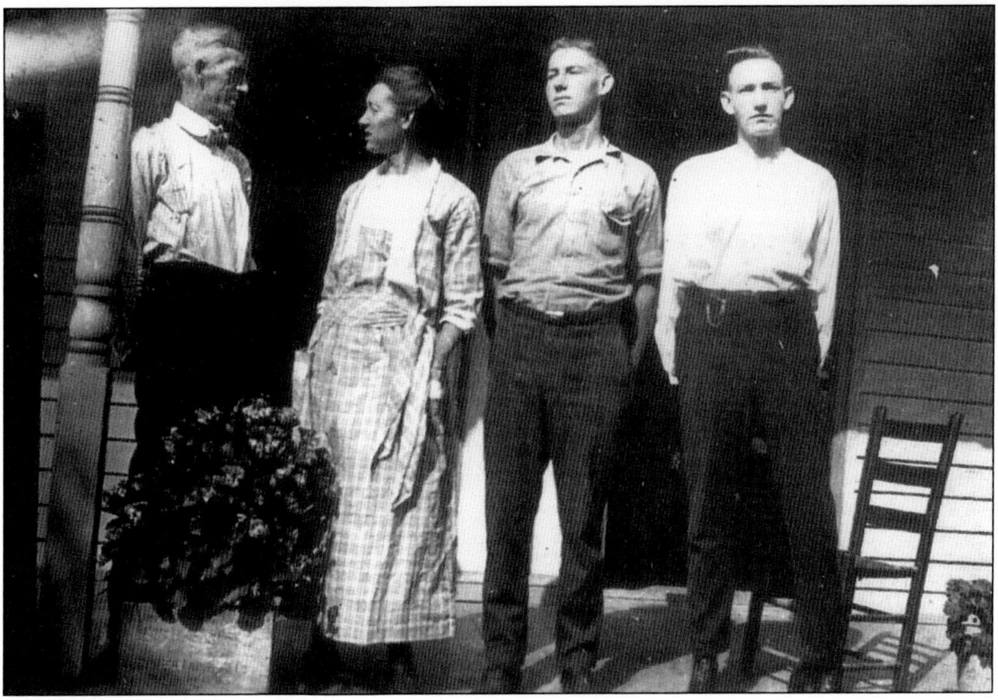

This photo shows, from left to right, George W. Kent, the son of Joshia and Elizabeth Floyers Kent; Adelia Powell Kent; Leslie Carl Kent; and Josh Kent. A story often told about George was that during the World War II maneuvers, a soldier dived under his jeep during a practice "attack" and was joined by Kent. When asked why he was there, Kent replied that if the soldier were safe there then he would be, too.

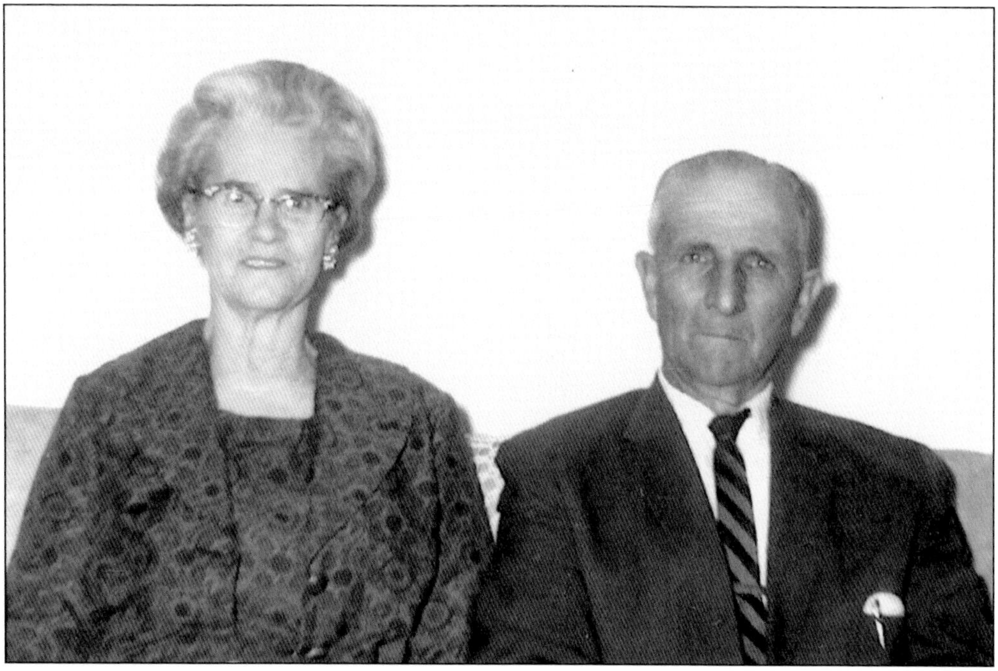

Dora Mai Burgess Kirby and John Lee Kirby, pictured here, lived on Big Branch. John, son of Bill and Martha Kirby, was a farmer.

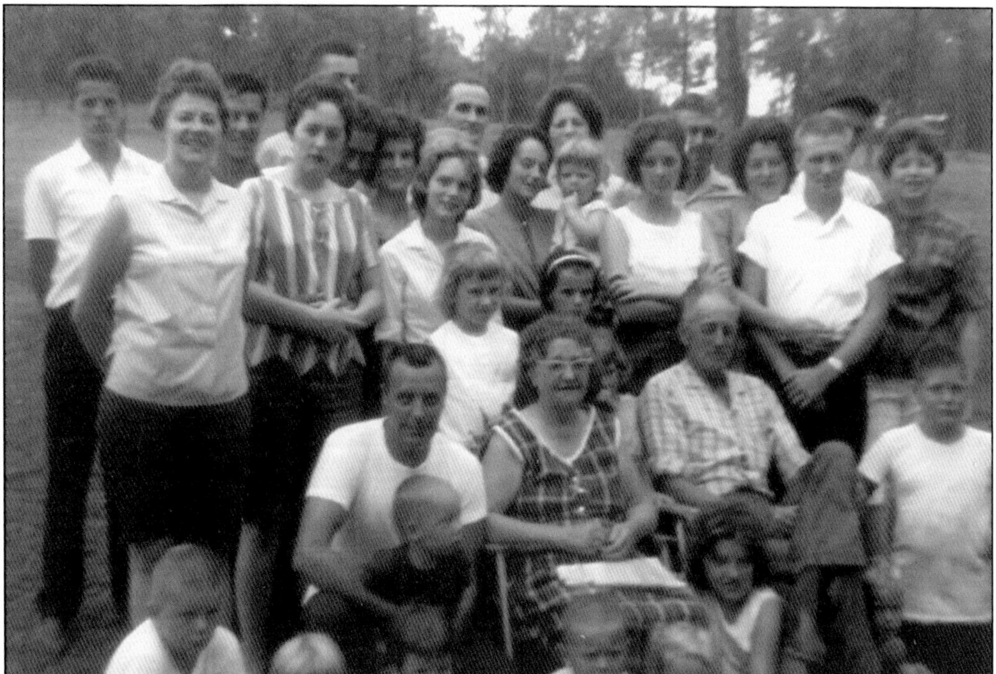

The Dewey Albert and Daisy Elizabeth Mathis Lynn Family Reunion drew a crowd for this photo. The Lynns had six daughters—Reba Estelle Lynn Noblett, Lillian Lorelle Lynn Alcorn, Lois Evelyn Lynn Satterfield, Wilma Jean Lynn Brewington, Georgia Ellen Lynn Lewis, and Nan Roberta Lynn Alcorn.

Ralph and Jo Miller Maddux celebrated their 50th wedding anniversary at the Granville Community Center in 1994. They had two daughters, Martha Maddux Williford and Nancy Maddux Lafever. Ralph owned and operated the first Harley-Davidson dealership in Cookeville for 18 years. Jo was a schoolteacher in Putnam County. Hannah Hall is in the background.

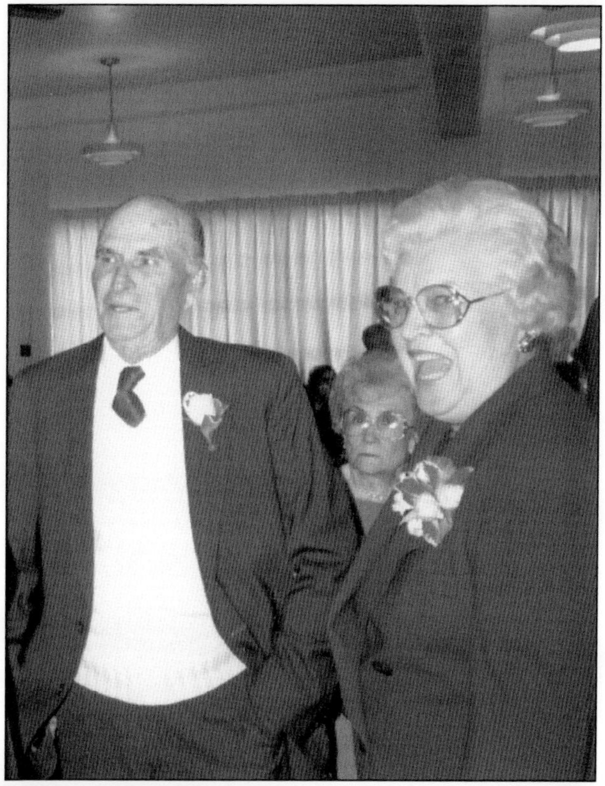

This home, originally known as the Maddux home, was referred to as the Freeman home after Ethel Maddux married Dr. Luther Freeman and they made their home here. Pictured in the yard, from left to right, are ? Sadler; Emily Sadler, beside the house; Altie Maddux McClarin, beside the tree; Ethel Maddux, seated; Martha Stanton Maddux; Lucille Gleason, an orphan; and Robert Fain Maddux.

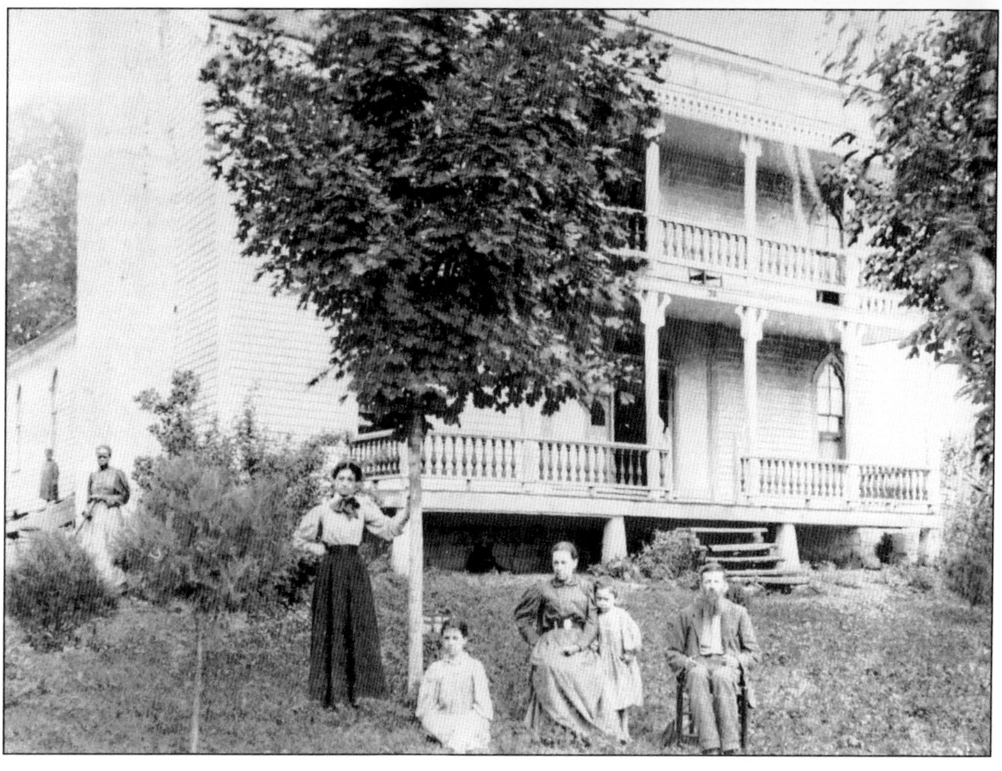

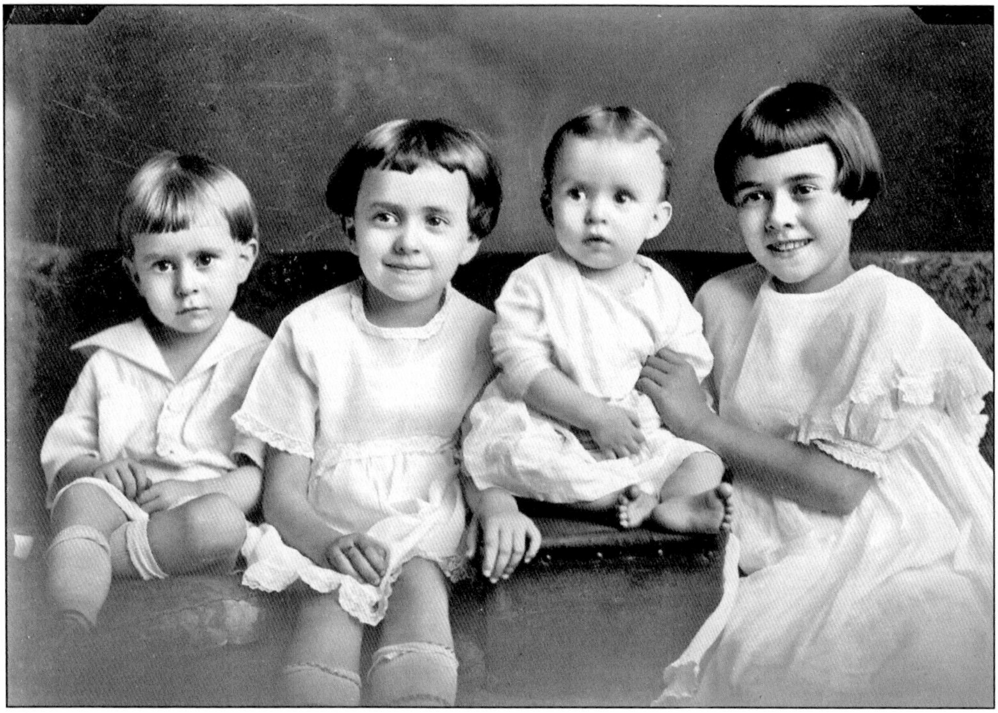

This 1919 portrait shows four of the children of Thomas Jefferson and Maggie Burton Maddux. They are, from left to right (with married names in parentheses), Thomas Burton Maddux, Mary Freeman Maddux (Morrell), Ralph Maddux, and Beasley Maddux (Breeding).

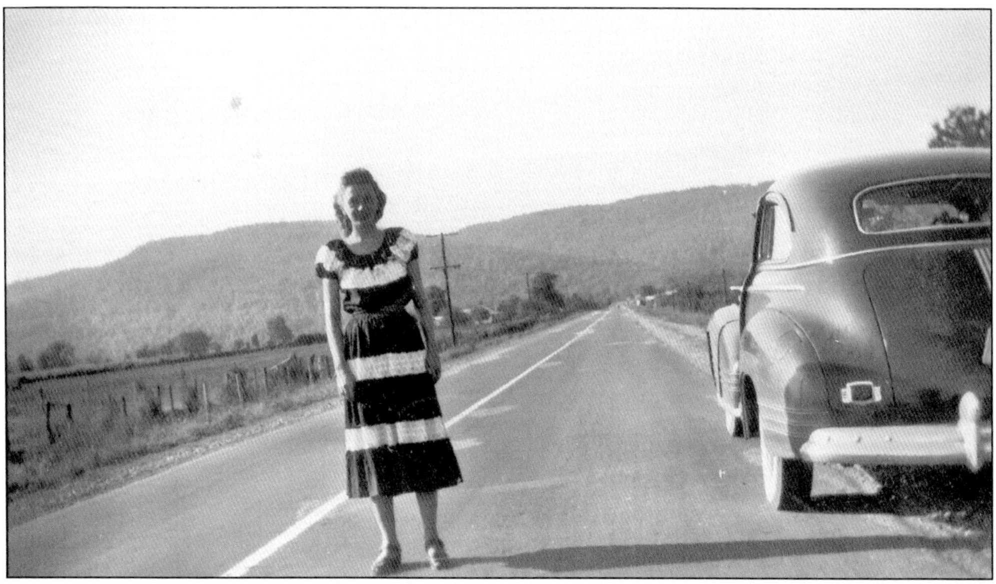

Katherine Manier was the daughter of George Webster and Lula Mae Burgess Manier and was raised on the Richmond Hargis farm across the river. She had one brother, Wade Douglas, and one daughter, Janie.

George Washington and Martha Lou Bryant Mathis lived in Mathis Hollow, which is in Huff Hollow. Their 11 children were Daisy Elizabeth, Raymond, Lillian Lucille, Walter Hamlett, Virgie Mae, Hester Naomi, Albert Wendell, Joseph Clarence, Clara Estelle, Garlin Junior, and Herman Lee Mathis.

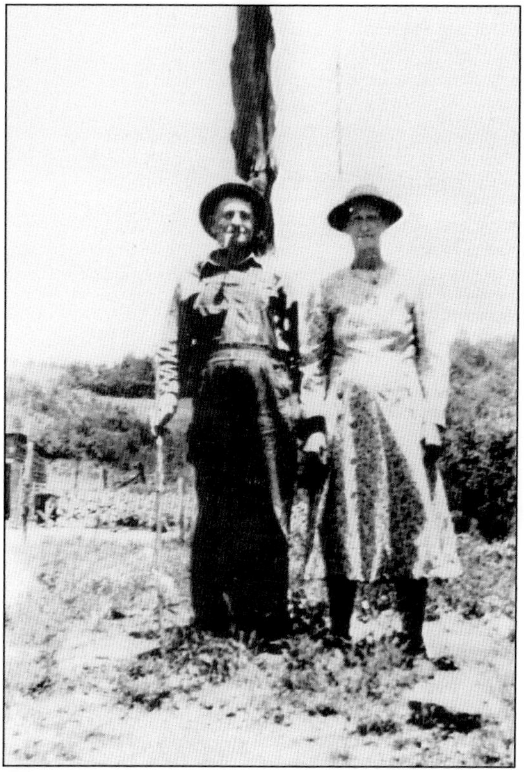

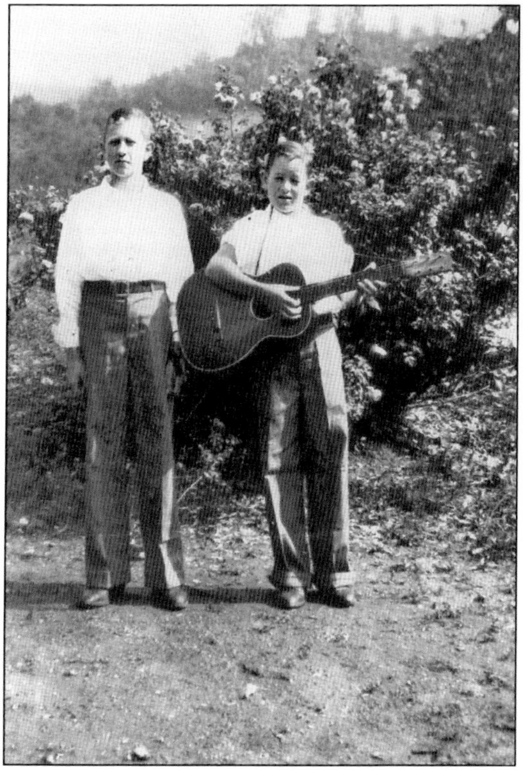

Garlin J. Mathis, on the left, was also called "Matchum." He married Manda Lou Clark. On the right is Herman Lee Mathis, nicknamed "Jack," who married Johnnie Helen Frey. They were the youngest sons of George W. and Martha Bryant Mathis.

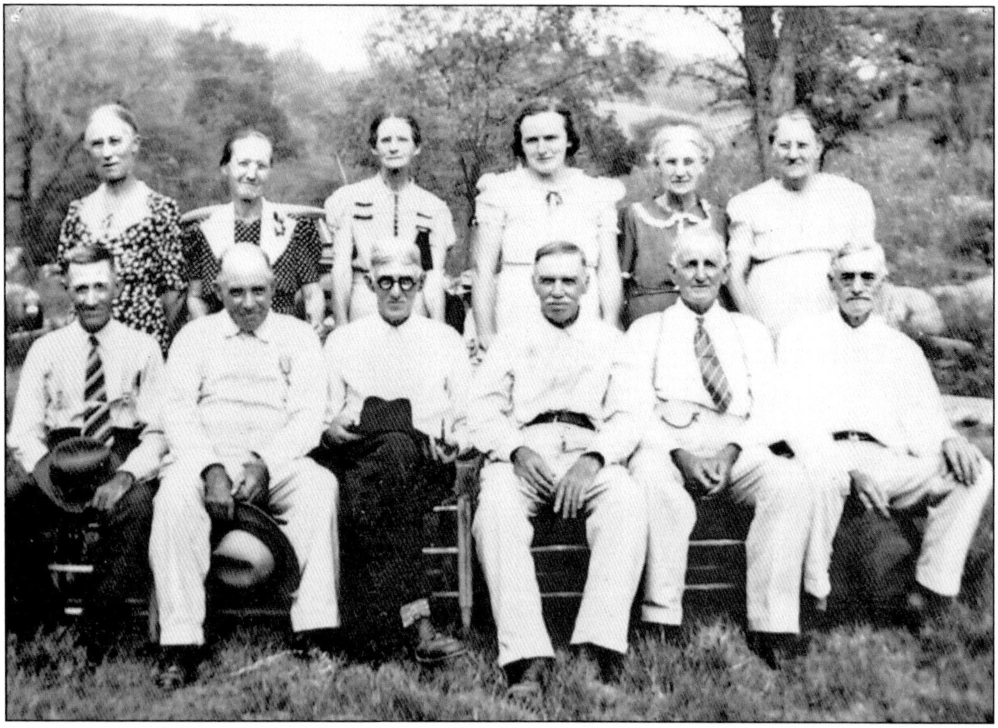

George McKinley was one of the earliest settlers in Granville and received a large land grant. His children and their spouses, from left to right, are Thomas C. and Willie Kinniard McKinley, Homer and Daisy Jared McKinley, Matt and Ada Stout McKinley, Hugh Hill and Lois Carter McKinley, Tom and Tinnie McKinley Apple, and Eddie and Fame McKinley Stanton.

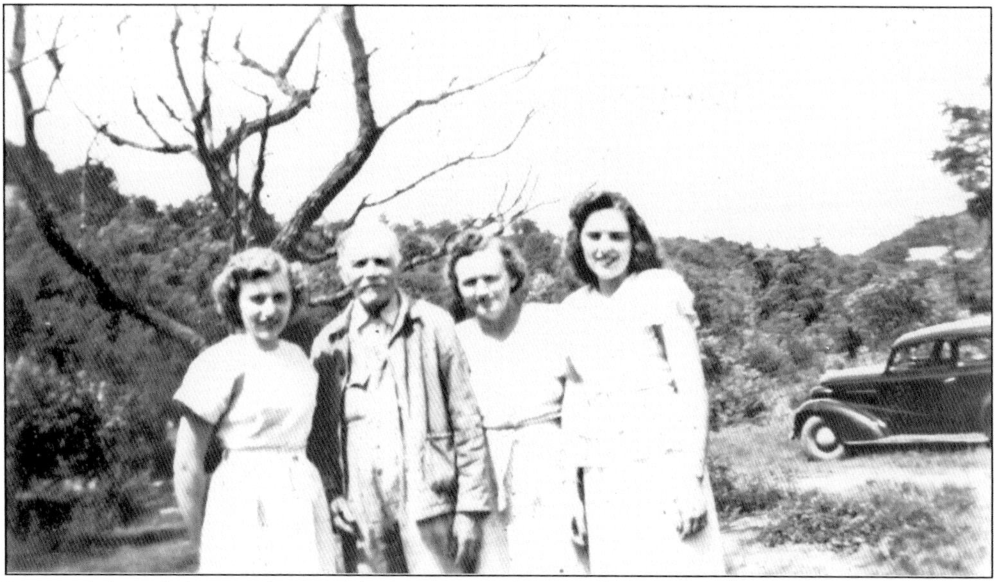

Pictured from left to right are Ida Sue McKinley, Hugh McKinley, Lois Carter McKinley, and Tommie Jean McKinley. The McKinley family lived in Lambert Hollow, where Hugh was a farmer.

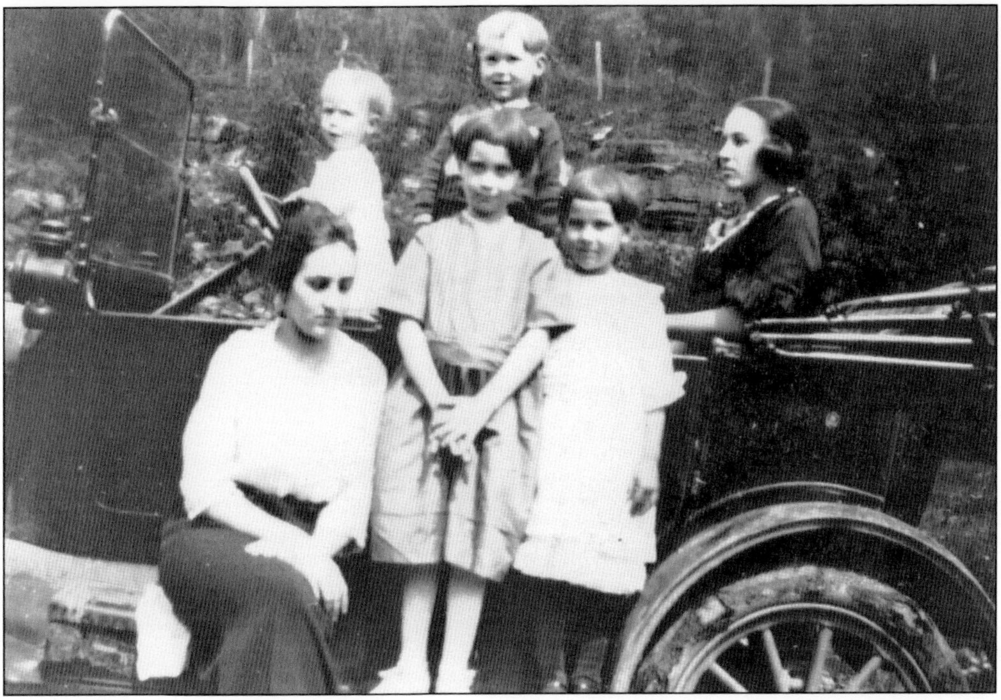

This 1919 Model T Ford could be purchased new for $495. This car, owned by the Thomas C. and Willie Kinniard McKinley family, holds their children. Pictured, from left to right, are (front row) Ola, Elise, and Ada; (back row, in car) Bob, Bill, and Ethel.

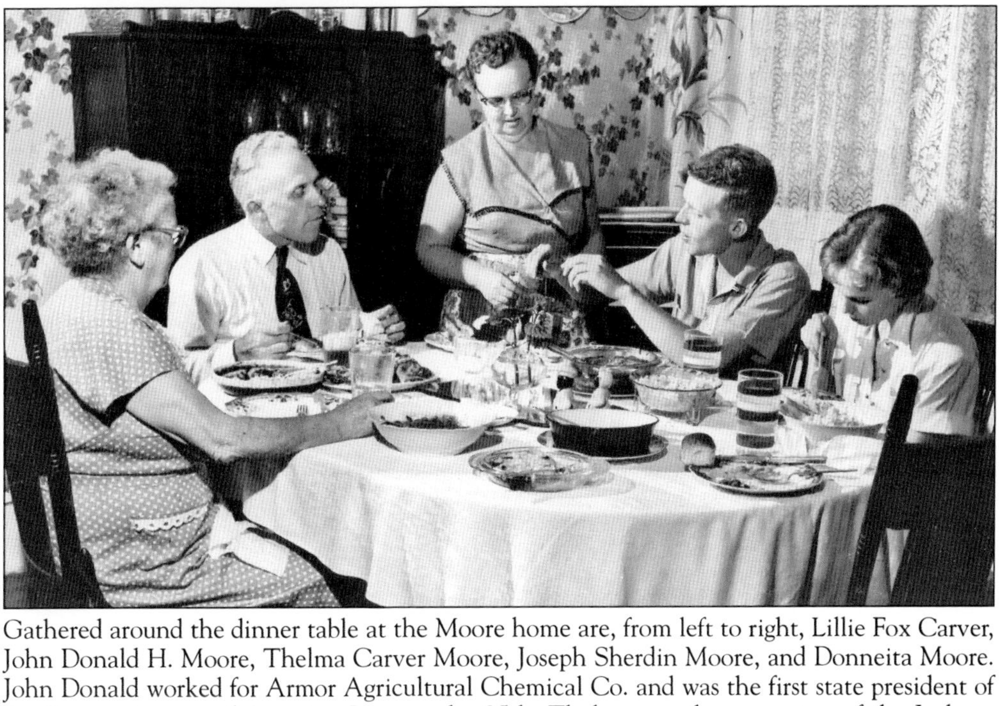

Gathered around the dinner table at the Moore home are, from left to right, Lillie Fox Carver, John Donald H. Moore, Thelma Carver Moore, Joseph Sherdin Moore, and Donneita Moore. John Donald worked for Armor Agricultural Chemical Co. and was the first state president of the Future Farmers of America; Joe was the 25th. Thelma was the supervisor of the Jackson County School System for 25 years.

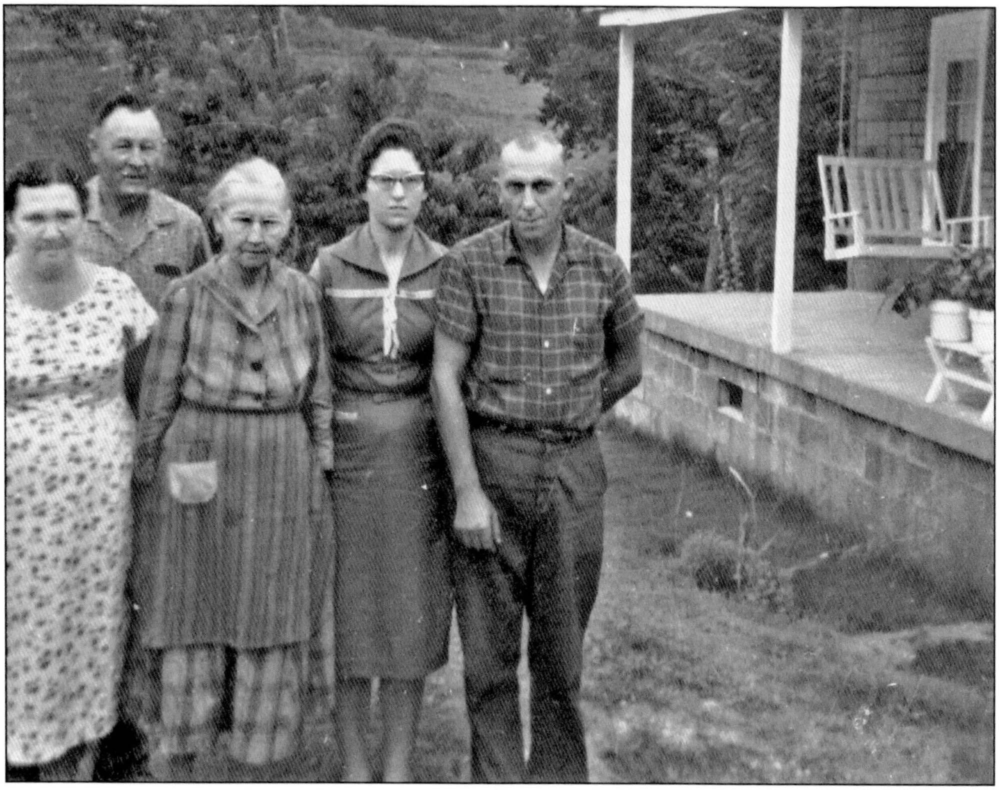

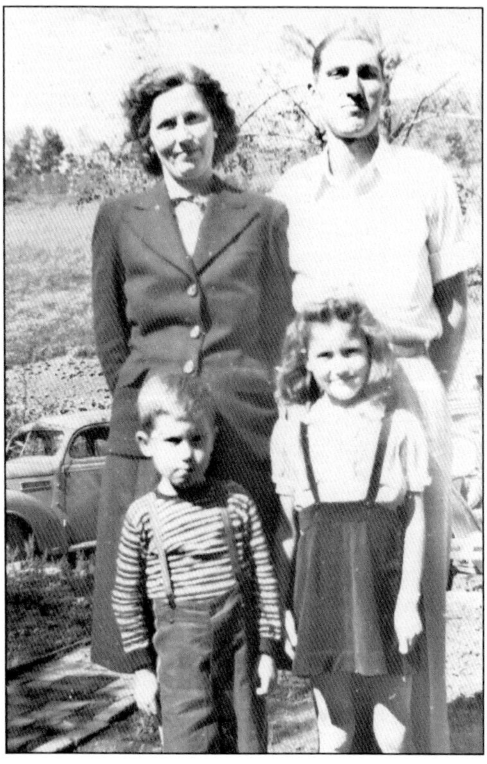

Eura Ann Hargis Montgomery was the wife of Noah Montgomery. Pictured here, from left to right, are Bonnie Montgomery, Eura, Thelma Guess Montgomery, and Frank Montgomery. A cousin, Ben, is standing behind the Montgomerys.

This 1946 snapshot shows Nellie Harris and John Frank Pruett with their children, Bob and Frankie, standing in front of them. The Pruett family lived in Huff Hollow and the Liberty community. John was the son of Benton and Lillie Clark Pruett, and Nellie was the daughter of Charlie and Vista Apple Harris.

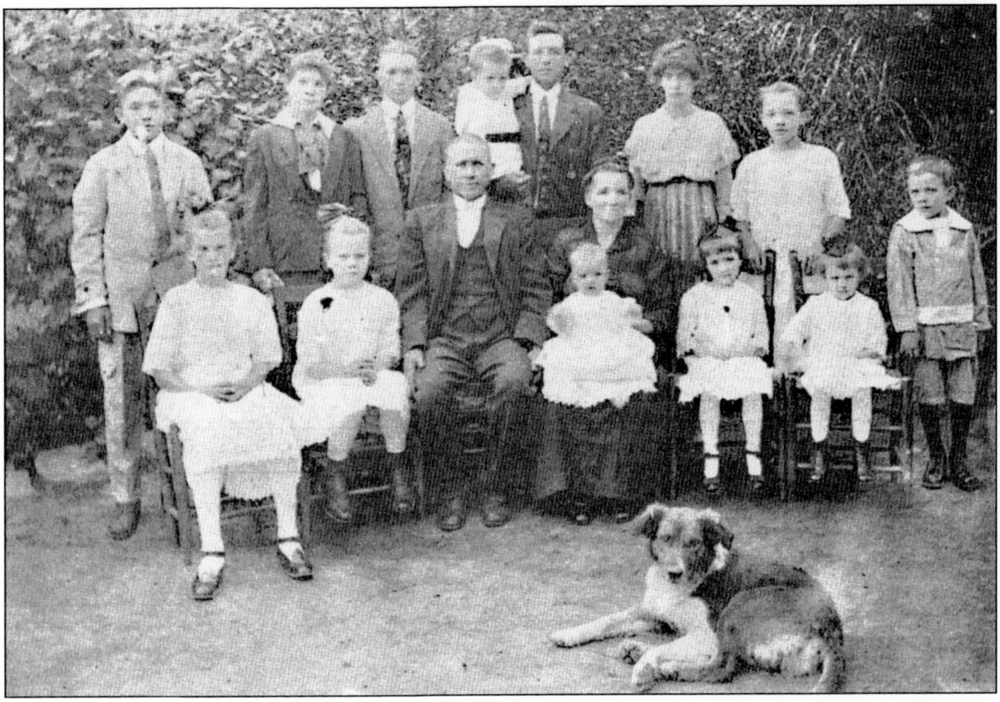

Jonas Bradford and Mary Flatt Ragland are surrounded by their family in this portrait. Those in the photograph are not specifically identified. The list of names attached to the picture includes Carmel, Annie, Herbert, Bee, Lillian, George, Elena, Vada, Clara, Ella, and Eugene.

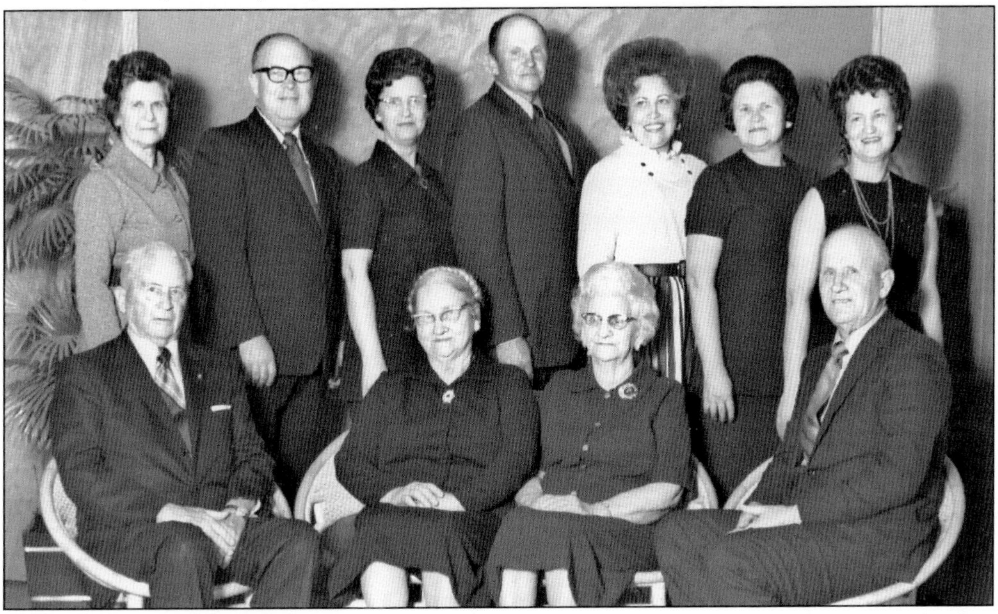

Sidney Alphaeus Ragland first married Vallie A. Kirby, and they had four children. After her death in 1907, he married her sister, Sarah Ann Kirby, and they went on to have ten children together. Pictured here are, from left to right, (front row) Vernon, Bessie May, Ma Ann, and Lester Patterson; (back row) Neva Ethel, Guy Dibrell, Zora Nell, Harvey Verble, Bobbye Ann, Lona Doris, and Reba Elise.

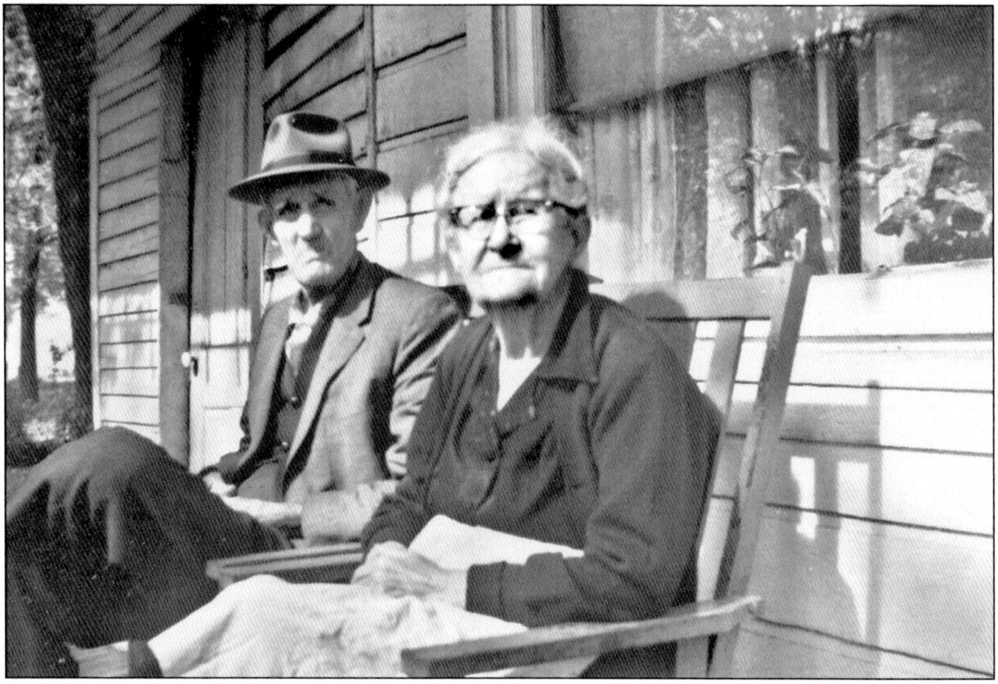

Charlie W. and Martha M. Thomas Ramsey are shown in this photo sitting on their front porch on Clover Street in Granville. Charlie operated the Granville Ferry and the Granville Warehouse for many years, in addition to working on the telephone lines. Martha operated the Granville telephone switchboard.

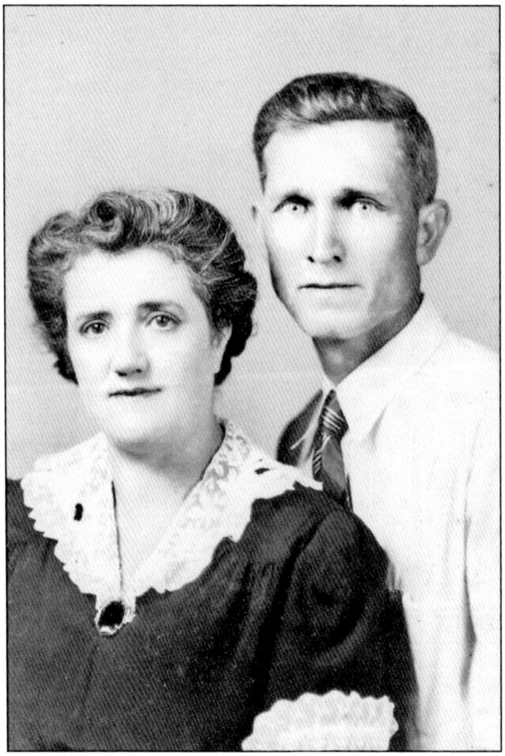

This portrait of Lucille Burgess and William Alvin Reynolds was taken in the late 1930s. William was the son of Abraham Warrick and Nancy Almedia "Allie" Kirby Reynolds. Lucille was the daughter of Andrew Jackson and Elnora Roberts Burgess. They had one son, Arnold, and two grandchildren, Pat and Mike. William was a farmer and lived on Big Branch.

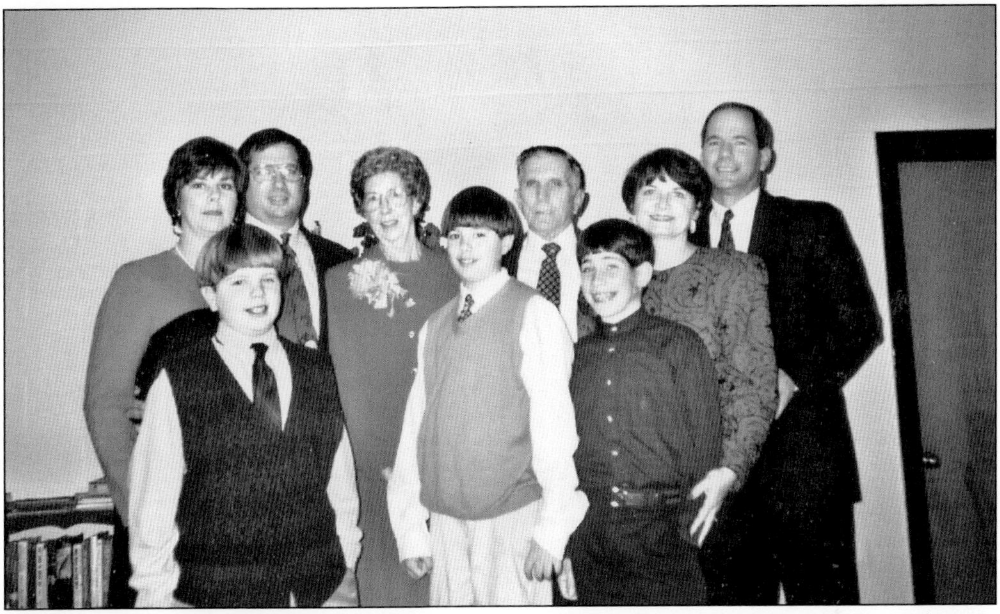

Arnold and Helen Fields Reynolds celebrated their 50th wedding anniversary on December 22, 1996. Both were educators; Arnold served as Sunday school superintendent of Granville Methodist Church for 33 years and was president of the Granville Community Club and the Granville Cemetery Association. Shown here, from left to right, are (front row) David, James, and John; (back row) Barbara, Mike, Helen, Arnold, Paula, and Pat Reynolds. Arnold served with Patton's army in World War II.

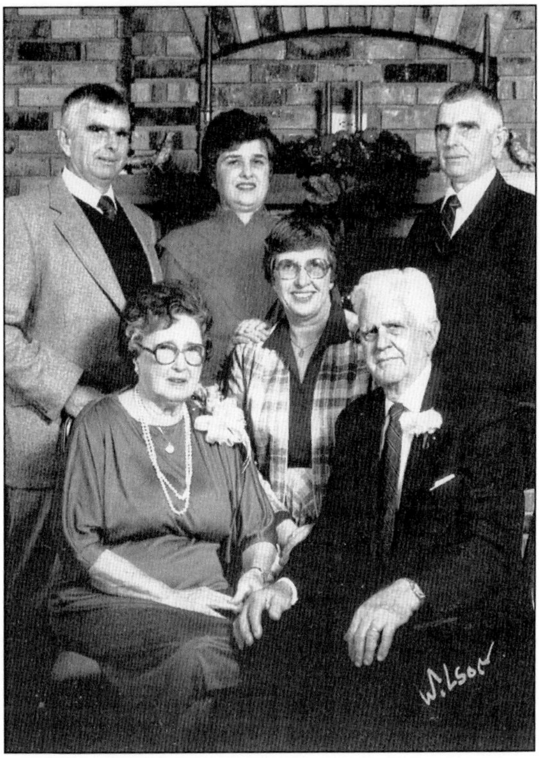

Vestle and Myrtle Reynolds were longtime educators in Jackson and Rutherford Counties. This family portrait, celebrating 50 years of marriage for the couple, includes, from left to right, (front row) Myrtle, Patsy Reynolds Yates, and Vestle; (back row) Sonny, Meta Sue, and Buddy Reynolds.

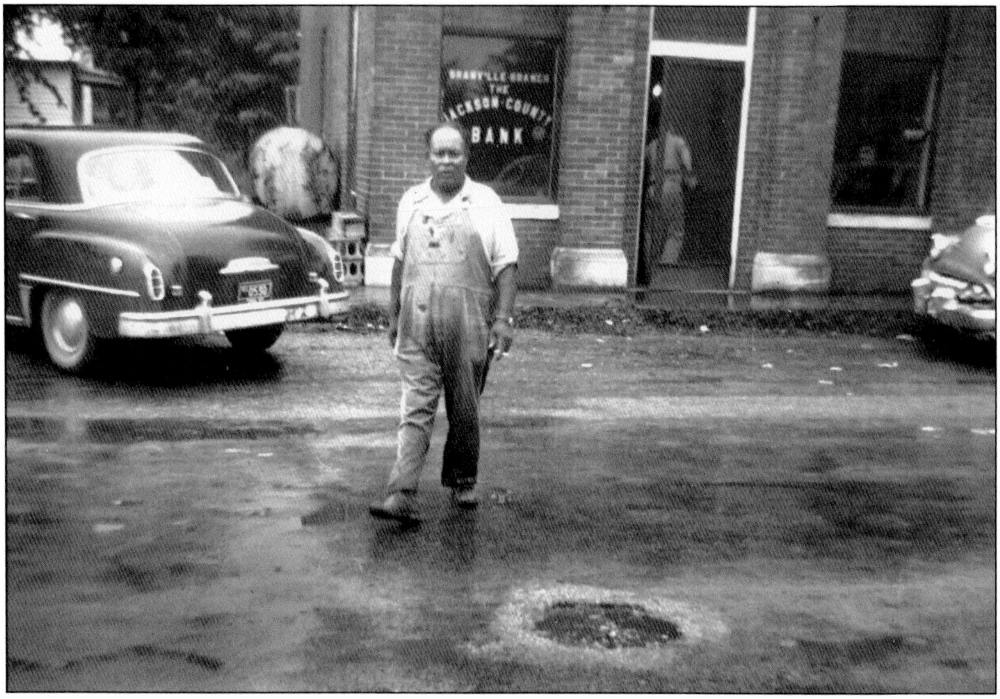

Henry Sadler crosses Clover Street in front of the Granville office of Jackson County Bank. He lived and worked on the Dr. Luther Freeman farm for many years.

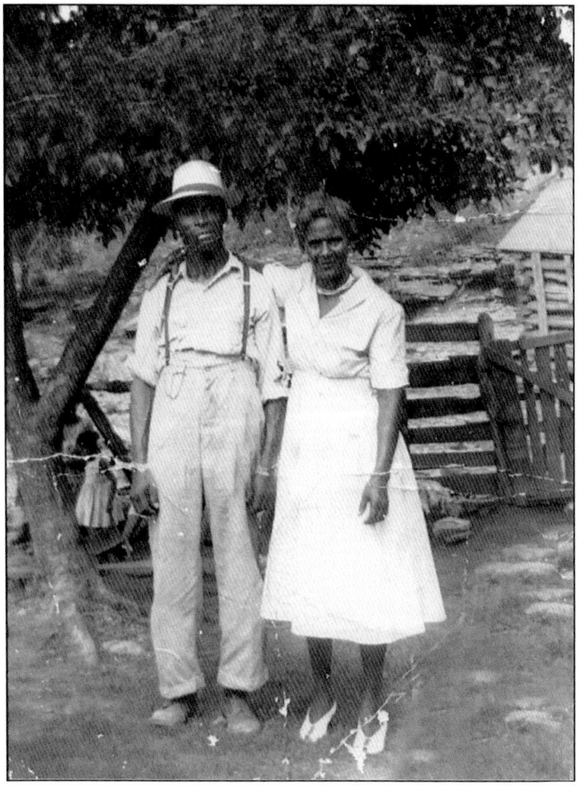

Ellison "Pete" and Ethel Ferrell Sadler, shown here, were married 62 years. They raised nine children together. This picture was taken on Dry Fork Road.

James Thayer Smith Sr., son of Col. James Webb Smith, married Alice Kelly of Granville. After his father's death, he took over the plantation in Holleman's Bend and later moved to Wilson County. James and Alice had seven children.

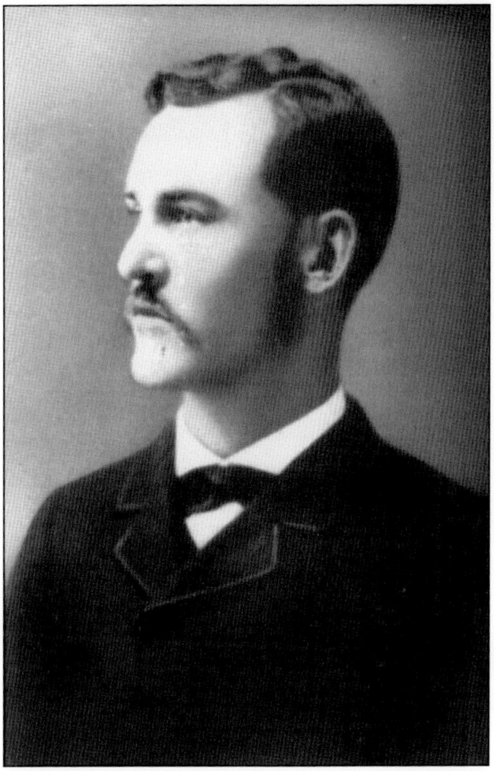

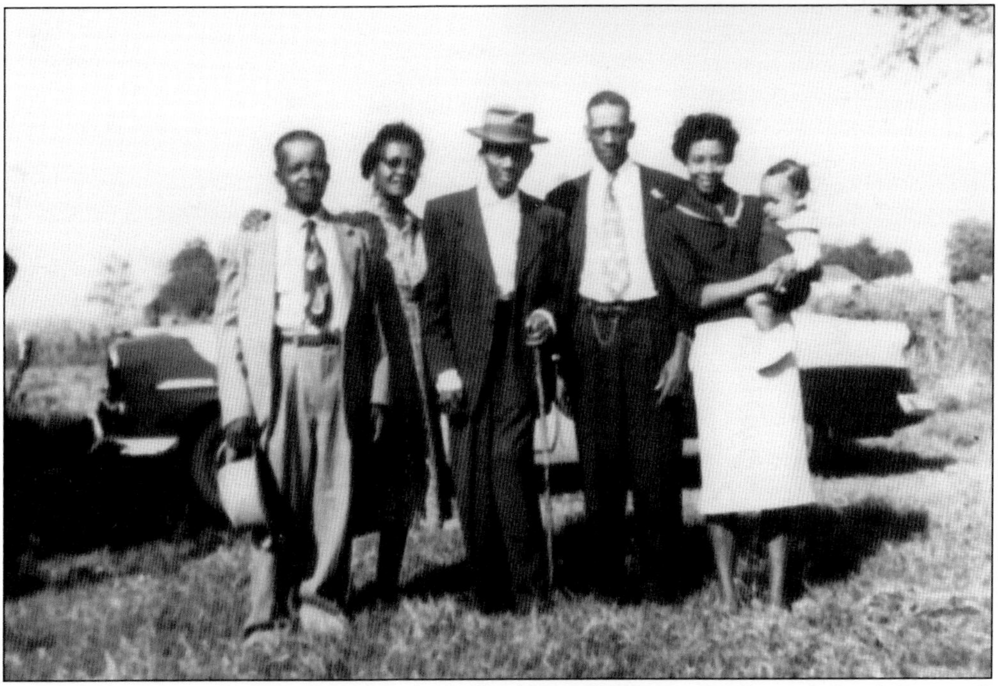

Tommie Stafford and family lived on the Roland Dowell Farm in Holleman's Bend. Pictured, from left to right, are William Stafford, Berchie Ann Stafford Pharris, Tommie Stafford, Henry Carlos Stafford, and Catherine Emogene Stafford White holding Gregory Paul White.

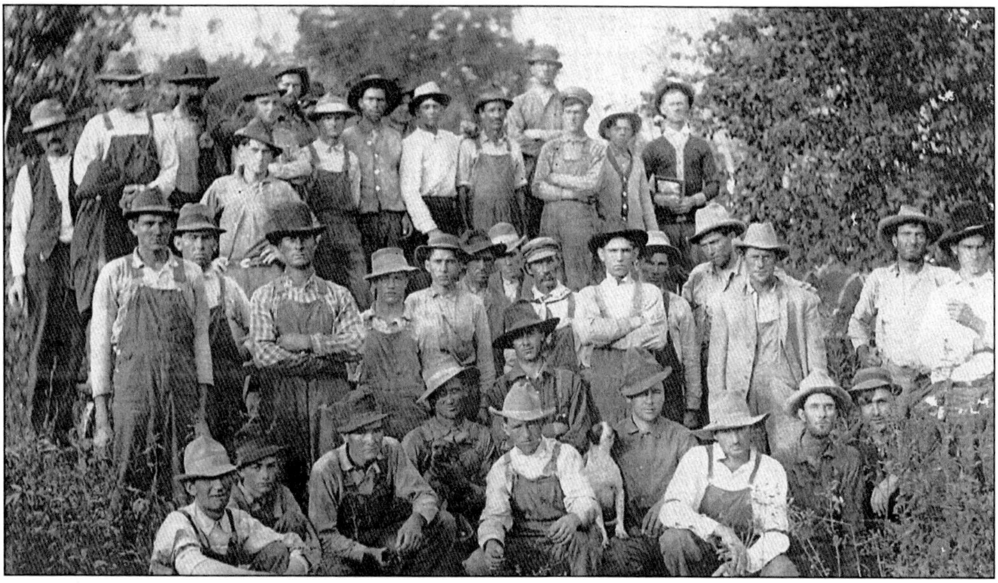

The Stidham family came to the Big Branch and Holleman's Bend areas from the mountains of North Carolina. The Stidham boys were Fernando, Alonzo, Pharo, Smith, Bruno, and Argo. The farm workers in this photo from the Stidham farm are not identified.

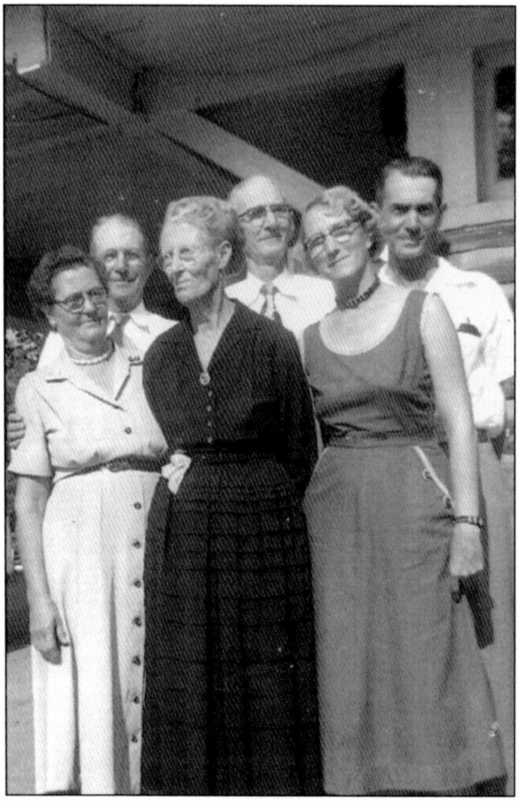

James Buchanan, son of William and Jane Stout, married Martha Veteto, daughter of William Polk and Mary Polly Keith Veteto, on February 14, 1883. The Stouts had 10 children. Pictured in this photo are, from left to right, (front row) Dora Lee Stout Elrod, Mary Jane Stout Jackson, and Anna Ruth Stout Huff; (back row) Austin May Stout, Clifford Dewey Stout, and William Webster "Bill" Stout. Children not pictured are Ova Bell Stout, Robert Taylor, Willis Morgan, and Lou Ella Stout Brown.

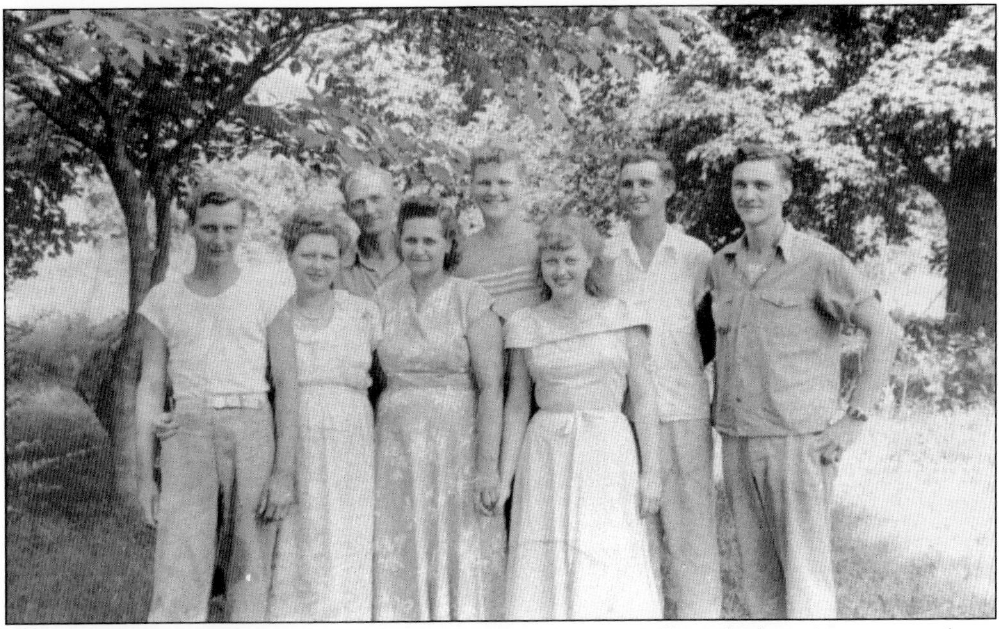

The marriage of Clifford Dewey Stout and Lina Sallie B. Huff resulted in the joining of two well-known Granville families. They produced six children. From left to right are (front row) Dewey Franklin, Virginia Nell, Sallie B., and Cyna Bell; (back row) Clifford, Joe Francis, William "Taylor," and Lonnie James Stout. Joe and Sue Dye Stout and their family still reside on the Stout farm on Martin's Creek.

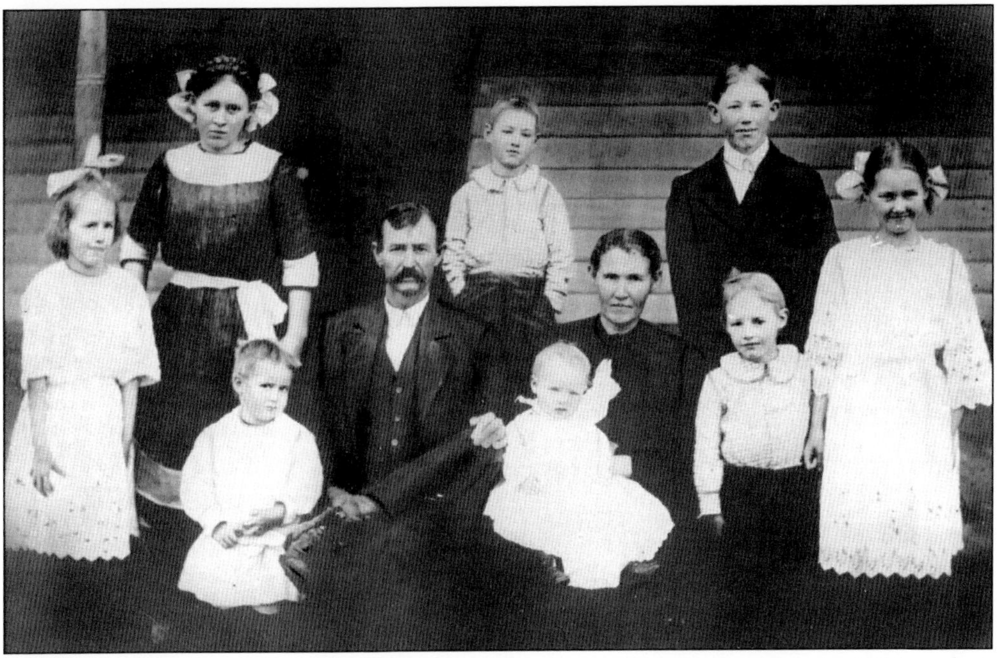

This James Thomas and Louella Neal Veteto family photograph was taken in 1914 at their Spring Fork home. Pictured, from left to right, are (front row) Willie, John Simmons, James Thomas, Louella holding Polly Marah, Bill Austin, and Nellie; (back row) Nora, Vestel, and Rowland Lewis Veteto.

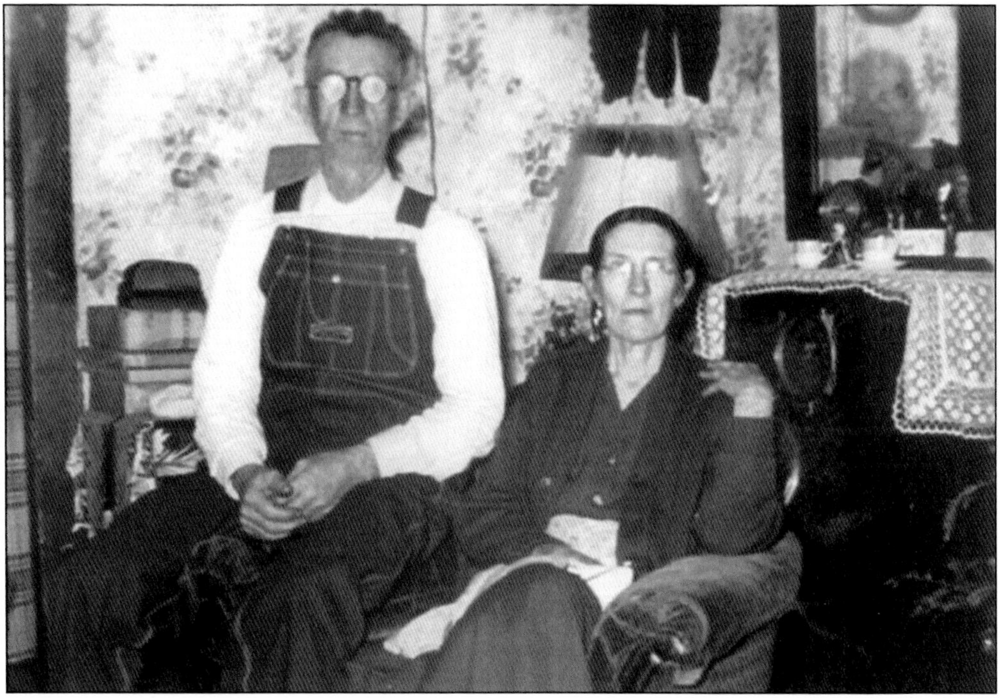

Married in 1908, William Harley "Bill" and Lela Ann Vinson Wade, pictured here, were the parents of seven children. Lela Ann was the daughter of Dave and Mettie Brown Vinson.

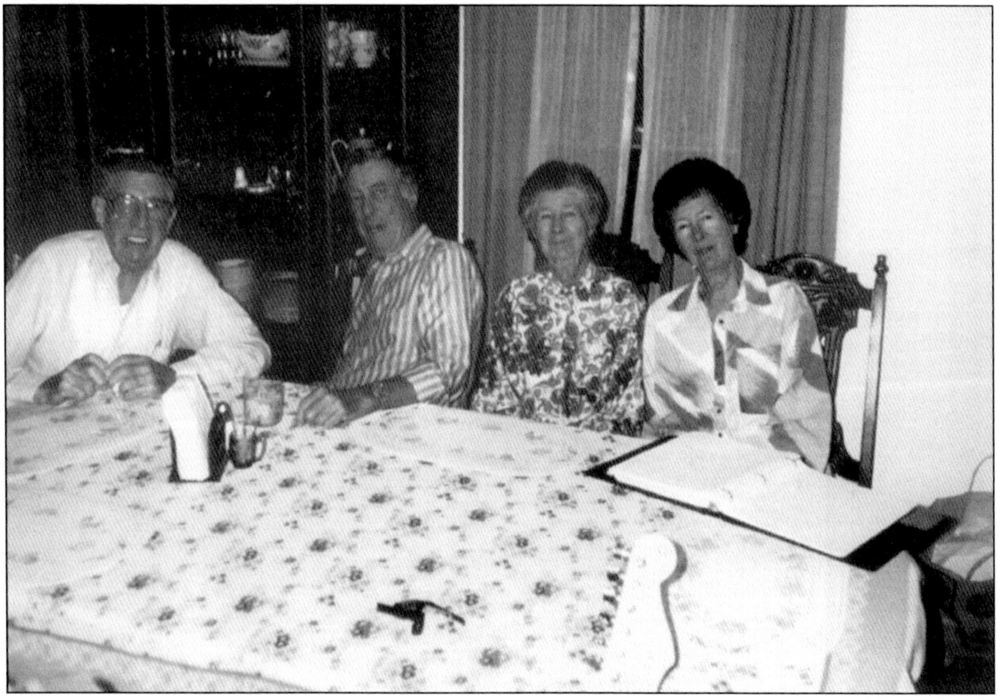

Pictured around the table are four of Bill and Lela Wade's children. From left to right are Billy, Donald, Ina Frances Wade Mathis, and Thelma Jean Williams. Bill and Leda were also the parents of Clara Vestel, Julia Maurine, and B.J. Wade.

Verble Wade, son of Robert Joshua and Nannie R. Meadows Wade, served three terms as the sheriff of Jackson County. Granville native Hugh Philpot also served as sheriff for Jackson County and local Paskel Fields served as sheriff's deputy.

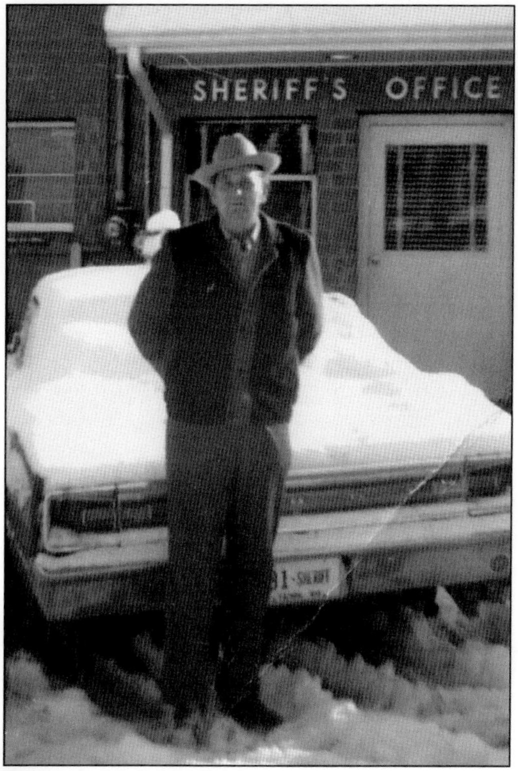

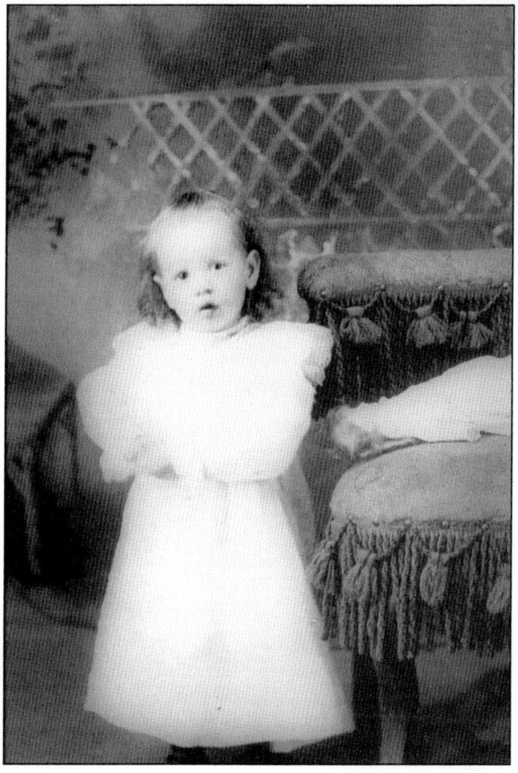

Mary Nell Ferrell was the daughter of Dr. Albert and Hannah Holleman Ferrell. She was an accomplished piano teacher in Granville. Mary Nell married John Watts, and they had two children, Glenn and Margaret. Even though Glenn lived and practiced medicine in Knoxville, he loved Granville and worked to preserve the family home here.

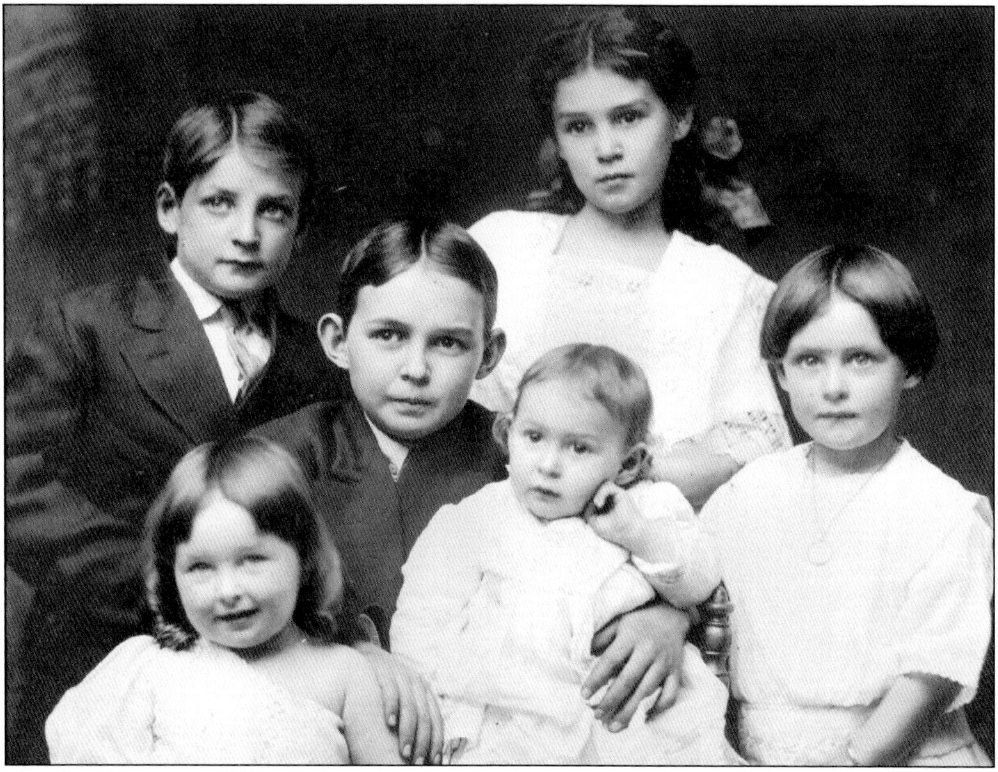

This family portrait of the Williamson children includes, from left to right, (front row) Louise "Peggy," Minnie Eva, and Anna Lee; (back row) Hugh Smith Jr., Will Herman, and Alva Dean.

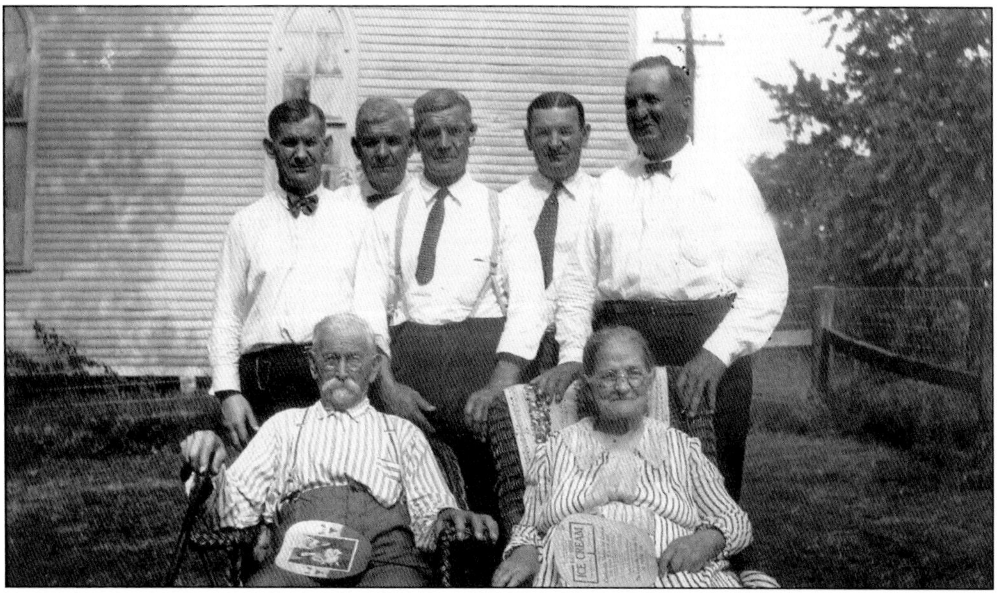

Joseph M. and Martha Ann Cooper Williamson made this picture with their sons in the yard next to the Granville Methodist Church. From left to right are (front row) Joseph and Martha Ann; (back row) Robert, W.C., Frank, Lex, and Hugh Smith Williamson.

On March 27, 1954, Patsy Williamson married Huber Edward Butler. Sharing the festivities in this photo is "Uncle Bill" William Claudius Williamson (seated), a prominent local business leader.

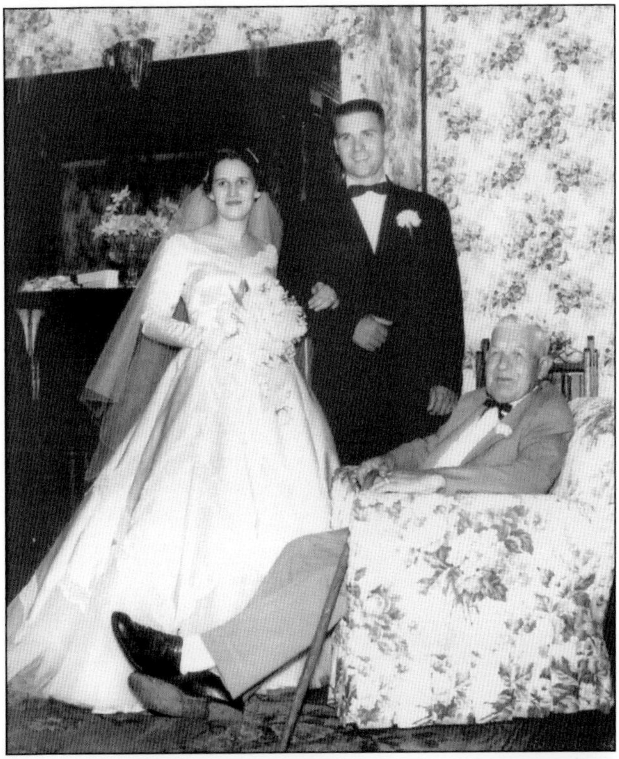

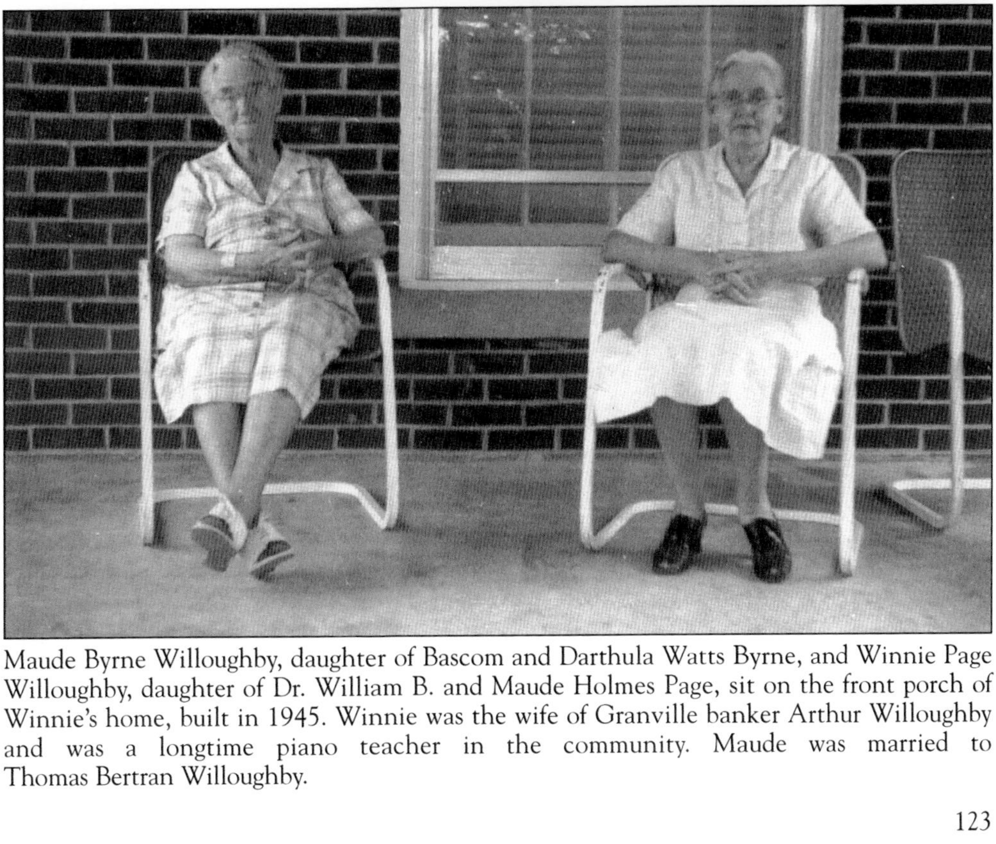

Maude Byrne Willoughby, daughter of Bascom and Darthula Watts Byrne, and Winnie Page Willoughby, daughter of Dr. William B. and Maude Holmes Page, sit on the front porch of Winnie's home, built in 1945. Winnie was the wife of Granville banker Arthur Willoughby and was a longtime piano teacher in the community. Maude was married to Thomas Bertran Willoughby.

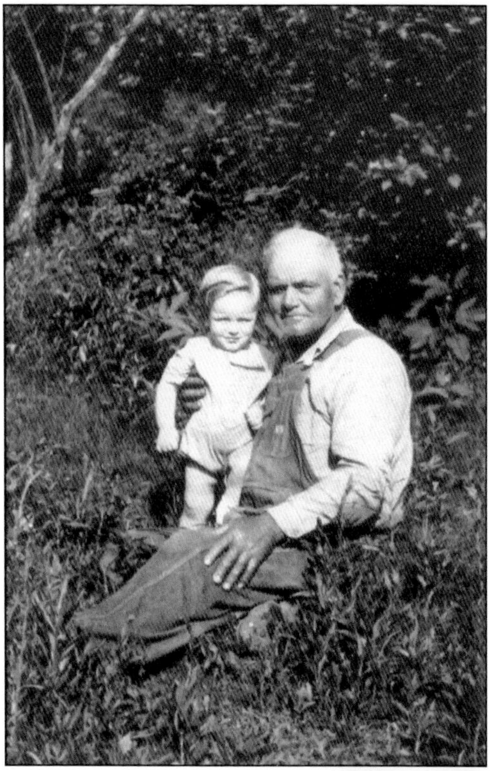

In 1891, Nancy Overstreet Woodard drove an ox-drawn wagon and forded the Cumberland River to bring two of her 16 children, Champion and Robert, to settle in the Brooks Bend area. This 1937 picture shows Champion Harrison Woodard with his grandson, Bobby Doyle Woodard, son of Harrison and Florence Massey Woodard.

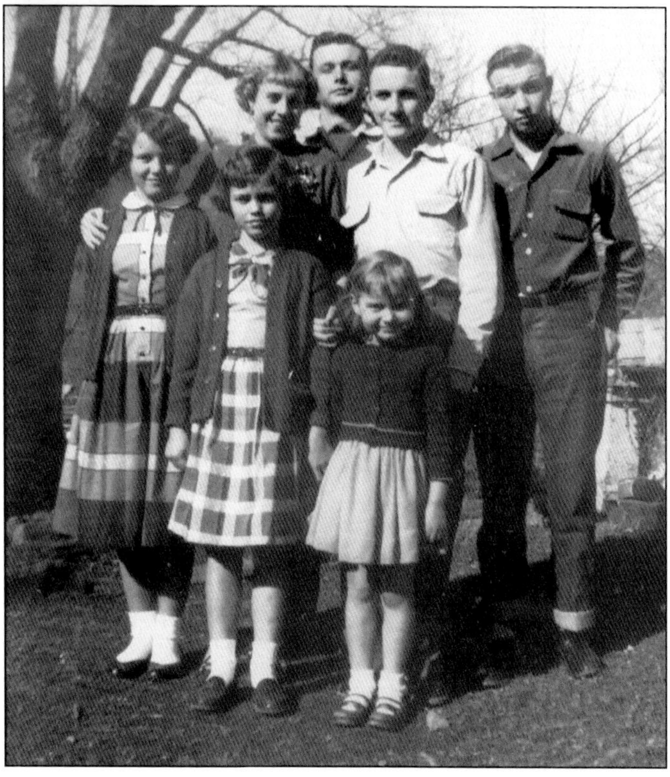

Grandchildren of Champion Harrison and Bertha Barnett Woodard are featured in this photograph taken in the early 1950s. From left to right are (front row) Virginia Mai Woodard (Moss), Linda Faye Woodard (Huffines), and Anna Sue Woodard; (middle row) Robbie Jean Maggart (Blair) and Bobby Doyle Woodard; (back row) Bernice Ray Woodard and Bradford Denson Woodford. Other grandchildren not pictured are Frank Lee Maggart, Glendon Carroll Woodard, Tommy Woodard Bush, and Regina Woodard (Carr).

Eight

The Journey Continues

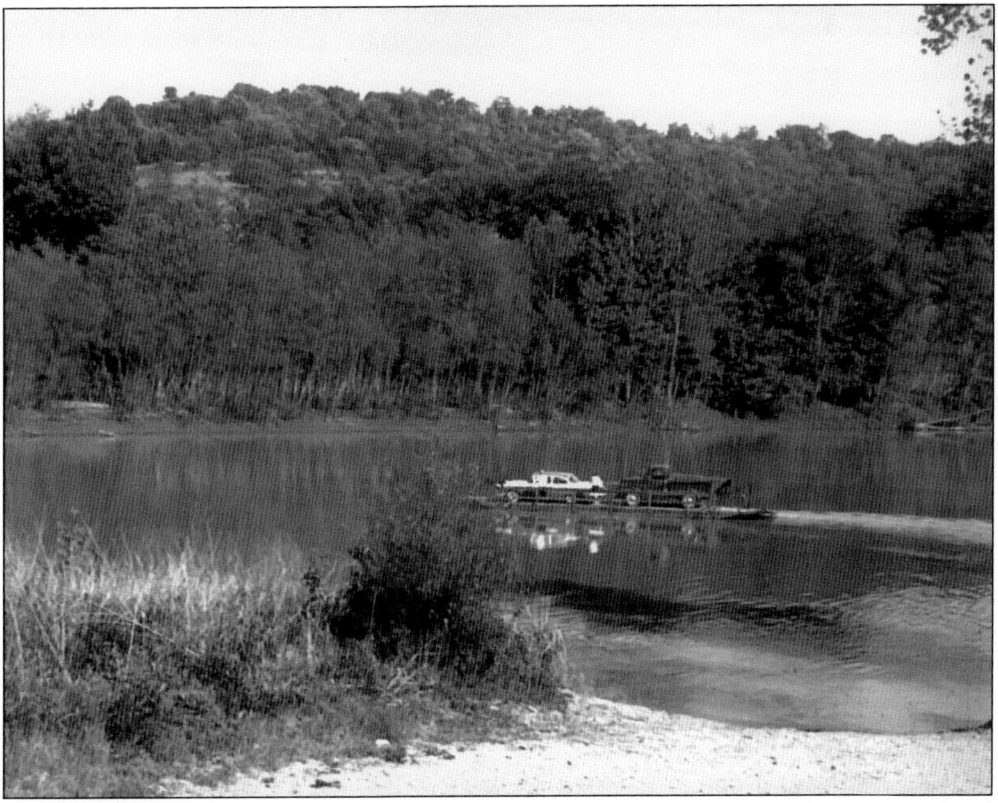

The last 100 years have brought many changes to Granville and produced many wonderful memories for the families here. Looking at this photo of the Granville Ferry carrying Harrison Woodard's 1952 Dodge truck and Wilse Maggart's 1957 Ford, one can almost see the passage of time, feel the tranquility of the water, and even yearn for a simpler life.

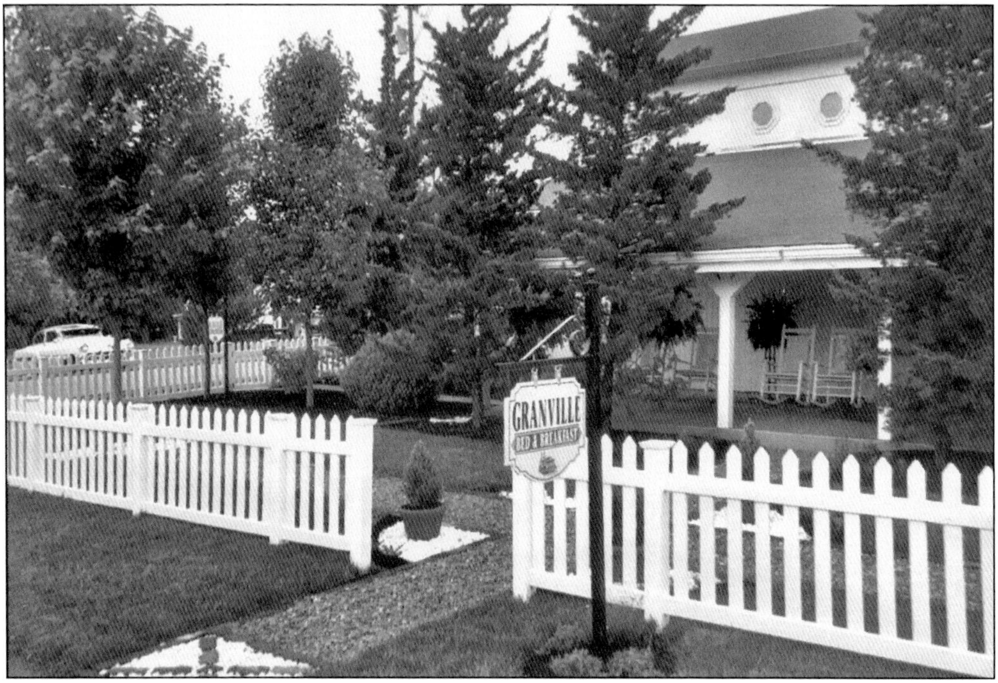

As life moves forward, small towns must progress or close up shop. In Granville, the journey continues. The area is popular for vacationers who come to fish, boat, camp, or just get away from it all. Located in a former bank building, the Granville Bed and Breakfast, pictured above, is a unique spot in which to escape. The side porch is perfect for relaxing.

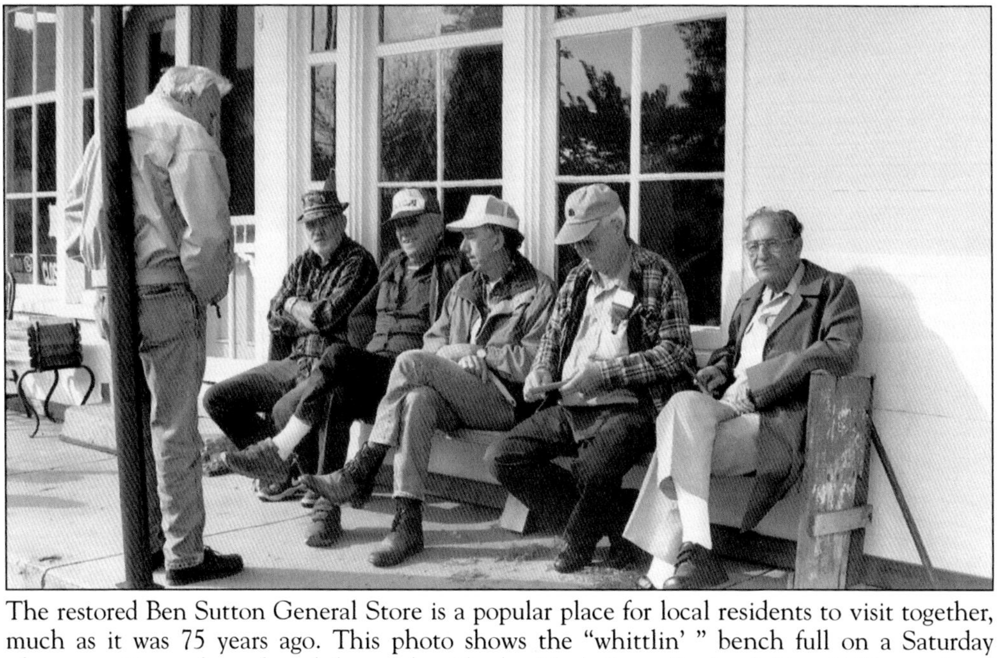

The restored Ben Sutton General Store is a popular place for local residents to visit together, much as it was 75 years ago. This photo shows the "whittlin' " bench full on a Saturday afternoon. Pictured are, from left to right, Charles Clark, Jonas Ragland, Donald Pharris, Loyd Clark, and Loyd Kelly Stout. Look closely and you will find elementary school pictures of these same men in chapter four.

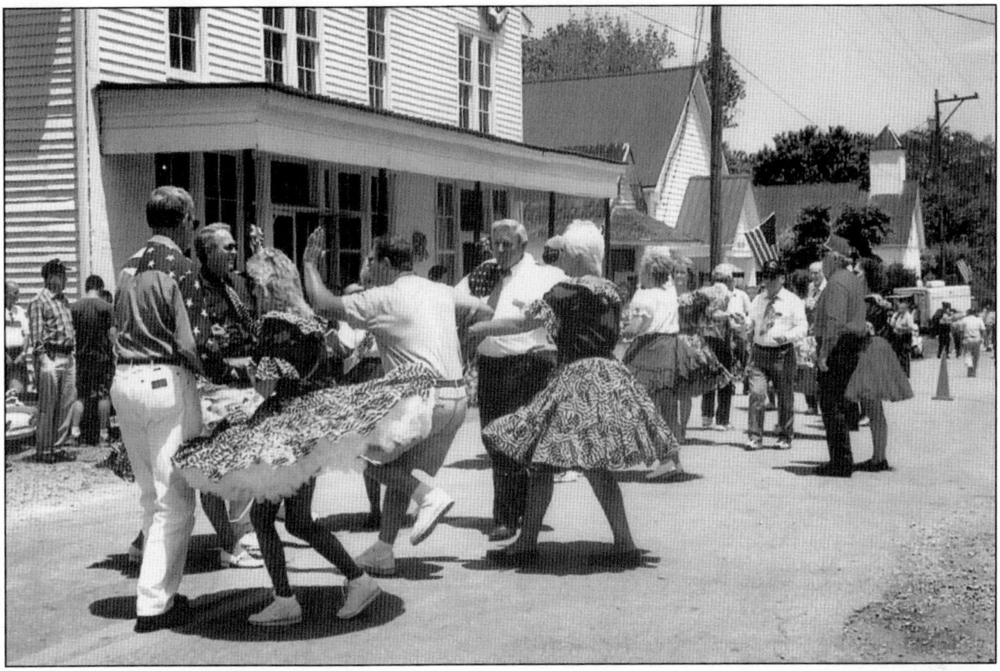

Each year, the last Saturday in May, Granville comes alive for Heritage Day. Square dancers perform in the street here. An antique car show, antique tractor show, craft demonstrations, music, and food booths are set up along Clover Street. Sponsored by the Granville Museum, Heritage Day celebrates local history with excitement and entertainment.

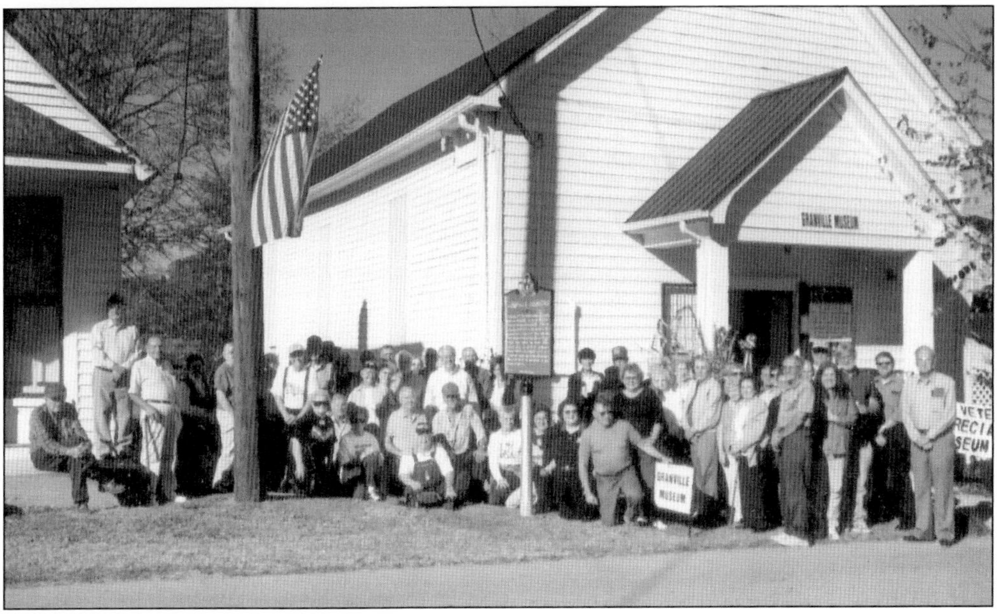

On November 3, 2001, a large crowd gathered for the dedication of the Granville Historical Marker by the Tennessee Historical Commission. Pictured in the background is the Granville Museum, opened in May 1999. The museum is dedicated to preserving the rich history of Granville and providing a place for a living history of the area to reside. Genealogical and historical information is stored there for viewing.

ACKNOWLEDGMENTS

The purpose of this book is to preserve the images of Granville's past for future generations. Memories, as well as factual histories, are lost as time and people pass on. The board members of the Granville Museum have spent countless hours researching and gathering photographs and information. The board owes a huge debt of gratitude to Kerry Fields, who loaned us the photographs of Vincent B. "Moe" DeNardo, the photographer of many of the street and community scenes included in this book. Additionally, many others searched through family photo albums, boxes, attics, and trunks for pictures and memorabilia. We received so many more pictures than we could ever use in a project this size. The additional photographs will be preserved in the Granville Museum to share with our visitors.

A special mention should be made of the following people with their sharp eyes and keen memories who assisted in the identification of people and places in Moe's photographs: Gerry Halfacre Anderson, Mildred Haile Carter, James Edward and Tommie Jean McKinley Clemons, Joe Moore, Helen Fields Reynolds, and Ogeal Halfacre Webster. We had help and support from many others also and regret that we cannot mention each and every one of them. They know who they are, and we want them to also please know that they are very valuable to us. The *Jackson County Tennessee Cemetery Inscriptions 1801–2003* by Larry Mabry and Reda Knight Bilbrey was a valuable resource used to verify spelling and genealogical information.

—Granville Pictorial History Book Committee
(Randall Clemons, Anna Stout Moffitt, and Patsy Reynolds Yates)

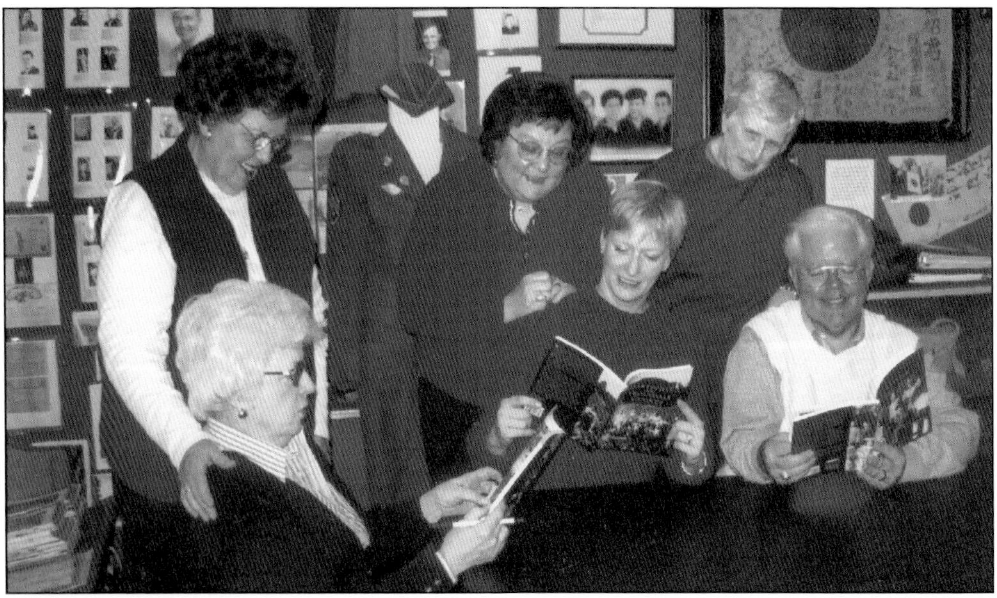

Volunteers and board members of the Granville Museum, Inc., met to review books in February 2004. A decision was made at that meeting to publish this volume. From left to right are (seated) Nancy Cook, Anna Stout Moffitt, and Randall Clemons; (standing) Tommie Jean Clemons, Suzanne Clemons Stafford, and Patsy Reynolds Yates.